FLORIDA STATE
UNIVERSITY LIBRARIES

MAY 4 1999

TALLAHASSEE, FLORIDA

JEWISH LAW FROM MOSES
TO THE MISHNAH

SOUTH FLORIDA STUDIES IN THE HISTORY OF JUDAISM

Edited by
Jacob Neusner
Bruce D. Chilton, Darrell J. Fasching, William Scott Green,
Sara Mandell, James F. Strange

Number 187
JEWISH LAW FROM MOSES
TO THE MISHNAH
The Hiram College Lectures on Religion
for 1999 and Other Papers

by
Jacob Neusner

JEWISH LAW FROM MOSES TO THE MISHNAH

The Hiram College Lectures on Religion for 1999 and Other Papers

by

Jacob Neusner

Scholars Press
Atlanta, Georgia

JEWISH LAW FROM MOSES TO THE MISHNAH
The Hiram College Lectures on Religion
for 1999 and Other Papers

by

Jacob Neusner

Copyright ©1998 by the University of South Florida

All rights reserved. No part of this work may be reproduced or transmitted in any form or by any means, electronic or mechanical, including photocopying and recording, or by means of any information storage or retrieval system, except as may be expressly permitted by the 1976 Copyright Act or in writing from the publisher. Requests for permission should be addressed in writing to the Rights and Permissions Office, Scholars Press, P.O. Box 15399, Atlanta, GA 30333-0399, USA.

Publication of this book was made possible by a grant from the Tisch Family Foundation, New York City. The University of South Florida acknowledges with thanks this important support for its scholarly projects.

Library of Congress Cataloging in Publication Data
Neusner, Jacob, 1932–
    Jewish law from Moses to the Mishnah : the Hiram College lectures on religion for 1999 and other papers / by Jacob Neusner.
        p.   cm. — (South Florida studies in the history of Judaism ; no. 187)
    Includes bibliographical references.
    ISBN 0-7885-0495-9 (cloth : alk. paper)
    1. Jewish law—History. 2. Judaism—History—Post-exilic period, 586 B.C.–210 A.D.   3. Rabbinical literature—History and criticism. 4. Judaism—History—Book reviews. I. Title. II. Series.
BM520.5.N48   1998
296.1'8—dc21   98-38441

Printed in the United States of America
on acid-free paper

Table Of Contents

Preface vii

The Hiram College Lectures on Religion for 1999

1. The Shape of Judaism 3
2. Systematizing Eden 21
3. Who Owns Eden? And: From the Bible to the Torah 43

Other Essays

4. What is "A Judaism"? 65
5. Religious Belief and Economic Behavior 85
6. The Theological Anthropology of Classical Judaism 103
7. Comparing Sources: Mishnah/Tosefta and Gospel 119
8. Vow-Taking, the Nazirites and the Law: Does James's Advice to Paul Accord with the Halakhah 137

Current Book Reviews

9. Halbertal's *People of the Book* 161
10. Nadler's *Faith of the Mitnagdim* 165
11. Shavit's *Athens in Jerusalem* 169
12. Brody's *Geonim* 173
13. Rubin's *Telling and Remembering* 177
14. Kaplan and Dresner's *Abraham Joshua Heschel* 181

Preface

By "Moses" I mean the Pentateuch, and by the Mishnah, ca. 200 C.E., the first of the two systematic presentations of the halakhah in formative Judaism, the other being the Tosefta (as demonstrated in acute detail in the *Religious Commentary*). At issue is the transformation of the Bible into the Torah, that is to say, the Hebrew Scriptures of ancient Israel into the systematic structure of religious belief and practice that we know as Judaism. I owe the title of these lectures to Professor E. P. Sanders, who called his critique of my *Judaism: The Evidence of the Mishnah* [1] *Jewish Law from Jesus to the Mishnah*, to which I first replied in *Judaic Law from Jesus to the Mishnah. A Systematic Reply to Professor E. P. Sanders*.[2] In that context these lectures respond in a more substantive and systematic reply. In my view Sanders does not so much misrepresent (Rabbinic) Judaism as misunderstand its character. His knowledge is simply superficial and uncomprehending, which is why he can reduce that massive religious construction to a small part of its mass.

What is at issue? Sanders represents Rabbinic Judaism as fundamentally an exercise in what he calls covenantal nomism. In my judgment, he is correct in his insistence that the theology of covenantal nomism pertains, but he grossly misunderstands the character of Rabbinic Judaism, which I do not believe he grasps in any significant dimension. That is because, in my view, the proper focus is elsewhere than in the category "nomism," which is formal and not substantive. He reduces Rabbinic Judaism to its external traits, especially its insistence on the rendering of theological conviction into concrete action. That is a typically Protestant reading of that Judaism – external and uncomprehending. That is why his grasp of the details of the law and of

---

[1] *Judaism. The Evidence of the Mishnah*. Chicago, 1981: University of Chicago Press. *Choice*, "Outstanding academic book list" 1982-3. Paperback edition: 1984. Second printing, 1985. Third printing, 1986. Second edition, augmented: Atlanta, 1987: Scholars Press for Brown Judaic Studies.
[2] Atlanta, 1993: Scholars Press for South Florida Studies in the History of Judaism.

the larger context established by them proves remarkably infirm, despite the certainty with which he presents his ideas. For my part, in these lectures and the researches on which they are based I represent Rabbinic Judaism as the systematization of the theology and law of the Hebrew Scriptures, the transformation of the narratives and rules into the design for the social order of holy Israel. That conception of matters is spelled out in the three lectures at hand. Both of us cannot be right, and I maintain, about Rabbinic Judaism he is wrong in his characterization of the structure and the system. I must stress what I mean by "wrong." That is not because covenantal nomism, as Sanders defines the term, does not play a role in Rabbinic theology. Sanders is wrong, simply wrong, because his reading of that theology – his understanding of the Judaism that is set forth in Rabbinic literature – is monumentally irrelevant to its critical concerns and generative issues.

"Our sages of blessed memory" claimed to set forth the Torah, the one whole Torah of Moses, our rabbi, formulated and transmitted both in writing (that is, the Hebrew Scriptures Christianity knows as the Old Testament) and in memory (that is, the traditions ultimately preserved in the Mishnah, Tosefta, two Talmuds, and Midrash-compilations of late antiquity). Then the Written Torah stands in judgment of the Oral Torah, just as (our sages would maintain, were they willing to use categories of others) the Old Testament stands in judgment of the New (as the Evangelists maintain in citing the Old to validate the New). Then the real issue is, is Judaism right? That is to say, does the Judaism of the Dual Torah, oral and written, state the intent and program of the Hebrew Scriptures, or does the Christianity of the Gospels, so rich in the exegesis of the ancient Scriptures, do so? Both cannot be right, and my claim here is that the sages read Scripture forward and produced the Torah, oral and written.

In the Hiram College Lectures on Religion, I take the logical next step. I ask whether and how the documents of the Oral Torah, halakhic as well as theological, carry forward the scriptural imperative, halakhic as well as theological. The answer to that question is contained in what follows. I appreciate the invitation to formulate my ideas in three systematic lectures, a convenient form for the succinct presentation of a large thesis.

These lectures mark the initial presentation of my thesis that the theology of Rabbinic Judaism, normatively set forth especially in the halakhah, or authoritative law constitutes the systematization, through the norms of the social order, of the laws and narratives of the ancient Israelite Scripture from Genesis through Kings. That thesis is here worked out on the basis of completed research and on-going work as well. The completed research is my systematic commentary to the halakhah from the perspective of its religious contents, on the one side, and my theological account of the sources of Rabbinic Judaism, on the other. The commentary is as follows:

> *The Halakhah of the Oral Torah: A Religious Commentary. Introduction. And* Volume I. *Between Israel and God.* Part One. *Thanksgiving: Tractate Berakhot. Enlandisement: Tractates Kilayim, Shebi'it, and 'Orlah.* Atlanta, 1997: Scholars Press for South Florida Studies in the History of Judaism.

> *The Halakhah of the Oral Torah: A Religious Commentary.* Volume I. *Between Israel and God.* Part Two. *Possession and Partnership. Tractates Ma'aserot and Terumot.* Atlanta, 1999: Scholars Press for South Florida Studies in the History of Judaism.

> *The Halakhah of the Oral Torah: A Religious Commentary.* Volume I. *Between Israel and God.* Part Three. *Possession and Partnership: Tractates Hallah, Ma'aser Sheni, and Bikkurim.* Atlanta, 1999: Scholars Press for South Florida Studies in the History of Judaism.

> *The Halakhah of the Oral Torah: A Religious Commentary.* Volume I. *Between Israel and God.* Part Four *Possession and Partnership: Tractates Pe'ah and Dema'i.* Atlanta, 1999: Scholars Press for South Florida Studies in the History of Judaism.

> *The Halakhah of the Oral Torah: A Religious Commentary.* Volume I. *Between Israel and God.* Part Five. *Transcendent Transactions: Meeting God without the Land. Tractates Sheqalim, Arakhin, and Ta'anit.* Atlanta, 1999: Scholars Press for South Florida Studies in the History of Judaism.

> *The Halakhah of the Oral Torah: A Religious Commentary.* Volume I. *Between Israel and God.* Part Six. *Transcendent Transactions: Where Heaven and Earth Intersect. Tractate Zebahim.* Atlanta, 1999: Scholars Press for South Florida Studies in the History of Judaism.

> *The Halakhah of the Oral Torah: A Religious Commentary.* Volume I. *Between Israel and God.* Part Seven. *Transcendent Transactions: Where Heaven and Earth Intersect. Tractate Menahot.* Atlanta, 1999: Scholars Press for South Florida Studies in the History of Judaism.

> *The Halakhah of the Oral Torah: A Religious Commentary.* Volume I. *Between Israel and God.* Part Eight. *Transcendent Transactions: Where Heaven and Earth Intersect. Tractates Tamid and Yoma.*

Atlanta, 1999: Scholars Press for South Florida Studies in the History of Judaism.

The Halakhah of the Oral Torah: A Religious Commentary. Volume I. *Between Israel and God.* Part Nine. *Transcendent Transactions: Where Heaven and Earth Intersect. Tractates Hagigah, Bekhorot and Me'ilah.* Atlanta, 1999: Scholars Press for South Florida Studies in the History of Judaism.

The Halakhah of the Oral Torah: A Religious Commentary. Volume I. *Between Israel and God.* Part Ten. *Transcendent Transactions: Where Heaven and Earth Intersect. Tractates Temurah, Megillah, and Rosh Hashanah.* Atlanta, 1999: Scholars Press for South Florida Studies in the History of Judaism.

The Halakhah of the Oral Torah: A Religious Commentary. Volume II. *Within Israel's Social Order.* Part One. *Civil Society. Repairing Damage to, Preserving the Perfection of, the Social Order. Tractates Baba Qamma, Baba Mesia, and Baba Batra.* Atlanta, 1999: Scholars Press for South Florida Studies in the History of Judaism.

The Halakhah of the Oral Torah. A Religious Commentary. Volume II. *Within Israel's Social Order.* Part Two. *Protecting the Commonwealth: Idolators, Sinners and Criminals and the Courts. Tractates Sanhedrin-Makkot and Shebuot.* Atlanta, 1999: Scholars Press for South Florida Studies in the History of Judaism.

The Halakhah of the Oral Torah. A Religious Commentary. Volume II. *Within Israel's Social Order.* Part Three. *Protecting the Commonwealth: Idolators, Sinners and Criminals and the Courts Tractates Keritot and Horayot. The Outsider. Tractate Abodah Zarah.* Atlanta, 1999: Scholars Press for South Florida Studies in the History of Judaism.

The Halakhah of the Oral Torah: A Religious Commentary. Volume III. *Inside the Walls of the Israelite Household.* Part One. *At the Meeting of Time and Space. Tractates Shabbat and Erubin.* Atlanta, 1999: Scholars Press for South Florida Studies in the History of Judaism.

The Halakhah of the Oral Torah: A Religious Commentary. Volume III. *Inside the Walls of the Israelite Household.* Part Two. *At the Meeting of Time and Space. Tractates Pesahim, Sukkah, Mo'ed Qatan, and Besah.* Atlanta, 1999: Scholars Press for South Florida Studies in the History of Judaism

The Halakhah of the Oral Torah: A Religious Commentary. Volume III. *Inside the Walls of the Israelite Household.* Part Three. *Sanctification in the Here and Now. The Table and the Bed. Tractates Hullin, Qiddushin, and Ketubot.* Atlanta, 1999: Scholars Press for South Florida Studies in the History of Judaism

The Halakhah of the Oral Torah: A Religious Commentary. Volume III. *Inside the Walls of the Israelite Household.* Part Four. *Sanctification and the Marital Bond. Tractates Nedarim, Nazir and Sotah.* Atlanta, 1999: Scholars Press for South Florida Studies in the History of Judaism

The Halakhah of the Oral Torah: A Religious Commentary. Volume III. *Inside the Walls of the Israelite Household.* Part Five. *The Desacralization of the Household. The Bed. Tractates Gittin and Yebamot.* Atlanta, 1999: Scholars Press for South Florida Studies in the History of Judaism

The Halakhah of the Oral Torah: A Religious Commentary. Volume III. *Inside the Walls of the Israelite Household.* Part Six. *The Desacralization of the Household.. Foci of Uncleanness. The Table. Tractate Kelim.* Atlanta, 1999: Scholars Press for South Florida Studies in the History of Judaism

The Halakhah of the Oral Torah: A Religious Commentary. Volume III. *Inside the Walls of the Israelite Household.* Part Seven. *The Desacralization of the Household. Foci of Uncleanness. The Table. Tractates Uqsin and Tohorot.* Atlanta, 1999: Scholars Press for South Florida Studies in the History of Judaism

The Halakhah of the Oral Torah: A Religious Commentary. Volume III. *Inside the Walls of the Israelite Household.* Part Eight. *The Desacralization of the Household. Sources of Uncleanness, Dissemination of Uncleanness. Tractates Ohalot and Makhshirin.* Atlanta, 1999: Scholars Press for South Florida Studies in the History of Judaism.

The Halakhah of the Oral Torah: A Religious Commentary. Volume III. *Inside the Walls of the Israelite Household.* Part Nine. *The Desacralization of the Household. Animate Sources of Uncleanness. Tractates Zabim and Niddah.* Atlanta, 1999: Scholars Press for South Florida Studies in the History of Judaism.

The Halakhah of the Oral Torah: A Religious Commentary. Volume III. *Inside the Walls of the Israelite Household.* Part Ten. *Animate Sources of Uncleanness. Tractates Negaim, Tebul Yom, and Yadayim.*

Atlanta, 1999: Scholars Press for South Florida Studies in the History of Judaism.

The Halakhah of the Oral Torah: A Religious Commentary. Volume III. *Inside the Walls of the Israelite Household.* Part Eleven. *Purification from the Pollution of Death. Tractates Parah and Miqvaot.* Atlanta, 1999: Scholars Press for South Florida Studies in the History of Judaism.

The theological account, focused principally on the aggadic or narrative and exegetical documents, is published as follows:

The Theology of the Oral Torah. Revealing the Justice of God. Kingston and Montreal, 1998: McGill-Queens University Press.

The on-going research, under way or planned, is as follows:

Eden Restored. The Theology of the Halakhah. Atlanta, 2000: Scholars Press for South Florida Studies in the History of Judaism.

Jewish Law from Moses to the Mishnah. Reading Forward from Scripture to the Generative Premises of the Halakhah.

The Bible as Torah

The Three Stages in the Formation of Judaism. From Scripture to the Talmud

The Integrity of the Oral Torah: The Common Theology of the Aggadah and Halakhah. Ten Cases

What, Exactly, Did Our Sages Mean by "the Oral Torah"? An Inductive Answer to the Question of Rabbinic Judaism

It is a pleasure to acknowledge the hospitality of Hiram College on the occasion of my presentation of these three lectures. For generous research support over the years I also express my on-going thanks to the University of South Florida and Bard College. No scholar in the humanities enjoys more generous or appreciative academic sponsorship than I.

I have included other recent papers of mine, prepared for various purposes, including the following: "Religious Belief and Economic Behavior," originally an address at University College, Worcester, England, under the auspices of Bishop Peter Selby; "Comparing Sources," originally an address at Bard College; "Vow-Taking," an address for the institute for Advanced Theological Studies of Bard College at Orlando, November, 1998. "What is a Judaism" is a

Preface

programmatic statement, aimed at guiding the analysis of the systemic qualities of bodies of data that cohere as what I call "a Judaism." As usual, I try to read all important books that appear in my field of specialization and to review them, and to that program, represented here by reviews of Halbertal, Shavit, and Brody, I add reviews of three other books of considerable interest.

JACOB NEUSNER
University of South Florida and Bard College
c/o Department of Religious Studies
University of South Florida
107 Cooper Hall
Tampa FL 33620-5550

THE HIRAM COLLEGE LECTURES
ON RELIGION FOR 1999

1

The Shape of Judaism

Jacob Neusner
University of South Florida and Bard College

Let me state at the very outset the proposition of these lectures. It is in two parts, theological and halakhic, that is to say, legal. First, comes the theological part. The theology of the Oral Torah tells a simple, sublime story.

[1] God created a perfect, just world called Eden and in it made man in his image, equal to God in the power of will. This world he sanctified.

[2] Man in his arrogance sinned and was expelled from the perfect world and given over to death. God gave man the Torah to purify his heart of sin and to make possible atonement for sin.

[3] Man educated by the Torah in humility can repent, accepting God's will of his own free will. When he does, man will be restored to Eden and eternal life.

Second, comes the halakhic part. The law of Judaism set forth in the Pentateuch and elaborated in the Mishnah, Tosefta, halakhic exegetical works, and two Talmuds, systematically translates the theological story into the norms of conduct that would define the society of holy Israel, that is, the people that accepted the Torah and God's dominion at Sinai.

The upshot is simple: Jewish law from Moses to the Mishnah tells the story of how the Bible, meaning, the Hebrew Scriptures of ancient Israel, was transformed into the Torah of the living faith, Judaism, a way of life, world view, and account of the social entity, Israel, formed by those destined to eternal life. Now back to the beginning.

The Judaism reached that statement that proved normative from the beginning of the Common Era nearly to our own day undertook to translate into a systematic social structure the laws and stories of the Hebrew Scriptures of Ancient Israel (known more commonly as "the Old Testament"). That Judaism, known as "rabbinic" because of the title conferred on its religious authorities, or "Talmudic" because of its definitive statement at the end of its formative period, the Talmud of Babylonia, set forth a single apologetics for itself. Its authorities claimed to possess a tradition from Sinai formulated and transmitted orally from Moses through the prophets to the sages of the Rabbinic writings themselves. Thus their's is a dual Torah, written and oral. Not only so, but the sages of the Rabbinic writings, from the Mishnah, a second century philosophical law code, through the Talmud of Babylonia of the seventh century, authoritatively interpreted Scripture, the written part of the Torah within the Rabbinic system.

Viewed not historically – historical fact has slight bearing upon the description, analysis, and interpretation of religious structures and their social systems – but phenomenologically, that claim will be sustained in these lectures. Here – sages allege – is the message of Sinai, translated into the norms of an entire society, that is to say, the law and theology of the sages in the Oral Torah. In these lectures I propose to show that the sages' claim is sustained by the documents that sages set forth to define those norms. Specifically, I argue that the halakhah, or law, of the Mishnah and related documents, embodies in rules of conduct specific responses to Scripture's account of Man – Adam and Eve – and their fall from Eden, on the one side, and Scripture's portrait of Israel and its loss of the Land of Israel, on the other. Hence, I propose to show how the sages of Judaism turned what Christianity knows as "the Bible" into what Judaism calls "the Torah."

I. The Theology of the Oral Torah

Let us begin with an overview of the theology that animates the documents, read whole and complete, of the Oral Torah of the first six centuries of the Common Era, from the Mishnah through the Talmud of Babylonia. The theology of the Oral Torah conveys the picture of world order based on God's justice and equity. The categorical structure of the Oral Torah encompasses the components, God and man; the Torah; Israel and the nations. The working-system of the Oral Torah finds its dynamic in the struggle between God's plan for creation –to create a perfect world of justice – and man's will. That dialectics embodies in a single paradigm the events contained in the sequences, rebellion, sin, punishment, repentance, and atonement; exile and return; or the disruption of world order and the restoration of world order. None of these categories and propositions is new; anyone familiar with the principal components of the faith and piety of Judaism, the Written Torah, the Oral Torah, and the liturgy of home and synagogue, will find them paramount.

Let me set forth a somewhat more elaborate synopsis of the same story in these few, still-simple propositions, the four principles of the theology of the Oral Torah.

1. God formed creation in accord with a plan, which the Torah reveals. World order can be shown by the facts of nature and society set forth in that plan to conform to a pattern of reason based upon justice. Those who possess the Torah – Israel – know God and those who do not – the gentiles – reject him in favor of idols. What happens to each of the two sectors of humanity, respectively, responds to their relationship with God. Israel in the present age is subordinate to the nations, because God has designated the gentiles as the medium for penalizing Israel's rebellion, meaning through Israel's subordination and exile to provoke Israel to repent. Private life as much as the public order conforms to the principle that God rules justly in a creation of perfection and stasis.
2. The perfection of creation, realized in the rule of exact justice, is signified by the timelessness of the world of human affairs, their conformity to a few enduring paradigms that transcend change (theology of history). No present, past, or future marks time, but only the recapitulation of those patterns. Perfection is further embodied in the unchanging relationships of the social commonwealth (theology of political economy), which assure that scarce resources, once allocated, remain in stasis. A further indication of perfection lies in the complementarity of the components of creation, on the one side, and, finally, the correspondence between God and man, in God's image (theological anthropology), on the other.
3. Israel's condition, public and personal, marks flaws in creation. What disrupts perfection is the sole power capable of standing on its own against God's power, and that is man's will. What man controls and God cannot coerce is man's capacity to form intention and therefore choose either arrogantly to defy, or humbly to love, God. Because man defies God, the sin that results from man's rebellion flaws creation and disrupts world order. The paradigm of the rebellion of Adam in Eden governs, the act of arrogant rebellion leading to exile from Eden thus accounting for the condition of humanity. But, as in the original transaction of alienation and consequent exile, God retains the power to encourage repentance through punishing man's arrogance. In mercy, moreover, God exercises the power to respond to repentance with forgiveness, that is, a change of attitude evoking a counterpart change. Since, commanding his own will, man also has the power to initiate the process of reconciliation with God, through repentance, an act of humility, man may restore the perfection of that order that through arrogance he has marred.
4. God ultimately will restore that perfection that embodied his plan for creation. In the work of restoration death that comes about by reason of sin will die, the dead will be raised and judged for their deeds in this life, and most of them, having been justified, will go on to eternal life in

the world to come. In the paradigm of man restored to Eden is realized in Israel's return to the Land of Israel. In that world or age to come, however, that sector of humanity that through the Torah knows God will encompass all of humanity. Idolators will perish, and humanity that comprises Israel at the end will know the one, true God and spend eternity in his light.

Now, recorded in this way, the story told by the Oral Torah proves remarkably familiar, with its stress on God's justice (to which his mercy is integral), man's correspondence with God in his possession of the power of will, man's sin and God's response.

If we translate into the narrative of Israel, from the beginning to the calamity of the destruction of the (first) Temple, what is set forth in both abstract and concrete ways in the Oral Torah, we turn out to state a reprise of the narrative of the Hebrew Scriptures, the Authorized History laid out in Genesis through Kings and amplified by the principal prophets. Specifically, I shall try to show, principal components of the halakhah of Rabbinic Judaism recapitulate and respond to the narrative of Genesis 1ff., the story of the fall of Man. Scripture's account of Man's fall from grace imposes upon the human condition the tragic vision of paradise lost.[1] The narrative of how things begin compels the question, how to restore Eden? The sages respond, Israel will build in the Land of Israel a social order to embody Eden, to restore humanity to Eden in the embodiment of holy Israel in the Land.

Now the ancient sages of Judaism are not the only heirs of Israelite Scripture to identify as the critical issue of Scripture the fall of Man. Responding to the picture set forth in Genesis, and, really from Genesis through Kings, the greatest intellects of Christianity and of Judaism through the history of the civilization framed by ancient Israelite Scripture have taken Man's fate as the critical issue of reflection. Specifically, profound theological minds, whatever the medium they have chosen to convey their conception of Man's fate and responsibility therefor, have reworked Scripture's vision of Man. That vision focused upon Adam and Eve created for eternity in Eden but fallen from grace by reason of rebellion against God's will. For its part, the halakhah of the Oral Torah, based upon deep foundations in the Written Torah, provides for the formation of an entire social order meant to realize in the here and now the reconciliation of God and Man, now through Israel's restoration of Eden in the Land. Then Eden forms the metaphor and the model, the fall the mythic provocation, the halakhah in detail embodies

---

[1] In these pages "Man," stands for man and woman, and I interchangeably use mankind or humanity. Then "man," with a small m, refers to the male of the species, alongside "women" to the female.

The Shape of Judaism

the systematic response, its theology of social regeneration and restoration defines the systemic center.[2]

The theology of the halakhah, the corpus of law set forth by ancient Judaism in the Written Torah (a.k.a., "the Old Testament") and the consequent Oral Torah comprised by the Mishnah, Tosefta, and two Talmuds, commences with one such vision of Eden and its aftermath as the meaning of Man. With Eden as its starting point, I shall show, the halakhah draws out the deepest implications of the narrative of Scripture and its laws, moving forward from them point by point; the halakhah then reads Scripture as the account of loss and restoration. It is unique in that it makes provision for the restoration of Eden by Man. In line with Scripture's plain message, the halakhah explores the requirements of the restoration within the social formation of Israel in the Land of Israel. The halakhah of the Oral Torah systematically transforms particular topics into occasions for profound reflection upon principles, most of them to do with the sanctification of life. That is to say, the halakhah brings about transformation of the here and the now and occasion (place and time and event, mostly in nature) into the embodiment, the exemplification, of the abstract ground of being. Involved is relationship of realms of the sacred: the rules of engagement between and among God, Land, Israel, time, place, circumstance. In these pages I shall show that the halakhah sets forth a systematic and coherent response to the tragic situation of Man, a response that works itself out in the governance of practical matters of time, place, and circumstance.

Specifically, through the provision of norms of conduct and conviction such as Scripture itself sets forth or logically invites, the halakhah lays out an account of how the entire social order may be constructed to realize Eden once more. That restoration comes about not in the end of days when the Messiah comes, but in the here-and-now of the workaday world. It is there that Israelite Man formed by the discipline of the Torah overcomes his natural propensity willfully to rebel against God. Within the social order of an enlandised Israel moral man constructs a godly society. That reading of the Written Torah and translation of its law into the canons of ordinary life speaks in the acutely-present tense to portray for Man a worthy future well within Man's own capacities to realize: "the Torah was given only to purify the heart of man," and "God wants the heart," as the Talmud frames matters.

---

[2]In the companion work, *Judaic Law from Moses to the Mishnah*, I argue that the basic structure and system of the halakhah of the Oral Torah represents a close and accurate reading of the Written Torah, with special reference to Genesis through Kings.

That theology of the halakhah viewed whole and in detail as an exercise in the restoration of Eden is the proposition set forth in these pages. Here I shall show that, like the Apostle Paul's masterpiece, his Letter to the Romans, with its tragic vision ("...as sin came into the world through one man and death through sin...", reminiscent of Fourth Ezra's "Oh Adam, what hast thou done!"), like Augustine's *City of God*, like Michelangelo's Last Judgment in the Sistine Chapel, and like John Milton's *Paradise Lost*, – to name just four counterparts to the halakhah – the halakhah of the Oral Torah responds to the human condition set forth in Scripture's account the loss of Eden and the fault and fall of Man. To all the heirs of Scripture Genesis records the nature and destiny of Man and sets the issues for reflection. But among all scripturally-founded constructions out of the vision of Man's tragedy the Oral Torah's stands quite by itself.

That is because of its immediacy and practicality. The halakhah embodies the unique mode of thought conducted by the great sages of Judaism in its formative age, its concrete practicality, its insistence upon deed as the medium of deliberation. The Judaic sages thought deeply but valued thought only by reason of its practical power to change Man: "study of the Torah takes priority, because study leads to concrete deed," they decided. That is why the halakhah – much of it a matter of theory at the time at which it was given the formulation we now have, from ca. 200 to ca. 600 C.E. – forms an account of how the very social fabric of Man may be formed of a tapestry of right deeds to yield Eden within the very material of the ordinary and the everyday.

For sages deliberation alone did not do, though, as we shall see, their account of deeds to be done in the quest for human regeneration rests upon deep layers of profound reflection indeed. Like Plato in the *Republic*, the sages conducted their thought through legislating the design of Israel's social order. Unlike Plato they actively aimed to realize in everyday affairs the principles of their theory of matters. Augustine told the story of the social order through history, Scripture's history. For their part the Judaic sages wrote their *City of God* in law. In contemplating issues strikingly congruent to those addressed in the salvific program of Paul in Romans,[3] it was through not theoretical theological reflections but practical rulings on the construction of the holy society that they conducted their inquiry into the logic of Man's fate and what is required for his redemption. And, in the nature of their

---

[3]Within the theology of the halakhah set forth here, one could make the case that the halakhah represents a systematic theological Auseinandersetzung with Romans, but to spell out exactly how that is so would prove disproportionate to what is at stake in these pages.

The Shape of Judaism

writings, sages produced few word-pictures, though their halakhic writings adhered to a remarkably powerful aesthetics, both in form and in intellectual elegance.

Note the contrast. The great tragic theologians of Christianity, Paul and Augustine, produced profound reflection. The counterpart artists, Michelangelo and Milton, conveyed the Fall through art and poetry, through eye and ear and intellect responding to the tragic moment of Eden and its aftermath. But none but the Judaic sages conceived of responding to the generalities of the human condition by defining the particular character of an entire social order, its norms of conviction and conduct, its culture embodied in rules of behavior and belief. In their mind, the very character of the community as constructed by concrete laws would form a commentary upon Man and the loss of Eden – a response to Eden but also a remedy for the rebellion that reduced Man to his and her present estrangement from God. Had they wished to argue that the salvation of Man from the condition of the sin that brought about the fall would come about through law – the laws of the Torah in particular – they could not have framed a more compelling, and, in their context, a more eloquent statement than they did through the logic and exegesis of the halakhah.

The sages of the halakhic, or legal, system for the practical conduct of holy Israel's social order in the Mishnah and Talmuds defined as the remedy for the rebellion at Eden the practicalities of quotidian life of an entire community. Israel would embody the City of God, for Mankind Israel would accomplish corporately what for Paul's Christianity one man is supposed to have done. In the Torah, as they portrayed the Torah, the system of norms of behavior meant to realize within the social order the norms of belief set forth by the sages of Judaism responded to the tragedy of the Fall – the starting point of the entire system – and the promise of restoration – the climax of its structure. This they did by defining the labor of social renewal, relating the rules of regeneration in the exact sense.

How, exactly, in the halakhah do sages set forth their account of the Fall and Man's hope? Like their counterparts among all heirs of Scripture, the Judaic sages accounted for creation and the condition of humankind, beginning to end, by appealing to the Torah's narrative of Man, from Genesis forward. How does the sages' Judaism seek to restore Eden and to put Adam and Eve back into Paradise? This it does by treating Israel, the people, as surrogates for and continuators of Man but with the difference marked by the Torah. Israel, formed by those who will love God and carry out his will, as Adam and Eve did not possess the potential to restore Eden. This they can and should do by turning Israel, first of all the enlandised part in the Land of Israel, into Eden, now defined as the sector of humanity and the segment of the territory of humanity that are fully permeated by God's will in the Torah, as God's choice for the renewed Eden. That account of Israel as Adam's successor, the Land as the stead of Eden, carries us far from the mundane realities of contemporary politics and wars. The sages' Judaism set forth a system that treats the holy people Israel as counterpart but ultimately opposite to Adam. Adam lived in Eden but rebelled against God and was driven out. Israel lived in the Land of Israel and for a brief moment, upon entry, Israel recapitulated Eden. But as the Torah (Scripture) says in the authorized history from Genesis through Kings, Israel rebelled against God and was driven out. But what distinguishes Israel from Adam is that Israel possessed the Torah, which held the power to transform the heart of man and so turn man from rebellion to loving submission. And when the Israelite man, regenerate in the Torah, fully conformed to the Torah, then Israel would recover its Eden, the Land of Israel.

This account of matters is not merely implicit in the Written Torah from Genesis through Kings but made explicit in the sages' own writings. That statement is made in so many words. Here the Land of Israel to Israel is like Eden to Adam, and the story of the two are the same, with the difference that Israel, driven from the Land, can return through the way of the Torah. Here is one version of how the metaphor of Eden is invoked for Israel – as the narrative of Scripture read as a continuity itself portrays matters:

1. A. R. Abbahu in the name of R. Yosé bar Haninah commenced [discourse by citing this verse]: "'But they are like a man, they have transgressed the covenant. There they dealt treacherously against me "(Hos. 6:7).
   B. "They are like a man, specifically, this refers to the first man [Adam]. [We shall now compare the story of the first man in Eden with the story of Israel in its land.]
   C. "Said the Holy One, blessed be He, 'In the case of the first man, I brought him into the garden of Eden, I commanded him, he violated my commandment, I judged him to be sent away and driven out, but I mourned for him, saying "How..."'[which begins the book of Lamentations, hence stands for a lament, but which also is written with the consonants that also yield, Where are you].
   D. "'I brought him into the garden of Eden,' as it is written, 'And the Lord God took the man and put him into the garden of Eden' (Gen. 2:15).
   E. "'I commanded him,' as it is written, 'And the Lord God commanded...' (Gen. 2:16).
   F. "'And he violated my commandment,' as it is written, 'Did you eat from the tree concerning which I commanded you' (Gen. 3:11).
   G. "'I judged him to be sent away,' as it is written, 'And the Lord God sent him from the garden of Eden' (Gen. 3:23).
   H. "'And I judged him to be driven out.' 'And he drove out the man' (Gen. 3:24).

The Shape of Judaism

I. "'But I mourned for him, saying, How….' And He said to him, 'Where are you' (Gen. 3:9), and the word for 'where are you' is written, 'How….'

J. "'So too in the case of his descendants, [God continues to speak,] I brought them into the Land of Israel, I commanded them, they violated my commandment, I judged them to be sent out and driven away but I mourned for them, saying, How….'

K. "'I brought them into the Land of Israel:' 'And I brought you into the land of Carmel' (Jer. 2:7).

L. "'I commanded them: ' 'And you, command the children of Israel' (Ex. 27:20). 'command the children of Israel' (Lev. 24:2).

M. "'They violated my commandment:' 'And all Israel have violated your Torah' (Dan. 9:11).

N. "'I judged them to be sent out:' 'Send them away, out of my sight and let them go forth' (Jer. 15:1).

O. "'….and driven away:' 'From my house I shall drive them' (Hos. 9:15).

P. "'But I mourned for them, saying, How…:' 'How lonely sits the city [that was full of people! How like a widow has she become, she that was great among the nations! She that was a princess among the cities has become a vassal. She weeps bitterly in the night, tears on her cheeks, among all her lovers she has none to comfort her; all her friends have dealt treacherously with her, they have become her enemies]' (Lamentations 1:1-2)."

Lamentations Rabbati IV.i.1

Israel represents the new Adam, God's way of correcting the errors of the initial creation. The Land of Israel stands for the new Eden. Just as Adam entered a perfect world but lost it, so Israel was given a perfect world – in repose at the moment of Israel's entry – but sinning against God, lost it. The difference, however, is that Israel has what Adam did not have, which is the Torah, a point that does not enter here except by indirection. The Torah's theory of who is man and what God wants of man leave no unclarity. What God craves is man's willing submission to God's will, made known in the Torah, beginning with the drama, for which the halakhah legislates, of the proclamation of God's unity: *Hear, Israel, the Lord our God is unique. And you shall love the Lord your God with all your heart, with all your soul, and with all your might.*

The restoration of Israel to the Land then forms a chapter in the story of the redemption of all of mankind. The last things are to be known from the first. In the just plan of creation man was meant to live in Eden, and Israel in the Land of Israel in time without end. The restoration to the Land will bring about that long and tragically-postponed perfection of the world order, sealing the demonstration of the justice of God's plan for creation. Risen from the dead, having atoned through death, man will be judged in accord with his deeds. Israel for its part, when it repents and conforms its will to God's, recovers its Eden. So the consequences of rebellion and sin having been overcome, the struggle of man's will and

God's word having been resolved, God's original plan will be realized at the last. The simple, global logic of the system, with its focus on the world order of justice established by God but disrupted by man, leads inexorably to this eschatology of restoration, the restoration of balance, order, proportion – eternity. Holy Israel, the people defined theologically and not politically, then assembles at prayer and expresses the hope that, in the end of days, God will call all humanity to his worship, as, even now, he has called holy Israel. Then everyone will acknowledge the sovereignty of the one and only God and accept his dominion.

But the halakhah legislates not for the Messiah's time but for ours. Its norms prove immediate and speak to the acutely present moment. When we ask, when and how is this supposed to take place? we find our way to the practical halakhah set forth by the sages of ancient Judaism. The time is the present, the hour immediate. In accord with the Judaic sages' account of the consequence of building the social order in accord with the halakhah of the Torah, Man – Adam and Eve – thereby would find the counterpart in Israel, and Eden, in the Land of Israel. How then does the past figure? Like Man, Israel at the moment of its creation entered the Land and found perfection like Eden's: all things arrayed in perfect repose. But Israel, like Man, had sinned and had lost the Land, its Eden. So the story of Joshua and Judges matches the tale of Genesis 1-3. But the revelation of Sinai intervenes. That is why it follows, through realizing the law of the Torah, Israel would regain its Paradise. For, granted what Man had missed, which is the Torah, and guided by the Torah, holy Israel would restore Eden. This it would do in the Land that God had given it for Eden but that had been lost to sin. And the Torah, setting forth the halakhah, the rules for the social order of restored Eden, would make of Israel, even sinful Israel, ever so capable of rebellion against God's will just as Adam was, a worth occupant of the Eden that the Land was meant to be, had been for a brief moment, and would once again become.

So much for the large theory of matters, yielding the theology of the halakhah. That theology holds together the details of the rules of concrete behavior together and frames of them a systematic statement of how holy Israel through the correct conduct of ordinary life will restore Man to Eden through Israel's formation in the Land. That is what is at stake in the halakhah: the formation of the entire social order through legal norms to regain Paradise. To revert to the counterpart exercises introduced at the outset – Paul, Augustine, Michelangelo, and Milton – the halakhah therefore would form the medium of a profound theological reflection written for the suffering faithful, such as in brief Paul produced. And – I cannot overstress – that observation vastly transcends generalities and rises to the specificities of ordinary affairs. In light of Paul's insistence upon the inadequacy of the law to deal with the condition of Man's sinfulness, it was as though they read Romans, with its contrast of salvation by faith and by Torah.

It was through the halakhah that the sages chose to show that, in the very context of the crisis of Man's fall, the Torah would bring about in the here and now of everyday life that very regeneration that, in Paul's system, faith was meant to accomplish. In light of the workaday world for which sages legislated, moreover, it was as if they had read the City of God and undertook to show the Bishop of Hippo how to accomplish in the visible and tangible world the realization of the promise of citizenship in an unseen city. And, were they to have spread forth before the poet the artful language that conveys the halakhah in the Mishnah, they might have said to him, "Here, here is Paradise recovered, these are its natural sounds, the Mishnah to be memorized like your poem" and to the artist, "Paint this – this picture of the world in repose, of Man regenerate, of Eden restored: 'Paint what Balaam found himself impelled to see: "For from the top of the mountain I see him, from the hills I behold him; lo, a people dwelling alone (Num. 23:9).""" Paul, Augustine, Michelangelo, Milton worked in solitary splendor to frame a vision. Only the sages of Judaism undertook to render palpable and tangible Man's hope for his restoration in Eden.

II. Eden and the Land

"Thus the heavens and the earth were finished and all the host of them. And on the seventh day God finished his work that he had done, and he rested on the seventh day from all his work that he had done. So God blessed the seventh day and sanctified it, because on it God rested from all his work that he had done in creation."
Genesis 2:1-3

By Eden Scripture means, that place whole and at rest that God sanctified, creation in perfect repose. In the halakhah Eden then stands for not a particular place but nature in a defined condition, at a particular moment: creation in Sabbath repose, sanctified. Then a place in repose at the climax of creation, at sunset at the start of the seventh day, whole and at rest, embodies, realizes Eden. How does the halakhah localize that place? Eden is the place to the perfection of which God responded in the act of sanctification at the advent of the seventh day. Where is that place? Here as elsewhere, the halakhah accommodates itself to both the enlandised and the utopian condition of Israel, the people. So, on the one hand, that place is the Land of Israel. The halakhah of the Oral Torah finds in Scripture ample basis for identifying with the Land of Israel that place perfected on the Sabbath. It is the Land that claims the right to repose on the seventh day and in the seventh year of the septennial cycle.

But it is the location of Israel wherever that may be. We begin with enlandised Israel, that is, the Land of Israel, at the moment at which, then and there, Eden was made real: when Israel entered into the Land at the moment of perfection. That moment recovered, Eden is restored – the correct starting point, therefore, for a theology of the halakhah that claims the whole holds together as a systematically-restorationist theology.

That is the explicit position of the halakhah of Shebi'it, the prohibitions of the Seventh Year, the halakhah in the Mishnah that elaborates the Written Torah's commandment, at Lev. 25:1-8:

> "When you enter the land that I am giving you, the land shall observe a Sabbath of the Lord. Six years you may sow your field and six years you may prune your vineyard and bather in the yield. But in the seventh year the land shall have a Sabbath of complete rest, a Sabbath of the Lord; you shall not sow your field or prune your vineyard. You shall not reap the aftergrowth of your harvest or gather the grapes of your untrimmed vines; it shall ba a year of complete rest for the land. But you may eat whatever the land during its Sabbath will produce – you, your male and female slaves, the hired-hand and bound laborers who live with you, and your cattle and the beasts in your land may eat all its yield."

Sages thus find in Scripture the explicit correlation of the advent of the Sabbath and the condition of the Land, meaning, "the land that I am giving you," which is to say, the Land of Israel. After six years of creation, the Land is owed a Sabbath, as much as is Man. A second, correlative commandment, at Dt. 15:1-3, is treated as well: "Every seventh year you shall practice remission of debts. This shall be the nature of the remission: every creditor shall remit the due that he claims from his neighbor; he shall not dun his neighbor or kinsman, for the remission proclaimed is of the Lord. You may dun the foreigner, but you must remit whatever is due you from your kinsmen."

The Torah represents God as the sole master of creation, the Sabbath as testimony to God's pleasure with the perfection, and therefore sanctification, of creation. The halakhah of Shebi'it sets forth the law that in relationship to the Land of Israel embodies that conviction. The law set forth in the Mishnah, Tosefta, and Talmud of the Land of Israel systematically works through Scripture's rules, treating [1] the prohibition of farming the land during the seventh year; [2] the use of the produce in the seventh year solely for eating, that is to say, its purpose and function by its very nature; and [3] the remission of debts. During the Sabbatical year, Israel relinquishes its ownership of the Land of Israel. So the Sabbath involves giving up ownership, a point to which we shall return later in this chapter. At that time Israelites in farming may do nothing that in secular years effects the assertion of ownership over the land (Avery-Peck, *Yerushalmi Shebi'it*, p. 2). Just as one may not utilize land he does not own, in the Sabbatical year, the farmer gives up ownership of the land that he does own.

What links the Sabbatical Year to Eden's restoration? The reason is clear: the Sabbatical Year recovers that perfect time of Eden when the world was at rest, all things in place. Before the rebellion, man did not have to labor on the land; he picked and ate his meals freely. And, in the nature of things, everything belonged to everybody; private ownership in response to individual labor did not exist, because man did not have to work anyhow. These then represent the halakhah's provisions for the Seventh Year. Reverting to that perfect time, the Torah maintains that the land will provide adequate food for everyone, including the flocks and herds, even – or especially – if people do not work the land. But that is on condition that all claim of ownership lapses; the food is left in the fields, to be picked by anyone who wishes, but it may not be hoarded by the landowner in particular. Avery-Peck (Avery-Peck, *Yerushalmi Shebi'it*, p. 3).states this matter as follows:

> Scripture thus understands the Sabbatical year to represent a return to a perfected order of reality, in which all share equally in the bounty of a holy land that yields its food without human labor. The Sabbatical year provides a model through which, once every seven years, Israelites living in the here-and-now may enjoy the perfected order in which God always intended the world to exist and toward which, in the Israelite world view, history indeed is moving...The release of debts accomplishes for Israelites' economic relationships just what the agricultural Sabbatical accomplishes for the relationship between the people and the land. Eradicating debt allows the Israelite economy to return to the state of equilibrium that existed at the time of creation, when all shared equally in the bounty of the Land.

The Priestly Code expresses that same concept when it arranges for the return of inherited property at the Jubilee Year to the original family-ownership:

> "You shall count off seven weeks of years, so that the period of seven weeks of years gives you a total of forty-nine years...You shall proclaim release throughout the land for all its inhabitants. It shall be a jubilee for you; each of you shall return to his holding and each of you shall return to his family"
> Leviticus 25:8-10

The Jubilee year is observed as is the Sabbatical year, meaning that for two successive years the land is not to be worked. The halakhah we shall examine in due course will establish that when land is sold, it is for the span of time remaining to the next jubilee year. That then marks the reordering of land-holding to its original pattern, when Israel inherited the land to begin with and commenced to enjoy its produce.

Just as the Sabbath commemorates the completion of creation, the perfection of world-order, so does the Sabbatical year. So too, the Jubilee year brings about the restoration of real property to the original division. In both instances, Israelites so act as to indicate they are not absolute owners of the Land, which belongs to God and which is divided in the manner that God arranged in perpetuity. Avery-Peck states the matter in the following way (Avery-Peck, *Yerushalmi*, p. 4):

> On the Sabbath of creation, during the Sabbatical year, and in the Jubilee year, diverse aspects of Israelite life are to return to the way that they were at the time of creation. Israelites thus acknowledge that, in the beginning, God created a perfect world, and they assure that the world of the here-and-now does not overly shift from its perfect character. By providing opportunities for Israelites to model their contemporary existence upon a perfected order of things, these commemorations further prepare the people for messianic times, when, under God's rule, the world will permanently revert to the ideal character of the time of creation.

Here we find the halakhic counterpart to the restorationist theology that the Oral Torah sets forth in the aggadah. Israel matches Adam, the Land of Israel, Eden, and, we now see, the Sabbatical year commemorates the perfection of creation and replicates it. (Later in this chapter we shall see that the same conception of relinquishing ownership of one's real property operates to facilitate everyday activities on the Sabbath.)

The Sabbatical year takes effect at the moment of Israel's entry into the Land. That repeated point of insistence then treats the moment of the entry into the Land as the counterpart to the moment of repose, of perfection at rest, of Creation. Observing the commandments of the Sabbatical year marks Israel's effort at keeping the Land like Eden, six days of creation, one day of rest, and so too here:

Sifra CCXLV:

I.2. A. "When you come [into the land which I give you, the land shall keep a Sabbath to the Lord]":
    B. Might one suppose that the sabbatical year was to take effect once they had reached Transjordan?
    C. Scripture says, "into the land."
    D. It is that particular land.

Now comes the key point: the Sabbatical year takes effect only when Israel enters the Land, which is to say, Israel's entry into the Land marks the counterpart to the beginning of the creation of Eden. But a further point will register in a moment. It is when Eden/the Land enters into stasis, the families receiving each its share in the Land, that the process of the formation of the new Eden comes to its climax; then each Israelite bears responsibility for his share of the Land. That is when the Land has reached that state of order and permanence that corresponds to Eden at sunset on the sixth day:

> E. Might one suppose that the sabbatical year was to take effect once they had reached Ammon and Moab?
> F. Scripture says, "which I give you,"
> G. and not to Ammon and Moab.
> H. And on what basis do you maintain that when they had conquered the land but not divided it, divided it among familiars but not among fathers' houses so that each individual does not yet recognize his share –
> I. might one suppose that they should be responsible to observe the sabbatical year?
> J. Scripture says, "[Six years you shall sow] your field,"
> K. meaning, each one should recognize his own field.
> L. "...your vineyard":
> M. meaning, each one should recognize his own vineyard.
> N. You turn out to rule:
> O. Once the Israelites had crossed the Jordan, they incurred liability to separate dough-offering and to observe the prohibition against eating the fruit of fruit trees for the first three years after planting and the prohibition against eating produce of the new growing season prior to the waving of the sheaf of new grain [that is, on the fifteenth of Nisan].[4]
> P. When the sixteenth of Nisan came, they incurred liability to wave the sheaf of new grain.
> Q. With the passage of fifty days from then they incurred the liability to the offering of the Two Loaves.
> R. At the fourteenth year they became liable for the separation of tithes.

The Sabbatical takes over only when the Israelite farmers have asserted their ownership of the land and its crops. Then the process of counting the years begins.

In relationship to God, the Land of Israel, as much as the People of Israel, emerges as a principal player. The Land is treated as a living entity, a participant in the cosmic drama, as well it should, being the scene of creation and its unfolding. If the perfection of creation is the well-ordered condition of the natural world, then the Land of Israel, counterpart to Eden, must be formed into the model of the initial perfection, restored to that initial condition. So the Sabbath takes over and enchants the Land of Israel as much as it transforms Israel itself. Newman expresses this view in the following language (Newman, *Shebi'it*, p. 15):

---

[4]Bold-face type signifies the origin of the designated, coherent composition in the Mishnah or the Tosefta, then its insertion whole into Sifra.

> For the priestly writer of Leviticus, the seventh year, like the seventh day, is sanctified. Just as God rested from the work of creation on the seventh day and sanctified it as a day of rest, so too God has designated the seventh year for the land's rest. Implicit in this view is the notion that the Land of Israel has human qualities and needs. It must 'observe a Sabbath of the Lord' because, like the people of Israel and God, it too experiences fatigue and requires a period of repose. The Land of Israel, unlike all other countries, is enchanted, for it enjoys a unique relationship to God and to the people of Israel. That is to say, God sanctified this land by giving it to his chosen people as an exclusive possession. Israelites, in turn, are obligated to work the Land and to handle its produce in accordance with God's wishes...

The counterpart in the matter of the remission of debts works out the conception that all Israelites by right share in the Land and its gifts, and if they have fallen into debt, they have been denied their share; that imbalance is righted every seven years.

The halakhah outlines where and how man participates in establishing the sanctity of the Sabbatical year, expanding the span of the year to accommodate man's intentionality in working the land now for advantage then. It insists that man's perceptions of the facts, not the facts themselves, govern: what looks like a law violation *is* a law violation. In these and other ways the halakhah of Shebi'it works out the problematics of man's participation in the sanctification of the Land in the Sabbatical year. The topic of the law, restoring the perfection of creation, then joins with the generative problematics of the halakhah to make the point that Israel has in its power to restore the perfection of creation, the ordering of all things to accord with the condition that prevailed when God declared creation good. God, therefore sanctified creation and declared the Sabbath. The particular topic served as the obvious, indeed the ideal, medium to deliver in the context of that message of restoration the critical statement. It is that Israel by a fulfilled act of will bore within its power the capacity to attain the perfection of the world. That is because to begin with Israel's perception of matters – and its actions consequent upon those perceptions – made all the difference.

God pays the closest attention to Israel's attitudes and intentions. Otherwise there is no way to explain the priority accorded to Israelite perception of whether or not the law is kept, Israelite intention in cultivating the fields in the sixth year, and other critical components of the governing, generative problematic. God furthermore identifies the Land of Israel as the archetype of Eden and model of the world to come. That is why God treats the Land in its perfection just as he treats Eden, by according to the Land the Sabbath rest. He deems the union of Israel and the Land of Israel to effect the sanctification of the Land in its ascending degrees corresponding to the length of the term of Israel's possession. And, finally, God insists, as the ultimate owner of the Land, that at regular intervals, the possession of the Land be relinquished, signaled as null, and that at those same intervals ownership of the produce of the Land at least in potentiality be equally shared among all its inhabitants.

2

Systematizing Eden

Jacob Neusner
University of South Florida and Bard College

How is the narrative of Eden and the fall, extending to the formation of Israel as the medium of mankind's regeneration, translated into a system for the governance of the social order? Within the metaphor of Eden and Adam, the Land stands for Eden, Israel the holy people for Adam. Then God relates to Israel through the Land and the arrangements that he imposes upon the Land, beginning with the point of intersection, rules governing the use of the fruit of the trees of the Land. We cannot come closer to the realization of the metaphor of Eden than that! In that context God relates to the Land in response to Israel's residence thereon. But God relates to the Land in a direct way, providing for the Land, as he provides for Israel, the sanctifying moment of the Sabbath. So a web of relationships, direct and indirect, hold together God, Land, and Israel. That is for the here-and-now, all the more so for the world to come. And if that is how God relates to Israel, Israel relates to God in one way above all, and that is, by exercising in ways that show love for God and acceptance of God's dominion the power of free will that God has given man. That brings us to a natural companion of the halakhah of Shebi'it, which is that of 'Orlah – the necessary second step in this exposition of how the halakhah effects the restoration of Eden.

I. Remembering the Fruit of the Forbidden Tree
The Halakhah of the Use of the Produce of a Fruit Tree
in the Fourth Year after its Planting

Devoted to the prohibition of the use of the produce of a fruit tree for the first three years after its planting and the restriction as to the use of that same tree's produce in the fourth year after its planting, the halakhah of 'Orlah elaborates the Torah's commandment, at Lev. 19:23-25:

> "When you come to the land and plant any kind of tree for food, you shall treat it as forbidden. For three years it shall be forbidden, it shall not be eaten. In the fourth year all its fruit shall be set aside for jubilation before the Lord, and only in the fifth year may you use its fruit, that its yield to you may be increased: I am the Lord your God."

The produce of the fourth year after planting is brought to Jerusalem ("for jubilation before the Lord") and eaten there. But the main point of the halakhah centers upon the prohibition of the fruit for the first three years.

In the halakhah, the role of man in precipitating the effect of the prohibition takes priority. Man has a role in bringing about the prohibition of the law, but man cannot by his intentionality change the facts of the case. How does the Israelite farmer's intentionality govern? It is man's assessment of the use of the tree that classifies the tree as a fruit-tree or as a tree of some other category, e.g., one meant for lumber. If man deems the tree planted for fruit, then the prohibition applies. But man cannot declare as a fruit-tree, so subjecting the produce to the prohibition for three years from planting, one that does not bear fruit at all. Man's actions reveal his original intentionality for the tree, e.g., how the tree is planted.

Here is an explicit statement, in connection with the exegesis of the halakhah, that intentionality dictates whether or not a tree that can bear fruit actually is covered by the prohibition. Trees not used for fruit are not affected by the prohibition, so the farmer may use the lumber even in the first three years from planting; and parts of trees not intended for fruit are not subject to it either, so may be pruned off and used for fuel. But intention cannot classify what nature has already designated for one or another category. In the following, Simeon b. Gamaliel refines the law by insisting that man's intention conform to the facts of nature. That is to say, if one planted a tree for lumber or firewood but it is not appropriate for such a use, then his intentionality is null.

7.   A.   "...trees for food":
      B.   this excludes the case of **planting trees for fence posts or lumber or firewood.**
      C.   **R. Yosé says, "Even if he said, 'The side of the tree facing inward is to be used for food and the side outward is to be used as a fence, the side of the tree inward is liable to the laws of 'orlah, and the side of the tree facing outward is exempt"** [M. Orlah 1:1A-D].
      D.   Said Rabban Simeon b. Gamaliel, "Under what circumstances? When he planted it as a fence for lumber or for firewood, a use appropriate for those trees. But when he planted it as a fence, for lumber, or for

Systematizing Eden

firewood in a case not appropriate for that species, the tree is liable to the laws of 'orlah" [T. Orl 1:1C-H].
E. How do we know the law given just now?
F. Scripture says, "all kinds of trees."

The matter of appropriateness will recur many times, since the intense interest of the halakhah in the correct classification of things comes to expression in an interesting notion. A thing has its inherent, intrinsic purpose, and when it serves that purpose, it is properly used; when not, it is improperly used. How does that make a difference? What is edible is food, and produce that may serve for food or for fuel, if it is of a sacred status, cannot be used for anything but food. So intentionality meets its limits in the purpose that a thing is supposed to serve, that is to say, intentionality is limited by teleology. That explains why, also, if the farmer planted the tree for firewood and changed his mind, then the change of his intentionality effects a change in the status of the tree:

G. **If he planted it for firewood and then gave thought to use the tree for food, how do we know that it is liable?**
H. **Scripture says, "And you will plant every kind of fruit tree."**
I. **From what point do they count the years of the tree for purposes of determining liability to 'orlah?**
J. **From the time that it is planted [T. Orl. 1:1I-L].**

The connection of the tree to the land dictates liability; a fruit-tree planted in an unperforated pot is exempt from the law. The law extends not only to the whole fruit but also to defective produce and parts of the fruit. And what is interesting, when the farmer initially plants the tree marks the starting point for reckoning the three years, not when he decided to use it for fruit rather than lumber. In that case, the actuality takes over and sets aside the intentionality. The farmer's initial intent may classify the tree as other-than-a-fruit-tree, but the potentiality as a fruit-tree persists, so when the farmer's second thoughts take over. the initial status of the tree, not the intervening one, is what counts, a very profound way of seeing the matter, rich in potential consequences that are not explored here.

The power of the metaphor of Eden emerges, we shall now see, in specificities of the law. These turn out to define with some precision a message on the relationship of Israel to the Land of Israel and to God. If we turn to Sifra, a systematic exegesis of the book of Leviticus in dialogue with the halakhah of the Mishnah, at Sifra CCII:I.1, our attention is drawn to a number of quite specific traits of the law of 'Orlah, and these make explicit matters of religious conviction that we might otherwise miss. The first is that the prohibition of 'orlah-fruit applies solely within the Land of Israel and not to the neighboring territories occupied by Israelites, which means that, once again, it is the union of Israel with the Land of Israel that invokes the prohibition:

Sifra CCII:

I.1. A. "When you come [into the land and plant all kinds of trees for food, then you shall count their fruit as forbidden; three years it shall be forbidden to you, it must not be eaten. And in the fourth year all their fruit shall be holy, an offering of praise to the Lord. But in the fifth year you may eat of their fruit, that they may yield more richly for you: I am the Lord your God" (Lev. 19:23-25).]
B. Might one suppose that the law applied once they came to Transjordan?
C. Scripture says, "...into the land,"
D. the particular Land [of Israel].

What that means is that some trait deemed to inhere in the Land of Israel and no other territory must define the law, and a particular message ought to inhere in this law.

This same point registers once more: it is only trees that Israelites plant in the Land that are subject to the prohibition, not those that gentiles planted before the Israelites inherited the land:

Sifra CCII:

I.2. A. "When you come into the land and plant":
B. excluding those that gentiles have planted prior to the Israelites' coming into the land.
C. Or should I then exclude those that gentiles planted even after the Israelites came into the land?
D. Scripture says, "all kinds of trees."

A further point of special interest requires that the Israelite plant the tree as an act of deliberation; if the tree merely grows up on its own, it is not subject to the prohibition. So Israelite action joined to Israelite intention is required:

Sifra CCII:

I.4. A. "...and plant...":
B. excluding one that grows up on its own.
C. "...and plant...":
D. excluding one that grows out of a grafting or sinking a root.

The several points on which Sifra's reading of the halakhah and the verses of Scripture that declare the halakhah alert us to a very specific religious principle embedded in the halakhah of 'orlah.

First, as with Shebi'it, the law takes effect only from the point at which Israel enters the land. That is to say, the point of Israel's entry into the Land marks the beginning of the Land's consequential fecundity. In simpler language, the fact that trees produce fruit matters only from

Systematizing Eden

Israel's entry onward. To see what is at stake, we recall that the entry of Israel into the Land marks the restoration of Eden. The Land bears fruit *of which God takes cognizance* only when the counterpart-moment of creation has struck. The halakhah has no better way of saying, the entry of Israel into the Land compares with the moment at which the creation of Eden took place. In this way, moreover, the law of Shebi'it finds its counterpart. Shebi'it concerns telling time, marking off seven years to the Sabbath of creation, the one that affords rest to the Land. The halakhah of 'Orlah also means telling time. Specifically, 'Orlah-law marks the time of the creation of produce from the moment of Israel's entry into the land. Israel's entry into the Land marks a new beginning, comparable to the very creation of the world, just as the Land at the end matches Eden at the outset.

Second, Israelite intentionality is required to subject a tree to the 'orlah-rule. If an Israelite does not plant the tree with the plan of producing fruit, then the tree is not subject to the rule. If the tree grows up on its own, not by the act and precipitating intentionality of the Israelite, the 'orlah-rule does not apply. If an Israelite does not plant the tree to produce fruit, the 'orlah-rule does not apply. And given the character of creation, which marks the norm, the tree must be planted in the ordinary way; if grafted or sunk as a root, the law does not apply.

Third, the entire issue of the halakhah comes down to Israelite restraint in using the produce of the orchards. What is the counterpart to Israelite observance of the restraint of three years? And why should Israelite intentionality play so critical a role, since, Sifra itself notes, the 'orlah-rule applies to trees planted even by gentiles? The answer becomes obvious we ask another question: Can we think of any other commandments concerning fruit-trees in the Land that – sages say time and again – is Eden? Of course we can: "Of every tree of the garden you are free to eat; but as for the tree of knowledge of good and evil, you must not eat of it" (Gen. 2:16). But the halakhah of 'orlah imposes upon Israel a more demanding commandment. Of *no* tree in the new Eden may Israel eat for three years. That demands considerable restraint. Israel must exceed the humble requirement of obedience in regard to a fruit-tree that God assigned to Adam, the Land imposes obligations far in excess of those carried by Eden. And the issue devolves upon Israel's will or attitude, much as Eden turned tragic by reason of Man's rebellious will.

That is because Israel's own intentionality – not God's – imposes upon every fruit-bearing tree – and not only the one of Eden – the prohibition of three years. That is the point of the stress on the effects of Israel's desire for the fruit. So once Israel wants the fruit, it must show that it can restrain its desire and wait for three years. By Israel's act of will, Israel has imposed upon itself the requirement of restraint. Taking the entry-point as our guide, we may say that, from the entry into the Land and for the next three years, trees that Israelites value for their fruit and plant with the produce in mind must be left untouched. And, for all time thereafter, when Israelites plant fruit-trees, they must recapitulate that same exercise of self-restraint, that is, act as though, for the case at hand, they have just come into the Land.

To find the context in which these rules make their statement, we must ask that details, not only the main point, carry the message. So we ask, why three years in particular? A glance at the narrative of Creation provides the obvious answer. Fruit trees were created on the third day of creation. Then, when Israel by intention and action designates a tree – any tree – as fruit-bearing, Israel recapitulate the order of creation and so must wait for three years, as creation waited for three years. Then the planting of every tree imposes upon Israel the occasion to meet once more the temptation that the first Adam could not overcome. Israel now recapitulates the temptation of Adam then, but Israel, the New Adam, possesses, and is possessed by, the Torah. By its own action and intention in planting fruit trees, Israel finds itself in a veritable orchard of trees like the tree of knowledge of good and evil. The difference between Adam and Israel – permitted to eat all fruit but one, Adam ate the forbidden fruit, while Israel refrains for a specified span of time from fruit from all trees – marks what has taken place through Israel, in the Land of Israel, which is the regeneration of humanity. The enlandisement of the halakhah bears that very special message, and I can imagine no other way of making that statement through law than in the explicit concern sages register for the fruit-trees of the Land of Israel. No wonder, then, that 'orlah-law finds its position, in the Priestly Code, in the rules of sanctification.

So when Israel enters the Land, in exactly the right detail Israel recapitulates the drama of Adam in Eden, but with this formidable difference. The outcome ought not to be the same. By its own act of will Israel addresses the temptation of Adam and overcomes the same temptation, not once but every day through time beyond measure. Adam could not wait out the week, but Israel waits for three years – as long as God waited in creating fruit trees. Adam picked and ate. But here, too, there is a detail not to be missed. even after three years, Israel may not eat the fruit wherever it chooses. Rather, in the fourth year from planting, Israel will still show restraint, bringing the fruit only "for jubilation before the Lord" in Jerusalem. That signals that the once-forbidden fruit is now eaten in public, not in secret, before the Lord, as a moment of celebration. That detail, too, recalls the Fall and makes its comment upon the horror of the fall. That is, when Adam ate the fruit, he

Systematizing Eden

shamefully hid from God for having eaten the fruit. But when Israel eats the fruit, it does so proudly, joyfully, above all, publicly before the Lord. The contrast is not to be missed, so, too, the message. Faithful Israel refrains when it is supposed to, and so it has every reason to cease to refrain and to eat "before the Lord." It has nothing to hide, and everything to show.

And there is more. In the fifth year Israel may eat on its own, the time of any restraint from enjoying the gifts of the Land having ended. That sequence provides fruit for the second Sabbath of creation, and so through time. How so? Placing Adam's sin on the first day after the first Sabbath, thus Sunday, then calculating the three forbidden years as Monday, Tuesday, and Wednesday of the second week of creation, reckoning on the jubilation of Thursday, we come to the Friday, eve of the second Sabbath of creation. So now, a year representing a day of the Sabbatical week, just as Leviticus says so many times in connection with the Sabbatical year, the three prohibited years allow Israel to show its true character, fully regenerate, wholly and humbly accepting God's commandment, the one Adam broke. And the rest follows.

Here, then, is the message of the 'orlah-halakhah, the statement that only through the details of the laws of 'orlah as laid out in both parts of the Torah, written and oral, the halakhah could hope to make. By its own act of restraint, the New Adam, Israel, in detailed action displays its repentance in respect to the very sin that the Old Adam committed, the sin of disobedience and rebellion. Facing the same opportunity to sin, Israel again and again over time refrains from the very sin that cost Adam Eden. So by its manner of cultivation of the Land and its orchards, Israel manifests what in the very condition of humanity has changed by the giving of the Torah: the advent of humanity's second chance, through Israel. Only in the Land that succeeds Eden can Israel, succeeding Adam, carry out the acts of regeneration that the Torah makes possible.

But, I hasten to add, the halakhah presents as the norms for a social system not only what happened in Eden, with its tragic consequences, but also what happened with Israel in the Land of Israel, producing equally weighty results. Israel corrupted the perfected Land, losing out on Eden, as the narrative from Joshua through Kings conveys. So the halakhah will have to, and does, accommodate not only the restoration of Eden in the Land by the New Adam that is Israel, but also the recapitulation of the tragedy of Eden by Israel in the Land. The restorationist theology embodied in the halakhah does so, as we shall see in its presentation of the halakhah of atonement. And, when the halakhah speaks of sin and atonement, it delivers the same message of the priority of Israelite will, the consequentiality of Israelite intentionality, that we encounter time and again in the halakhic chapters of Eden and the Land. But this observation carries us way ahead of our story. Let us continue to dwell on what it means to build Eden in the Land.

II. The Order of the Species: Each According to its "Name"

An enlandised relationship, then, identifies the encounter between Israel and God with not only the right time and the right person but also the right place: the Land God has chosen for the People whom he has chosen. When it comes to the details, the Written Torah defines the conditions in which Israel is to work that particular Land, deriving its sustenance from the Land and its exceptional gifts. These are the rules of interior relationship that govern when in God's presence and by his act, holy Israel and the Land are (re)joined together. These rules turn out to establish for the Land the order and system that characterize Eden: all things properly classified, species by species. The halakhah of Kilayim elaborates upon Lev. 19:19:

> "You shall not let your cattle mate with a different kind; you shall not sow your field with two kinds of seed; you shall not put on cloth from a mixture of two kinds of material."

Further, Deuteronomy 22:9-11 figures:

> "You shall not sow your vineyard with a second kind of seed, otherwise the crop from the seed you have sown and the produce of the vineyard may not be used; you shall not plow with an ox and an ass together; you shall not wear cloth that combines wool and linen."

Lev. 19:2 places into the context of the sanctification of Israel the considerations of meticulous division among classes or species of the animal and vegetable world that define the tractate's topic. Sanctification takes place in the context of Gen. 1:1-2:4, the orderly creation of the world, species by species. The act of sanctification of creation took place when all things were ordered, properly in place, each according to its kind. Creation takes place when chaos is brought under control and ordered, that is when the world is made perfect and ready for God's act of sanctification. Mandelbaum observes, "The point of the laws of the Priestly Code in Leviticus...is to prevent the confusion of those classes and categories that were established at the creation. P thus commands man to restore the world from its present condition of chaos to its original orderly state, and so to make the world ready once again for sanctification."[1]

---

[1] Mandelbaum, *Kilayim*, p. 3.

Systematizing Eden

From one viewpoint Kilayim takes God's perspective on the Land, imagining the landscape as seen from on high. God wants to see in the Land an orderly and regular landscape, each species in its proper place. He wants to see Israel clothed in garments that preserve the distinction between animal and vegetable exactly where that distinction operates for fabrics. He wants to see animals ordered by their species, just as they were when Noah brought them into the ark (Gen. 7:14). What that means is that grapes and wheat are not to grow together, oxen and asses are not to be yoked together, and wool and linen – animal and vegetable fibers – are not to be worn in a single garment together.

But from another viewpoint, it is the perspective of not God but man, Israel in particular, that dictates matters. For who bears responsibility for restoring the perfection of creation? The Priestly Code wants the land to be returned to its condition of an unchanging perfection. But the Mishnah, Mandelbaum states, has a different view:

> The Mishnah underlines man's power to impose order upon the world, a capacity unaffected by historical events. In spite of the occurrence of catastrophes and disasters, man retains the ability to affect the world around him through such ordinary activities as sowing a field. While the Priestly Code thus has man confront confusion by reconstructing the ideal order of creation, the Mishnah regards man as imposing his own order upon a world in a state of chaos, and, so, in effect, as participating in the process of creation.[2]

Man has the power to do in the Land of Israel what God did in creating the world at Eden, that is, establish order, overcome chaos, perfect the world for the occasion of sanctification. The law thus embodies in the topic at hand the view prevailing throughout the halakhah, as formulated at M. Kel. 17:11: "Everything is according to the measure of the man." The halakhah that elaborates the commandments on the present topic set forth in Scripture makes man God's partner in overcoming chaos and establishing order. It is man's perspective that governs, man's discernment that identifies chaos or affirms order.

Now if we ask ourselves, how in a religious system that deems man created in God's image, after God's likeness, do we account for the law's stress on man's view, an answer immediately presents itself. Man's perspective governs, how man sees the Land determines whether or not the law is obeyed, for two reasons. The first is that, with man created "in our image, after our likeness," man's and God's perspectives are the same. If man discerns the confusion of species, so would God, and if man does not, then neither would God. But when the halakhah leaves matters relative to appearance to man, the actualities of mixed seeds no longer

---

[2] Mandelbaum, *Kilayim*, p. 4.

matter, or matter so much as appearances. And that requires a second reason as well. For if God cares that "you shall not sow your field with two kinds of seed and that you shall not sow your vineyard with a second kind of seed," surely the actuality, not the appearance, ought to prevail – unless another consideration registers. That consideration comes into play when we ask, how, through the shared engagement with the Land, do God and Israel collaborate, and to what end?

The answer to that question exposes the second, and I think, principal, explanation for the emphasis of the halakhah upon how man sees things, Israelite man being the subject throughout. Israel is in charge of the Land. Israel not only bears responsibility for what happens in the land, but also bears the blame and the penalty when matters are not right. Israel relates to God through Israel's trusteeship of the Land. The tractates that deal with the enlandisement of the relationship of Israel to God, Kilayim and the others, present Israel as the trustee of the Land and, as we see in the present tractate, assign to Israel the task of cultivating the Land in a manner appropriate to the perfection of creation at the outset. No wonder, then, that Israel's view of matters must prevail, for Israel bears full responsibility on the spot for how things will appear to Heaven.

That fact – Israel's responsibility to farm the Land in accord with the orderly rule of Eden – makes Israel not only the custodian of the Land but also partner in that vast labor of reform that, in the end, will bring about the restoration of Adam to Eden. Adam was responsible only for not eating the produce of a single tree; he did not have to labor, for a harvest, he need only reach up and pick the fruit. Israel for its part had to work the Land and bore responsibility for the appearance of the whole of it. For, we recall, it is God's plan at the end to bring to life all Israel and in the world or age to come to restore all Israel to the Land of Israel, completing the return to Eden but with the difference made by the Torah: Israel back to the Land of Israel compares to Adam in Eden in all but one aspect. Armed with the Torah, Israel will not rebel as Adam did. That is why, the restorationist teleology maintains, the world to come will endure: chaos overcome, order will prevail. How Israel cultivates the Holy Land entrusted to it then makes all the difference, field by field in its correct configuration.

The restoration of Adam to Eden takes place, at the end, in and through the restoration, to the Land of Israel, of Israel, the particular embodiment of that part of Adam, or humanity, that knows God through the Torah. So all matters cohere. In assigning to Israel the task of farming the country in a manner appropriate to the principles of creation, therefore, the halakhah asks Israel to do its concrete part in restorationist teleology: to make the end like the beginning, Eden recovered. Once God

Systematizing Eden

has assigned the Land to Israel and instructed Israel on how to attain and preserve its condition of perfection as at creation, then Israel's perspective, not God's, must govern, because, for Israel, the stakes are very high: the resurrection of the dead to life, the restoration of Israel to the Land. But the halakhah concerns the here and now, and that brings us to the Sabbath of creation, which Israel celebrates, in the Land and otherwise, every seventh day.

III. The Sabbath of Creation in the Here and Now

The Sabbath marks the goal and climax of creation, the moment of perfection. To restore Eden by recapitulating its principal qualities, the halakhah of Shabbat-Erubin identifies the time of Eden with the Sabbath day and the space of Eden with the Israelite household. Then Eden forms the metaphor that governs the Israelite household on the seventh day. The lines of structure and order that organize the Israelite household's interior construction mark the confluence of time, space, and circumstance. At a particular time, the space encompassed by the household is demarcated, closed off entirely so that the circumstance of the conduct of life therein is deeply affected. At that point the Israelite household comes to spatial realization, keeping within all who belong, walling off the rest. In concrete terms, on the Sabbath, an invisible wall descends to differentiate the private domain of the household from public domain of marketplace and street – and other private domains – and to close off the one from the other. And, at that time, in that space, the ordinary foci of workaday activities – cooking and eating, working and resting – become radically re-configured: no cooking, no working, only eating and resting in perfect repose. And that is Paradise, or, as the sages say, one-sixtieth of the taste of the Garden of Eden.

The Israelite household at rest on the Sabbath day recapitulates the celebration of God at the moment of the conclusion and perfection of creation. Then the Israelite household, like creation at sunset marking the end of the sixth day of creation, is sanctified: separated from the profane world and distinguished as God's domain. With all things in place and in order, at the sunset that marks the advent of the seventh day, the rest that marks the perfection of creation descends. The sanctification takes place through that very act of perfect repose that recapitulates the one celebrated at the climax of creation. Like God at the celebration of creation, now man achieves perfect, appropriate rest. That takes place when time, circumstance, but space, too, come together. The advent of the Sabbath marks the time, the household, the space, and the conduct of home and family life, the circumstance. Sages then make through the halakhah of the Sabbath the first and most important statement of their system. It is the statement that celebrates God's repose by bringing about the stasis of creation, the perfection of the Creator's work, all evoked every time the word "Sabbath" resonated with the sounds of the beginnings, the melodies of the restoration.

The issue of residence therefore becomes critical to an account of how Israel meets God within the walls of the Israelite household, because on the Sabbath one is to remain in place, meaning, within the limits of private domain. But the transformation of private domain – what is private, what is shared – on the Sabbath forms the generative problematic of the halakhah – that, and the meaning of "eating in his place." Private domain defines the critical focus of the halakhah. To effect that shift in concern, bringing people within the walls of the courtyards and alleyways in which they are imagined to reside, realizes the intent of the Written Torah when it says, "Remain every man of you in his place." Consequently, activities in public domain are severely circumscribed by the prohibition against carrying therein, as well as by the one that prohibits unlimited travel.

The halakhah formulates matters at two levels; on the surface it attends to minutia of carrying from one domain to the other (Shabbat) and to the detailed, richly instantiated definition of private domain (Erubin). But at the heart of matters profound reflection on the meaning of what is private and what is shared takes place. The tractate in detail therefore addresses the problem, how can Israelites on the Sabbath move about from one private domain to another, so arranging matters that shared and common ownership of private domain secures for all parties the right to carry in the space held in common? One answer is, since where one eats, there one resides, prepare a symbolic, or fictive, meal, the right to which is shared by all. All householders thereby commingle their property rights, so that will then form of various private domains a single common estate. Another answer is, establish a boundary around the entire set of private domains, one that like a wall forms of them all a single property. The medium by which the one or the other procedure is carried out is called an *'erub*, a medium of commingling, thus referring to either the symbolic, shared meal or the equally fictive demarcation line, as the case requires: a meal of commingling, or a boundary-marker for commingling ownership of private property. In play throughout the exposition of the halakhah of Erubin are these propositions that have already come to full exposition in the halakhah of Shabbat: [1] one may not transport objects from private to public domain, but [2] there are types of domain that are neither the one nor the other, specifically, the courtyard linking a number of private properties, and the alleyway onto which a number of courtyards debouch.

Systematizing Eden

The paramount question before us is, why do sages devote their reading of the law of Shabbat-Erubin above all to differentiating public from private domain? All of Erubin and a fair component of Shabbat focus upon that matter, which stands at the head of the first of the two tractates and at the conclusion of the second. And, to revert to the halakhah of Shabbat once more, the other principal focus, the definition of an act of labor that, when performed on the Sabbath, is culpable, defines yet another question that demands attention. Why do sages formulate the principle that they do, that the act of labor prohibited on the Sabbath is one that fully constitutes a completed act of labor – beginning, middle, and end – in conformity with the intentionality of the actor.

The answer to both questions derives from the governing theology of the Sabbath, the key to the restoration of Eden, first at regular, temporal intervals, and, ultimately, for all eternity. The Written Torah represents the Sabbath as the climax of creation. The theology of the Sabbath put forth in the Oral Torah's halakhah derives from a systematization of definitions implicit in the myth of Eden that envelopes the Sabbath. Sages' thinking about the Sabbath invokes in the formation of the normative law defining the matter the model of the first Sabbath, the one of Eden. The two paramount points of concern – [1] the systematic definition of private domain, where ordinary activity is permitted, and [2] the rather particular definition of what constitutes a prohibited act of labor on the Sabbath – precipitate deep thought and animate the handful of principles brought to concrete realization in the two tractates. "Thou shalt not labor" of the Commandments refers in a generic sense to all manner of work; but in the halakhah of Shabbat, "labor" bears very particular meanings and is defined in a quite specific, and somewhat odd, manner. We can make sense of the halakhah of Shabbat-Erubin only by appeal to the story of Creation, the governing metaphor derived therefrom, the sages' philosophical reflections that transform into principles of a general and universal character the case at hand.

Given the broad range of possible points of halakhic emphasis that the Written Torah sustains – the dual formulation of matters in the Ten Commandments that make remarkably slight impact here, rest for animals and slaves playing no role in the articulation of the law, we realize that sages made choices. Why the stress on space and activity? When approaching the theme and problem of the Sabbath, they chose to answer two questions: what does it mean to remain "in his place," and what constitutes the theory of forbidden activity, the principles that shape the innumerable rules and facts of the prohibition? Accordingly, we must ask a basic question. It is, what is it about the Sabbath of creation that captures sages' attention?

The foci of their thinking turn out to locate themselves in what is implicit and subject to generalization in the story of creation. The halakhah turns out to realize in detailed, concrete terms generalizations that sages locate in and derive from the story of creation. And what they find is a metaphor for themselves and their Israel, on the one side, and the foundation for generalization, out of the metaphor, in abstract terms susceptible to acute concretization, on the other. That is to say, the Sabbath of Eden forms the model: like this, so all else. And sages, with their remarkable power to think in general terms but to convey thought in examples and details, found it possible to derive from the model the principles that would accomplish their goal: linking Israel to Eden through the Sabbath, the climax of their way of life, the soul of their theological system.

Only when we know what is supposed to take place on the Sabbath – in particular in the model of the Sabbath that originally celebrated creation – to the exclusion of the model of the Sabbath that would focus the halakhah upon the liberation of slaves from Egypt (Deuteronomy's version) or the cessation of labor of the household, encompassing animals and slaves (Exodus's version) – only then shall we find the key to the entire matter of the Sabbath of the halakhah of the Oral Torah. Then we may identify the setting in which the rules before us take on meaning and prove to embody profound religious thinking. I find the halakhah that presents the model of how sages think about the Sabbath and accounts for the topical program of their thought – the fully articulated source of the governing metaphor – is Shebi'it. That tractate, as we have now seen, describes the observance of the Sabbath that is provided every seventh year for the Land of Israel itself. The Land celebrates the Sabbath, and then, Israel in its model. The Land is holy, as Israel is holy, and the Priestly Code leaves no doubt that for both, the Sabbath defines the rhythm of life with God: the seventh day for Israel, the seventh year for the Land.

For both, moreover, to keep the Sabbath is to be like God. And, specifically, that is when God had completed the work of creation, pronounced it good, sanctified it – imposed closure and permanence, the creation having reached its conclusion. God observed the Sabbath, which itself finds its definition as the celebration and commemoration of God's own action. This is what God did, this is what we now do. What God did concerned creation, what we do concerns creation. And all else follows. The Sabbath then precipitates the imitation of God on a very particular occasion and for a very distinctive purpose. And given what we have identified as sages' governing theology – the systematic account of God's perfect justice in creation, yielding an account and explanation of all else – we find ourselves at the very center of the system. The meeting of time

Systematizing Eden

and space on the seventh day of creation – God having formed space and marked time – finds its counterpart in the ordering of Israelite space at the advent of time, the ordering of that space through the action and inaction of the Israelites themselves.

Erubin, with its sustained exercise of thought on the commingling of ownership of private property for the purpose of Sabbath observance and on the commingling of meals to signify shared ownership, accomplishes for Israel's Sabbath what Shebi'it achieves for the Land's. On the Sabbath inaugurated by the Sabbatical Year the Land, so far as it is otherwise private property, no longer is possessed exclusively by the householder. So, too, the produce of the Land consequently belongs to everybody. It follows that the halakhah of Erubin realizes for the ordinary Sabbath of Israel the very same principles that are embodied in the halakhah of Shebi'it. That halakhah defines the Sabbath of the Land in exactly the same terms: the Land is now no longer private, and the Land's produce belongs to everybody. The Sabbath that the Land enjoys marks the advent of shared ownership of the Land and its fruit. Sharing is so total that hoarding is explicitly forbidden, and what has been hoarded has now to be removed from the household and moved to public domain, where anyone may come and take it.

Here we find the Sabbath of Creation overspreading the Sabbath of the Land, as the Priestly Code at Genesis 1 and at Leviticus Lev. 25:1-8, cited above, define matters. The Sabbatical year bears the message that on the Sabbath, established arrangements as to ownership and possession are set aside, and a different conception of private property takes over. What on ordinary days is deemed to belong to the householder and to be subject to his exclusive will on the Sabbath falls into a more complex web of possession. The householder continues to utilize his property but not as a sole proprietor does. The sole proprietor exercises his will without restraint; he alone dictates what is to be done with what he owns. But that is not the situation of the Israelite householder on the Sabbath. He gives up exclusive access thereto, and gains in exchange rights of access to other peoples' property. Private property is commingled; everybody shares in everybody's. The result is, private property takes on a new meaning, different from the secular one. So far as the householder proposes to utilize his private property, he must share it with others, who do the same for him. To own then is to abridge ownership in favor of commingling rights thereto, to possess is to share. And that explains why the produce of the Land belongs to everyone as well, a corollary to the fundamental postulate of the Sabbath of the Land.

What qualities of Eden then impress sages? With the halakhah as the vast corpus of facts, we focus upon two matters: [1] time and space, [2] time and activity. How is space demarcated at the specified time, how is activity classified at that same time? The former works itself out in a discussion of where people may move on the Sabbath and how they may conduct themselves (carry things as they move). The latter finds its definition in the model of labor that is prohibited. With Eden as the model and the metaphor, we take a simple sighting on the matter. First, Adam and Eve are free to move in Eden where they wish, possessing all they contemplate. God has given it to them to enjoy. If Eden then belongs to God, he freely shares ownership with Adam and Eve. And – all the more so – the produce of Eden is ownerless. With the well-known exception, all the fruit is theirs for the taking. So we find ourselves deep within the halakhah of Shebi'it.

For the halakhah of Shebi'it sets forth in concrete terms what is implicit in the character of Eden. In the Sabbatical Year the Land returns to the condition characteristic of Eden at the outset: shared and therefore accessible, its produce available to all. The Sabbatical Year recovers that perfect time of Eden when the world was at rest, all things in place. Before the rebellion, man did not have to labor on the land; he picked and ate his meals freely. And, in the nature of things, everything belonged to everybody; private ownership in response to individual labor did not exist, because man did not have to work anyhow. Reverting to that perfect time, the Torah maintains that the land will provide adequate food for everyone, including the flocks and herds, even if people do not work the land. But that is on condition that all claim of ownership lapses; the food is left in the fields, to be picked by anyone who wishes, but it may not be hoarded by the landowner in particular.

It is in this context that we read the halakhah of Shabbat-Erubin, with special reference to the division of the world into private and public domain, the former the realm of permitted activity on the Sabbath, the latter not. If we may deal with an 'erub-fence or an 'erub meal, how are we to interpret what is at stake in these matters? It in both instances is to render private domain public through the sharing of ownership. The 'erub-fence for its part renders public domain private, but only in the same sense that private domain owned by diverse owners is shared, ownership being commingled. The 'erub-fence signals the formation for purposes of the sanctification of time of private domain – but with the ownership commingled. So what is "private" about "private domain" is different on the Sabbath from in secular time. By definition, for property to be private in the setting of the Sabbath, it must be shared among householders. On the Sabbath, domain that is totally private, its ownership not commingled for the occasion, becomes a prison, the householder being unable to conduct himself in the normal manner in the courtyard beyond his door, let alone in other courtyards in the same alleyway, or in other alleyways that debouch onto the same street. And the halakhah, as we have seen, makes provision for those – whether Israelite or gentile – who do not offer their proprietorship of their households for commingling for the Sabbath.

What happens, therefore, through the 'erub-fence or 'erub meal is the re-definition of proprietorship: what is private is no longer personal, and no one totally owns what is his, but then everyone (who wishes to participate, himself and his household together) owns a share everywhere. So much for the "in his place" part of "each man in his place." His place constitutes an area where ordinary life goes on, but it is no longer "his" in the way in which the land is subject to his will and activity in ordinary time. If constructing a fence serves to signify joint ownership of the village, now turned into private domain, or constructing the gateway, of the alleyway and its courtyards, what about the meal? The 'erub-meal signifies the shared character of what is eaten. It is food that belongs to all who wish to share it. But it is the provision of a personal meal, also, that allows an individual to designate for himself a place of Sabbath residence other than the household to which he belongs.

So the Sabbath loosens bonds, those of the householder to his property, those of the individual to the household. It forms communities, the householders of a courtyard into a community of shared ownership of the entire courtyard, the individual into a community other than that formed by the household to which he belongs – now the community of disciples of a given sage, the community of a family other than that in residence in the household, to use two of the examples common in the halakhah. Just as the Sabbath redefines ownership of the Land and its produce, turning all Israelites into a single social entity, "all Israel," which, all together, possesses the Land in common ownership, so the Sabbath redefines the social relationships of the household, allowing persons to separate themselves from the residence of the household and designate some other, some personal, point of residence instead.

The main point of the law of private domain in Shabbat and Erubin seen in the model of Shebi'it then is to redefine the meaning of "private domain," where each man is to remain in "his" place. The law aims to define the meaning of "his," and to remove the ownership of the land and its produce from the domain of a householder, rendering ownership public and collective. Taking as our model Shebi'it, we note that in the year that is a Sabbath, the land is held to be owned by nobody and everybody, and the produce of the Land belongs to everyone and no one, so that one may take and eat but thank only God. It is no one's, so every may take; it is everyone's, so everyone may eat, and God alone is to be acknowledged. Since, on the Sabbath, people are supposed to remain within their own domain, the counterpart to Shebi'it will provide for the sharing of ownership, thus for extending the meaning of "private domain" to encompass all the partners in a shared locus. "Private domain," his place, now bears a quite different meaning from the one that pertains in profane time. The Sabbath recapitulates the condition of Eden, when Adam and Eve could go where they wished and eat what they wanted, masters of all they contemplated, along with God. Israel on the Sabbath in the Land, like Adam on the Sabbath of Eden that celebrates Creation, shares private domain and its produce.

Israel on the Sabbath in the Land like God on the Sabbath of Eden rests from the labor of creation. And that brings us to the question, What about that other principle of the Sabbath, the one set forth by the halakhah of Shabbat? The richly detailed halakhah of Shabbat defines the matter in a prolix, yet simple way. It is to be stated with emphasis: *on the Sabbath it is prohibited deliberately to carry out in a normal way a completed act of constructive labor, one that produces enduring results, one that carries out one's entire intention: the whole of what one planned, one has accomplished, in exactly the proper manner.* That definition takes into account the shank of the halakhah of Shabbat as set forth in the Mishnah-tractate, and the amplification and extension of matters in the Tosefta and the two Talmuds in no way revise the basic principles. Here there is a curious, if obvious, fact: it is not an act of labor that itself is prohibited (as the Ten Commandments in Exodus and Deuteronomy would have it), but an act of labor of a very particular definition.

What is striking is, no prohibition impedes performing an act of labor in an other-than-normal way. In theory, one may go out into the fields and plough, if he does so in some odd manner. He may build an entire house, so long as it collapses promptly. The issue of activity on the Sabbath therefore is removed from the obvious context of work, conventionally defined. Now the activity that is forbidden is of a very particular sort, modeled in its indicative traits after a quite specific paradigm. A person is not forbidden to carry out an act of destruction, or an act of labor that produces no lasting consequences. He may start an act of labor if he does not complete it. He may accomplish an act of labor in some extraordinary manner. None of these acts of labor are forbidden, even though, done properly and with consequence, they represent massive violations of the halakhah. Nor is part of an act of labor that is not brought to conclusion prohibited. Nor is it forbidden to perform part of an act of labor in partnership with another person who carries out the other requisite part. Nor does one incur culpability for performing an act of labor in several distinct parts, e.g., over a protracted, differentiated period of time. A person may not willingly carry out the entirety of an act of constructive labor, start to finish. The issue is not why not, since we know the answer: God has said not to do so. The question is, whence the particular definition at hand?

Clearly, a definition of the act of labor that is prohibited on the Sabbath has taken over and recast the commonsense meaning of the commandment not to labor on the Sabbath. For considerations enter that recast matters from an absolute to a relative definition. One may tie a knot – but not one that stands. One may carry a package, but not in the usual manner. One may build a wall, only if it falls down. And, as I have stressed, one may do pretty much anything without penalty – if he did not intend matters as they actually happened. The metaphor of God in Eden, as sages have reflected on the story of Creation, yields the governing principles that define forbidden labor. What God did in the six days of creation provides the model.

Let us review the main principles item by item. They involve the three preconditions. The act must fully carry out the intention of the actor, as creation carried out God's intention. The act of labor must be carried out by a single actor, as God acted alone in creating the world. An act of labor is the like of one that is required in the building and maintenance of God's residence in this world, the tabernacle. The act of labor prohibited on the Sabbath involves two considerations. The act must be done in the ordinary way, just as Scripture's account leaves no doubt, God accomplished creation in the manner in which he accomplished his goals from creation onward, by an act of speech. And, weightier still, the forbidden act of labor is one that produces enduring consequences. God did not create only to destroy, but he created the enduring world. And it goes without saying, creation yielded the obvious consequences that the act was completely done in all ways, as God himself declared. The act was one of consequence, involving what was not negligible but what man and God alike deemed to make a difference. Sages would claim, therefore, that the activity that must cease on the Sabbath finds its definition in the model of those actions that God carried out in making the world.

That such a mode of thought is more than a mere surmise, based on the congruence of the principles by which labor forbidden on the Sabbath spin themselves out of the Creation-story, emerges when we recall a striking statement. It is the one that finds the definition of forbidden labor in those activities required for the construction and maintenance of the tabernacle, which is to say, God's residence on earth. The best statement, predictably, is the Bavli's:

> People are liable only for classifications of labor the like of which was done in the tabernacle. They sowed, so you are not to sow. They harvested, so you are not to harvest. They lifted up the boards from the ground to the wagon, so you are not to lift them in

> from public to private domain. They lowered boards from the wagon to the ground, so you must not carry anything from private to public domain. They transported boards from wagon to wagon, so you must not carry from one private domain to another.
>
> Bavli Shabbat 4:2 I.4/49b

Sages found in the analogy of how, in theory, the tabernacle was maintained, the classifications of labor that pertain. In the tabernacle these activities are permitted, even on the Sabbath. In God's house, the priests and Levites must do for God what they cannot do for themselves – and the identification of acts of labor forbidden on the Sabbath follows.

The details of the halakhah then emerge out of a process in which two distinct sources contribute. One is the model of the tabernacle. What man may do for God's house he may not do for his own – God is always God, the Israelite aspires only to be "like God," to imitate God, and that is a different thing. The other is the model of the creation of the world and of Eden. Hence to act like God on the Sabbath, the Israelite rests; he does not do what God did in creation. The former source supplies generative metaphors, the like of which may not be done; thus acts like sowing, like harvesting, like lifting boards from public to private domain, and the like, are forbidden. The latter source supplies the generative principles, the abstract definitions involving the qualities of perfection and causation: intentionality, completion, the normality of the conduct of the action, and the like. The mode of analogical thinking governs, but, as we see, a double metaphor pertains, the metaphor of God's activity in creation, the metaphor of the priests' and Levites' activity in the tabernacle. Creation yields those large principles that we have identified: the traits of an act of labor for God in creation define the prohibited conditions of an act of labor on the Sabbath. By appeal to those two metaphors, we can account for every detail of the halakhah.

What then takes place inside the walls of the Israelite household when time takes over space and revises the conduct of ordinary affairs? Israel goes home to Eden. How best to make the statement that the Land is Israel's Eden, that Israel imitates God by keeping the Sabbath, meaning, not doing the things that God did in creating the world but ceased to do on the Sabbath, and that to restore its Eden, Israel must sustain its life – nourish itself – where it belongs? To set forth those most basic convictions about God in relationship to man and about Israel in relationship to God, I can imagine no more eloquent, no more compelling and appropriate, medium of expression than the densely detailed halakhah of Shebi'it, Shabbat, and Erubin. Indeed, outside of the setting of the household, its ownership, utilization, and maintenance, I cannot think of any other way of fully making that statement stick. In theory implausible for its very simplicity (as much as for its dense

Systematizing Eden

instantiation!), in halakhic fact, compelling, the Oral Torah's statement accounts for the human condition. Israel's Eden takes place at in the household open to others, on the Sabbath, in acts that maintain life, share wealth, and desist from creation.

The key words, therefore, are in the shift from the here and now of time in which one works like God, to the *then* and *there* when one desists from working, just as God did at the moment the world was finished, perfected, and sanctified. Israel gives up the situation of man in ordinary time and space, destructive, selfish, dissatisfied and doing. Then, on the Sabbath, and there, in the household, with each one in place, Israel enters the situation of God in that initial, that perfected and sanctified then and there of creation: the activity that consists in sustaining life, sharing dominion, and perfecting repose through acts of restraint and sufficiency.

3

Who Owns Eden?
And
From the Bible to the Torah

Jacob Neusner
University of South Florida and Bard College

This lecture is in two separate parts, the one completing the halakhic exposition begun at the end of Lecture One, the other addressing the final proposition of these lectures.

I. Who Owns Eden?

The key to the entire system of interaction between God and Israel through the Land and its gifts emerges in the halakhah of Ma'aserot and its companions, which deal – along the lines of Shebi'it and 'Erubin – with the difference between possession and ownership. God owns the world, which he made. But God has accorded to man the right of possession of the earth and its produce. This he did twice, once to Man in Eden, the second time to Israel in the Land of Israel. And to learn the lesson that Adam did not master, that possession is not ownership but custody and stewardship, Israel has to acknowledge the claims of the creator to the glory of all creation, which is the Land. This Israel does by giving back God's share of the produce of the Land at the time, and in the manner, that God defines. The enlandised components of the halakhah therefore form a single, cogent statement of matters.

If there is a single obstacle to obedience to God's will, it is man's natural inclination to take possession for ownership. For it is the attitude expressed in the claim of entire right of ownership – "my power and the might of my hand have gotten me this abundance" (Dt. 8:17) – that conveys the arrogance motivating rebellion such as took place to begin with in Eden. Someone who can do anything that he wants with a given object or person or property owns that object, person, or property. Someone whose will therefor is limited by the will of Another does not. Hence, for its part, the antidote to rebellion and sin, which is the Torah, would impose upon ownership of the Land the supererogatory obligation to acknowledge a divided right of ownership and possession, that is to say, a partner's claim. And for Israel in the Land, the partner is God. And at stake is Israel's demonstration that, this time around, Man acts with correct intentionality, responding to God's will with obedience, not rebellion.

Ma'aserot, the tractate concerning "tithes," discusses the entire set of agricultural dues, viewed generically: what the Israelite owes God out of the produce of the Land (and not in particular the tenth of the crop paid to this party, or the tenth of that tenth paid to that). The rules set forth here pertain to all the agricultural tithes and offerings and dictate the procedures – liability, timing, special problems – that pertain to them in general. The point of the halakhah, permeating all categories, is that when Israel asserts its rights of possession, God's interest in that same crop is provoked, and he lays claim to his share in the crop of Land that ownership of which is held in partnership between God and the Israelite farmer. Then the rest follows, a vast exercise in how the will of God and the will of the Israelite meet in concord, Israel obeying God's laws about the disposition of the abundance of the Land. The link to Eden is firm: Israel obeys laws concerning the disposition of the fruit of the Land in the way in which Adam did not obey those concerning the fruit of Eden.

The basic halakhic principle concerns not only Israel's relationship with God but also Israel's correspondence to God. In concrete terms the halakhah realizes the theological position of the Pentateuchal account, which makes explicit that God and Israel relate through the Land. That is where the conflict of wills – the free will of Israelite man, the commanding voice of the God who created all things – works itself out. And the point of conflict focuses upon the conduct of Israel in the Land. The halakhah accords to Israel possession, but not ownership of the Land, which God alone retains. God asserts his ownership when Israel proposes to exercise its rights of usufruct: when the tenant takes his share of the crop, he must also hand over to the Landowner (and to those designated by him to receive his share) the portion of the crop that owing. And until the tenant, in possession of the Land, does pay his rent, he may not utilize the crop as owners may freely do.

In his commentary to Mishnah-Tosefta Ma'aserot Jaffee states the religious principle in this language: "A supernatural claim to the tithes is made upon produce grown by Israelites at the precise moment at which they wish to use it...The farmer's appropriation of the produce offers an opportunity to explore issues involving the nature of ownership and the effects of human intentions in bringing out ownership. These reflections on the tension between the farmer's right to his produce and his duty to satisfy supernatural claims upon it before he eats it comprise the bulk of the tractate" (Jaffee, *Mishnah* , p. 13). The obligation to tithe represents God's limitation on rights of ownership of the Land. Israel possesses the Land, but God is the owner, in that God can evict Israel from the Land and has done so in the past, just as God evicted prior occupants.

It follows that the halakhah rests upon the principle that, while Israel possesses it, God owns the Land, and the agricultural offerings that Israel sets aside for those designated by God as his scheduled castes – the priest, the poor, the support of Jerusalem, for example – represent God's share of the crops. God and man lay claim to the produce of the Land. Only when the produce is shown by the actions of the farmer to be valuable to the farmer does God's claim emerge: "Only after produce has ripened may we expect the farmer to use it in his own meals or sell it for others for use in theirs. Thus God's claim to it is first provoked...from that point onward" (Jaffee, *Mishnah* , p. 4). That principle is expressed in the law that produce that is ownerless is not liable to tithing, e.g., produce of the Seventh Year and the like. In this connection Jaffee further states (Jaffee, *Mishnah* , p. 3):

> Produce is liable to the removal of tithes either at the time it is intended for use as a meal or at the time it is claimed as private property, whichever happens to come first....In both instances a human being has appropriated for his personal benefit produce against which God has a claim. God's claim is violated...whenever an Israelite farmer or householder prepares to use untithed produce as if he had full rights regarding its disposition. Whether he prepares it for a meal out in the field or brings raw food into his home for the use of his family, he has claimed rights of ownership that in fact are still God's. Accordingly, the Israelite must give to God his due before exercising his own property rights.

The farmer may use the produce as his own only when he has acknowledged God's claim, not eating the produce as if it were his own, but only after setting aside God's share. If the farmer prepares to make a meal of the produce in the field or claims to be sole owner, he loses his right to eat the food until he tithes (Jaffee, p. 4). Meeting God's claim, the farmer may then use the produce.

The system of obligatory tithing then is gets underway when the Israelite proposes to exercise his will over his domain and its produce. But at that point, it is not only God's will that comes into play. Every other party to the system then responds to the intentionality of the farmer. As Jaffee points out, priests cannot claim their dues whenever they choose, and God does not take an active role in determining when the produce must be tithed (Jaffee, p. 4). Human actions that reveal human intentions provoke God: when the farmer indicates that he plans to dispose of the fruit, God wants his share. Jaffee expresses this matter in the following language (Jaffee, *Mishnah* , p. 5):

> The fundamental theological datum of Maaserot...is that God acts and wills in response to human intentions. God's invisible action can be discerned by carefully studying the actions of human beings....the halakhah of Maaserot locates the play of God's power...in an invisible realm immune from the hazards of history...the realm of human appetite and intentions...God...acts and wills...only in reaction to the action and intention of his Israelite partner on the Land...Those who impose upon themselves the task of reconstructing the human and social fabric of Israelite life make effective the holiness of the Land and make real the claims of its God.

As we see, the halakhah spins out the implications of the distinction between possession and ownership. How do I claim that the present halakhic construction bears the burden of Eden? Just as, in connection with Shebi'it and 'Erubin, the halakhah underscores the ambiguous character of Israel's possession of its own domain, in the one case asserting God's ownership, in the other insisting upon the householder's relinquishing his control of his domain, so here too the same transaction characterizes Israel's relationship with God. Israel holds with open arms what God has given, thus the distinction between possession and ownership.

But the connection not only recapitulates what is already familiar but yields a further and fresh, if related, consideration. It is that, as in the account of Eden, God's will comes into conflict with Man's, showing them to be emotionally consubstantial, so here too, God and Man respond in the same way to the same facts. How is it that Israel and God relate in so concrete and specific a situation as is defined by the course of nature, the ripening of the crops? It is because, the halakhah takes for granted, God and Israel bear the same attitudes, feel the same emotions, form corresponding intentions. God and man are alike not only in intellect – the same rules of reasoning applying to both – but also, and especially, in attitude and emotion, in virtue in the classic sense. God commands Israel to love him, therefore God values and prizes the emotion of love. Man is commanded to love God. But that is not the only emotion shared by man and God. In the biblical biography of God, the tragic hero, God, will despair, love, hope, feel disappointment or exultation. The biblical record of God's feelings and God's will concerning the feelings of humanity – wanting human love, for example

– leaves no room for doubt. In this matter, the Rabbinic literature is explicit when it says, "the merciful God wants the heart." God commands that humanity love God with full heart, soul, mind and might, because God feels and values that same emotion. God's heart, not only his rationality, corresponds to man's. In that context we take up the halakhic position outlined in Ma'aserot. When the farmer wants the crop, so too does God. When the householder takes the view that the crop is worthwhile, God responds to the attitude of the farmer by forming the same opinion. The theological anthropology that brings God and the householder into the same continuum prepares the way for understanding what makes the entire Mishnaic system work.

The agricultural dues to which Ma'aserot in general makes reference are assigned to God's dependents, specifically the sacerdotal castes, priests and Levites, and the poor; and they are further used to support the holy city, Jerusalem, by securing an enhanced supply of food and an increased flow of funds to the city. In addition, obligatory and votive offerings for the Temple, both in specie (Temple coin) and the produce of nature (animals, wine, and grain), support the Temple buildings and the cycle of regular offerings that are maintained in the city. The upshot is, Israel in the holy Land, God's partners in the possession of the country and its abundance, give back to Heaven through designated castes, locations, and activities, God's share in the whole, and this the holy people do both in obedience to God's commandments and also on their own initiative.

The halakhah of Terumot constitutes a vast exegesis of a single religious principle: the Israelite has the power by an act of will confirmed (where required) by a concrete deed to sanctify what is common. The Israelite then is accorded by God the remarkable power to designate as holy, by reason of the Israelite's own uncoerced will, what is otherwise ordinary and not sacred. Not the only category of the halakhah to embody in concrete actions that considerable proposition, the halakhah of Terumot nonetheless forms a remarkably apt medium for delivering that message. That is because of the stress in the halakhah at hand on considerations of particularity: the householder's act of sanctification pertains to a very specific batch of produce, the consequence of sanctification invokes a very particular teleology inherent in the type of produce that has been sanctified. The upshot is, Israel's and God's purposes and power intersect. And, to revert to what we have learned in the halakhah of Ma'aserot, here possession shades over, if not to ownership, then to responsibility: for that which is subject to one's will, one is responsible, and that means, specifically, one must conform to God's will that which is subject to one's own will.

A critical component of the Israelite's relationship to God is his responsibility for preserving the sanctification of what belongs to God and is designated for God's clients. It is the thought, confirmed by deed, of the Israelite that what is secular is made sacred. Avery-Peck expressed that principle in the following language: "It is the common Israelite, the non-priest, who, while forbidden to eat holy produce, has the power to cause produce to be deemed holy." The active player in the designation and disposition of the portion of the crops to serve as heave-offering for the priest therefore is the Israelite householder or farmer, not the priest, and not God (except through the working of chance). Once God's interest in the crop has made the crop liable to the separation of the various tithes and offerings, it is the householder who takes over, and by an act of deliberation and intentionality, imparts the status of holiness to the portion of the crop he designates for the priesthood. And he bears full responsibility, also, for what happens to the designated produce until it is handed over to the priest. Avery-Peck (Avery-Peck, *Mishnah*, p. 3) frames the matter in this way:

> "The common Israelite is central in the process of sanctification. The holy heave-offering comes into being only if man properly formulates the intention to sanctify part of his produce and indicates that intention through corresponding words and actions.

All else flows from that basic principle. The Israelite householder has the power to initiate the entire process of sanctification, to transform the classification of produce and to subject that produce to the logic that inheres in its very character: its own teleology. The householder then restores to God his share in the crop and imposes upon God's share the discipline required by the logical character of that particular crop.

A productive corollary insists that the intentionality of the Israelite pertain to a very specific, differentiated corpus of produce. While holiness does not inhere in a given batch, so that the heave-offering of one batch may serve for several, nonetheless batches must be formed of like produce. That means that one's intentionality pertains to the species, not to the genus: olive oil, not olives in general, and so throughout. The particularity of the focus of intentionality cannot be overstated; the halakhah stresses the matter in a wide range of cases, e.g., they may not separate oil as heave-offering for olives which have been crushed, nor wine as heave-offering for grapes which have been trampled but the processing of which has not yet been completed.

On the other hand, when it comes to the actual identification of the portion of the crop to serve as heave-offering and so to be sanctified, the householder cannot act deliberately, choosing this part and not that, but must act in such a way that chance produces the selection. One cannot measure out or weigh out or count out the produce that is to be sanctified; rather, God indicates his choice through the workings of chance. That chance constitutes the expression of God's will is made explicit in various aggadic passages, and here the halakhah makes exactly the same statement. So man's intentionality arouses God's participation in the transaction, but God's role in making the selection then excludes man's participation in that chapter of the matter.

This brings us back to the correlative considerations, the specificity of intentionality, the teleology of that to which intentionality pertains. To state the matter in concrete terms: man's intentionality to sanctify an object must pertain to the particular object in mind, and God's intentionality for the sanctified object must be deemed equally specific. Man must sanctify a specific thing. God in creating that same specific thing did so for a particular purpose, and whoever gains the thing that man has sanctified must use that same thing in the manner that God has intended. The prerequisite of the act of sanctification – specificity – then finds its match in the teleology of that which is sanctified, man's intent, God's plan, matching for what is holy. What matches is the priority of an actor's plan.

Man's intent for a given object accordingly bears the power to classify as sacred that particular object. God's intent in making that same object controls the legitimate use of the object that is sanctified. So the plan or attitude or program of each party to the transaction – the householder's, God's – governs. But that takes place for each party in his own way. Man's intentionality dictates the classification of the object as God's (that is, as sanctified) and then, God's, the disposition, of the object now subjected to his ownership. That is where the teleology of things enters in. We may then say, once man has assigned ownership to God (through God's surrogates), God's plan in making an object, the teleology that inheres in that object, takes over. No wonder, then, that the halakhah so emphasizes the specificity of the transaction: this particular object (batch of produce), serving the natural purpose that inheres in this particular object, forming the transaction at which man and God intersect.

That somewhat complicated calculus yields a quite simple and now obvious proposition. In assigning to the status of sanctification a portion of the crop, the householder gives up his possession of, thus his right to subject to his own will, a batch of produce and assigns that which he gives up to God's domain, therefore makes the produce subject to God's will. God's will then extends to Israel in its way, to nature in its context. Stated in this way, the transaction in heave-offering represents an act of submission by man's to God's will that is very specific and concrete. The importance of the specificity of intentionality, on the one side, and the particularity of the teleology that governs the use of heave-offering, on the other hand, now merges. Israel and nature relate to God in accord with the same rules, in the same way, but in quite different dimensions.

Two distinct categories of the halakhah turn out to work together to make a single, quite remarkable statement, the one through the rules of sanctification through an act of will, the other through the disposition of that which has been sanctified in accord with the teleology that inheres therein. The message is the same: all things conform to the intention of the One who made them, each in its context and for its purpose. The obedience is not only the householder to the will of the senior partner, the Land-owner; it is also the conformity of the utilization of what has been sanctified to the purpose and intent of that same Actor. The householder conforms his will to God's. The produce likewise accords, in how it is legitimately utilized, to God's purpose. Designating produce as heave-offering and then utilizing it in an appropriate manner then, form a drama in which the actor and the acted upon – that is, the component of nature that is classified, sanctified – come together. Israel and nature, each in its way, carry out God's purpose, the one by the act of will, the other by the very character of its being. Israel by an act of will realizes God's will, nature, acted upon, bears witness to God by teleology's forming the criterion of legitimate utilization, that alone.

So the halakhah of Terumot returns us by a direct and smooth route to the issues of creation, once more realizing in concrete words and gestures the dynamics of the relationship between God and man – now: Israelite man, the householder – in creation. God has created the realm of nature, Eden and the Land (to invoke the principal locative categories of the aggadic-halakhic system, respectively). He did so with a purpose, and in each component of creation inheres the Creator's plan for that thing. And, we may now say, [1] when, through man's initiative, a component of creation is declared sacred, that particular thing subject to the intentionality of man must then realize the distinct and specific plan or purpose that defines the attitude of man. When then [2] man assigns to God a portion of the crop, that act of sanctification places that portion of the crop under God's plan and purpose in carrying out the act of creation. The rules that dictate the disposition of heave-offering therefore bring about a transaction in which wills work together, [2] God's and [1] man's, now to realize God's purpose in creation, on the one side, and demonstrate man's accord with that purpose, on the other.

Man by an act of will assigns to God his share in the produce of the Land, at which point that batch of produce becomes subject to God's will – meaning, the particular teleology of that produce, by species, not only genus. The act of sanctification then takes place when man by his act of will concerning what is subject to his possession declares subject to God's will that which, once made subject to God's will, must be utilized as God intended. Man then by the act of sanctification declares nature subject to God's initial purpose. In the setting of Terumot, which the system finds particularly appropriate for a statement of this character, Israelite man by an act of will declares subject to God's plan and program the produce of the Land that is God's share – a perfectly simple, rational, and right transaction reaffirming the order of nature. And that is a conception that the halakhah of Ma'aserot has not set forth, but for which that halakhah has prepared us. Israel in the Land has its role to play in restoring nature to its original perfection.

The fields yield their offering, the household its portion too. When the householder takes possession of his share of the crops, he also designates God's. Within the household itself, the householder does the same, but not for the same reason. At issue is God's share of the bread, but to understand what is at stake here and why God claims a portion – dough-offering – we must identify the exact point at which the obligation to separate God's share actually is incurred. For, in the model of our analysis of the halakhah of Ma'aserot, when we know *when* God's interest is provoked, we also know *why* – that is to say, what man does that elicits God's participation. Three principal considerations intersect: what constitutes bread that is liable to dough-offering, when liability takes effect, and where is the offering required? When we know the answers to these three questions, we may identify the religious conceptions that inhere in the halakhah. We start with the definition of bread: it is a baked food produce that is made of flour that, upon being moistened and kneaded and fermented, rises. What derives from flour that does not leaven is not liable to dough-offering and not classified as bread for purposes of Passover either.

Two criteria of liability coexist, one marking the beginning, the other the end, of the spell. First, people snack on dough without giving dough offering until the dough is made into a ball or is rolled out in a solid mass. But formal liability takes effect when a crust forms, which is to say, when the enzyme that brings about leavening dies.[1] These points of demarcation – when the liability commences, when the liability must be met – correspond to the points at which the crop in the field *may* be tithed, at the outset, and *must* be tithed, at the end of the harvesting-process. So the spell of liability commences with the mixture of flour and

---

[1] Obviously, the sages will not have used the language of contemporary science. But they certainly recognized when the leavening process ceased and knew the conditions for bringing it about, as their discussion here and at Pesahim makes quite apparent.

water and the working of the two into a mass, and it is fixed with the conclusion of the same process. The upshot is, the span of susceptibility coincides with the process of fermentation: the activation of the enzyme, at the outset, then the cultivation of the fermentation process, and finally the realization of the goal of that process in the forming of a crust, the conclusion of fermentation. And, to address the third question briefly, dough-offering must be presented out of dough made from grain that is eaten by Israel in the Land of Israel.[2] The Mishnah insists that the priests will not accept dough-offering from bread prepared overseas.

We may say that the critical criterion is [1] dough that has incurred liability within the Land of Israel and [2] that is consumed by Israelites in the Land. So there is a very specific point of intersection that dictates which dough is liable to dough-offering: [1] dough prepared from wheat and comparable flour, which, when mixed with yeast and water, has the power to ferment; [2] dough at the point at which the fermentation-process has realized its goal. The upshot is that the derivation of the grain by itself bears no consequence. But the processing of the flour produced by the grain, and the location of the Israelites who consume the bread form the critical criteria.

Dough that has formed a crust within the Land of Israel is liable, whatever the origin of the flour. In the priests' view dough-offering may not be brought from outside of the Land of Israel, but that is not because considerations of cultic cleanness pertain, which would exclude the produce of foreign lands, unclean as they are by definition. That is an explicit issue at M. Hallah 2:3, even though one may designate an unclean portion as dough-offering (Aqiba): just as he may designate dough-offering for a clean portion of dough, so he may designate dough-offering for an unclean portion of dough. This is then burned. So why the priests should reject dough-offering brought by Israelites from abroad is clear: it is when Israelites in the Land of Israel prepare dough that liability takes effect. Then the actuality of Israel dwelling on the Land, not the origin of the grain, determines: Israelites living in the Land of Israel separate dough-offering from the bread that they are going to eat, from the point at which the bread begins to ferment, and they are obligated to do so from the point at which the bread has ceased to ferment.

That the whole forms an exercise in thinking about the fermentation process is demonstrated, moreover, by the explicit insistence that just as flour produces dough subject to dough-offering only if a fermentation

---

[2]Not necessarily grown in the Land of Israel, but possibly from the interstitial territory of Syria, which is neither part of the Land of Israel nor part of the land of the gentiles.

process is possible, so flour produces unleavened bread valid for Passover only if a fermentation process is possible but is thwarted. So the bread that the Israelites in the Land of Israel eat to which God establishes his claim is comparable in its traits to the bread that the Israelites leaving Egypt, or commemorating their Exodus from Egypt, are required to eat – and that bread too is liable to dough-offering, as a matter of fact. At stake, then, is the fermentation-process itself: *Then God takes notice.* The process need not take place, but it must bear the potential to take place. So it may not affect the bread of the Exodus – which is liable to dough-offering – but it must affect the bread of Israel in the Land of Israel – also liable.

Having come this far, we may readily perceive the broad outlines of a simple message: bread in which God takes an interest is bread subject to living processes of nature: the life of the enzyme (as we should express matters). Leavening then is the key to the definition of bread. Taken as a natural process, leavening is animate, or is perceived as animate. It comes about "through the action of gas bubbles developed naturally or folded in from the atmosphere. Leavening may result from yeast or bacterial fermentation, from chemical reactions or from the distribution in the batter of atmospheric or injected gases.[3] Fermentation, required for wine or beer as much as for bread involves a process of frothing brought about by micro-organisms growing in the absence of air.

How then draw conclusions from natural processes of fermentation, perceived as the animation of the food? The calculus then is readily discerned: Israel's life in the Land of Israel is nourished through the transformation of grain into bread, that is, through the life-process that takes grain and makes it edible and life-sustaining. Then and there God lays his claim to a share: when Israel renews its life, meal by meal, its action in invoking the life-process of fermentation, start to finish, provokes God's reaction. That is because God too has a share in the transaction by which life is maintained – but (as the priests clearly maintained) only the transaction that takes place between Israel and the Land of Israel, there alone.

Does Israel have a say in the inauguration of the fermentation process and the engagement of God therein? To this exchange, this transfer and renewal of Israel's life in engagement with the living processes of nature, Israel's intentionality plays no role; the processes go forward willy-nilly. Then what about intentionality, e.g., that of the baker? In fact, that point is raised explicitly, in connection with M. Hallah 1:5. There the question is raised on whether a third party imposes upon grain the status of that which has been fully processed and is liable to be

---

[3]Samuel A. Matz, "Baking and Bakery Products," *Encyclopaedia Britannica* 2:597.

tithed. One authority maintains that he has imposed liability, even though the owner of the pile of grain does not know and approve of his action, the other denies it. That is in line with M. Hallah 1:7: As regards women who gave dough to the baker to make it into leaven for them – if the dough of each woman comprises less than the prescribed minimum volume subject to dough-offering , the dough is exempt from dough-offering. If the volume of all the women all together does meet the requisite amount to impose liability to dough-offering, the dough will be exempt, because it was the baker, not the woman, who owned the dough, who imposed liability. But contrary opinion registers as well.

Israel becomes responsible for the cultic cleanness of the produce only by an act of intentionality, but Israel becomes liable to hand over God's share of the produce willy-nilly. So it is with life. Let me explain, beginning with the question of why intentionality plays no role in the liability of the dough to dough-offering. The reason becomes clear when we recall the critical role human intentionality plays in the halakhah of Lev. 11:34, 37, worked out in tractate Makhshirin, the counterpart and opposite of the halakhah of Hallah. That halakhic category maintains that produce that is dry is insusceptible to uncleanness, that which is wet is susceptible; but the wetting down, to prove affective, must take place by intention. Thus, while what is deliberately wet down is subject to uncleanness, what is accidentally wet down is not. Here, by contrast, the mixing of the flour, salt, yeast, and water inaugurates a process through which, at the end, liability to the offering is incurred – whether the process came about deliberately or accidentally. A simple formulation involves a concrete case. A householder takes flour, which is dry and has not been deliberately wet down. Why not? Because once wet down, the flour moulders. The householder further takes yeast. And, putting the two together, the householder adds water. At that moment, when the process of kneading dough to bake bread commences (in contemporary language: with the irrigation of the yeast and the dough, the moment at which the dough congeals and the yeast buds and ferments, producing its sugar, its carbon dioxide, and its ethanol) – at that exact moment, the instant of animation, at which the bread begins to live, the householder goes on the alert for dangers to the bread – and so throughout.

That explains why the householder goes on the alert at the point at which he or she intentionally puts water on the dough. Then the flour, now dough, is susceptible to uncleanness. So in a cuisine based on bread (not potatoes, not rice, for example) what is at stake in "wetting down seed," based on the analogy of adding water to dry flour and yeast, is the point at which vegetation begins the process by which it becomes maximally edible and useful to the householder. Then – life bubbling away in the process of fermentation, deliberately inaugurated – the state of sanctification comes under threat from the source of uncleanness, such as corpse-uncleanness and its analogues, that the Torah has identified.

The moment of wetting grain down defines the hour of conflict between life and death, yielding sanctification or uncleanness – and this in concrete ways. Then, at the very time, the act done with deliberation precipitates the conflict. But that is only if the householder cares. If the householder does not intend the dough to congeal and the yeast to rise, in regard to susceptibility to uncleanness nothing of consequence happens. It is the Israelite's will and intention and the act that realizes them that endow with consequence what by nature happens willy-nilly. But so far as the process itself, it does not depend upon the householder's intentionality. The fermentation process that animates the flour and produces bread goes forward whether or not the householder intended it to. Nothing he does can stop it once it has started, and no call upon his alertness to prevent uncleanness is issued. That is why God's claim on the dough, for the dough-offering for the priesthood, does not depend upon man's intentionality – irrelevant to the process of animation, of bringing life to the inert flour – but upon God's own reason for engagement. That has to do with the maintenance of the processes of life, man's and nature's.

If I had to identify where the everyday meets the Eternal, I should choose the here and now of petty obsessions with tiny events and their intangible, animated histories, down to the moment of adding water to the yeast and dough when making bread: when life renews itself through the life-precipitating touch of water to the flour and the yeast. Here considerations of uncleanness and those of sanctification intersect. That is the point that precipitates concern with the forces of death, prime source of cultic uncleanness. Then, to preserve purity, Israel goes on the alert for the danger of pollution: at the moment when yeast, flour, and water ignite the processes of animation. So too for all of their counterparts: "if water be put on the seed," take care. Now we see the other half of the story. Unclean or otherwise, the dough congeals, the yeast ferments and yields gas, and so, life-processes having commenced, though death and its surrogates threaten. Then the householder goes on the alert – if he cares, if by an act of deliberation he has made life happen. And there too, by sharing the outcome of the fermentation with God, the householder acknowledges the opposite of death, which is life, embodied in the living processes by which the bread comes into being, and resulting in the presence, within the dough, of a portion subject to sanctification: donation to the priest in the present instance.

The particularity of dough-offering should now register. It is paid from bread made from grain from which the heave-offering has already been removed. So the critical point of differentiation – an offering from the mixture of flour, yeast, and water, taken from when fermentation starts to when it ends – takes on still greater consequence. Wine and beer ferment, but no counterpart offering from wine, over and above the heave-offering and tithes to which all produce is liable, is demanded, nor from beer. In the wine-olive-oil-wheat-culture of the Land of Israel, it is only wheat, in the course of its later processing, that becomes subject to a further offering of the present kind, one linked to its life-cycle. And that is because – so it seems to me – bread stands for life, consumed to be sure with oil and wine. Therefore it is the processing of flour into bread to sustain life where fermentation represents life that particularly registers. That marks the occasion for the affirmation of God's presence in all life-forms and processes: God lays his claim to his share, because God's claim upon the Israelite householder extends to the outer limits of vitality.

II. From the Bible to the Torah

The faithful of Judaism through the ages reach Scripture through oral tradition recorded here, never encountering an unmediated Scripture (whether historically or philologically or archaeologically, for example). Moses is always *rabbenu*, "our rabbi," and Isaiah, "Rabbi Isaiah." Jacob looked into the present and described the future, and Abraham, Moses, and the prophets met God on the afternoon of the ninth of Ab in the year we now number as 70 and rebuked him for what he had done through the Romans. These realizations do not draw upon easy sentimentality or resort to figurative conceits. People acted upon them every day, built their lives around them, met God in them. Their concrete actions, the deprivations they accepted and humiliations they turned into validation – these attest to the palpable reality, for holy Israel, of the vision of the dual Torah. Have they been, and are they today, right in reaching the Written Torah through the path set out by the Oral one?

Sages claimed in the Oral Torah, represented here by the Mishnah, Tosefta, Sifra, and other documents, to set forth the meaning of the Written Torah. This they did by translating into the norms of social conduct the conceptions set forth in the narratives of Scripture, beginning with Genesis. Speaking descriptively, standing back and seeing things whole, can we concur? Are sages right about the written part of the Torah, meaning, is what they say the Written Torah says actually what the ancient Israelite Scriptures say? Will those who put forth the books of Genesis through Kings as a sustained narrative and those who in that same context selected and organized the writings of the prophets, Isaiah, Jeremiah, Ezekiel, and the twelve, in the aggregate have concurred in sages' structure and system? Certainly others who lay claim to these same Scriptures did not concur. At the time the sages did their greatest theological work, in the fourth and fifth century C.E., their Christian counterparts, in the Latin, Greek and Syriac speaking sectors of Christianity alike, not only read Scripture in a very different way but also accused the rabbis of falsifying the Torah. How would the sages have responded to the charge?

That is certainly how sages want us to see matters, for that is how they present them. Implicit in the apologetics that forms an integral part of the theology of the Oral Torah two judgments take up a constant presence. When the faithful claim that the sages are right about Scripture, there is a formal argument that is set forth in vast detail in the Rabbinic writings. Specifically, nearly every proposition they set forth, the main beams of the structure of faith they construct – all sets securely and symmetrically upon the written Torah. Proof-texts constantly take the measure of the structure. That is why sages speak of the one whole Torah, in two media, correlative and complementary.

But beyond the formal argument, there is the substance of matters. Sages have not only history – the pivotal position of their writings in the sequence from *before* to *after* – but also hermeneutics on their side. In their reading of the written Torah whole, in canonical context, as a record of life with God, they are right to say their story goes over the written Torah's story. Start to finish, creation through Sinai to the fall of Jerusalem, all perceived in the light of the prophets' rebuke, consolation, and hope for restoration, Scripture's account is rehearsed in the Oral Torah. All is in proportion and balance. Viewed as a systematic hermeneutics, the sages' theology accurately sets forth the principal possibility of the theology that is implicit in the written part of the Torah – to be sure, in a more systematic and cogent manner than does Scripture.

Why do I maintain that the sages are right about Scripture? It is because, start to finish, the Oral Torah builds its structure out of a reading of the Written Torah. Sages read from the Written Torah forward to the Oral Torah. That is not only attested by the superficial character of proof-texting, but by the profound congruence of the theology of the Oral Torah with the course of the Scriptural exposition. Any outline of Scripture's account begins with creation and tells about the passage from Eden via Sinai and Jerusalem to Babylon – and back. It speaks of the patriarchal founders of Israel, the Exodus, Sinai, the Torah, covenants, Israel, the people of God, the priesthood and the tabernacle, the possession of the Land, exile and restoration. And so too has this outline of the Oral Torah's theology focused upon all of these same matters. True, sages proportion matters within their own logic, laying heaviest emphasis upon perfection, imperfection, and restoration of perfection to creation, focusing upon Israel, God's stake in humanity.

The theological structure and system appeal to the perfection of creation and account for imperfection by reference to the fall of man into sin by reason of arrogant rebellion and into death in consequence. They tell the story of the formation of holy Israel as God's party in humanity, signified by access to knowledge of God through God's self-manifestation in the Torah. They then present the exile Israel from and to the Land of Israel as the counterpart to the exile of Adam from Eden and the return of Israel to the Land. Therefore main beams of the Hebrew Scripture's account of matters define the structure of the Oral Torah's theology. The generative tensions of the Hebrew Scripture's narrative empower the dynamics of that theology.

A few obvious facts suffice. Take the principal propositions of Scripture read in sequence and systematically, meaning, as exemplary, from Genesis through Kings. Consider the story of the exile from Eden and the counterpart exile of Israel from the Land. Sages did not invent that paradigm. Scripture's framers did. Translate into propositional form the prophetic messages of admonition, rebuke, and consolation, the promise that as punishment follows sin, so consolation will come in consequence of repentance. Sages did not fabricate those categories and make up the rules that govern the sequence of events. The prophets said them all. Sages only recapitulated the prophetic propositions with little variation except in formulation. All sages did was to interpret within the received paradigm the exemplary events of their own day, the destruction of Jerusalem and Israel's subjugation in particular. But even at that they simply asked Scripture's question of events that conformed to Scripture's pattern. Identify as the dynamics of human history the engagement of God with man, especially through Israel, and what do you have, if not the heart of sages' doctrine of the origins and destiny of man. Review what Scripture intimates about the meaning and end of time, and how much do you miss of sages' eschatology of restoration? Details, amplifications, clarifications, an unsuccessful effort at systematization – these do not obscure the basic confluence of sages' and Scripture's account of last things (even though, as I said, the word "last" has its own meaning for sages).

Nor do I have to stress the form that sages impart to their propositions, nearly everything they say being joined to a verse of Scripture. That is not a formality. Constant citations of scriptural texts cited as authority serve merely to signal the presence of a profound identity of viewpoint. The cited verses are not solely pretexts or formal proof-texts. A hermeneutics governs, dictating the course of exegesis. In concrete terms, the theology I have outlined generates the exegesis we have encountered on nearly every page of this book. Sages cite and interpret verses of Scripture to show where and how the written Torah guides the oral one, supplying the specificities of the process of recapitulation. And what sages say about those verses originates not in the small details of those verses (such as Aqiba was able to interpret to Moses's stupefaction) but in the large theological structure and system that sages framed.

That is why I insist that the hermeneutics defined the exegesis, the exegesis did not define the hermeneutics – as I have shown many times in my systematic analysis of the various Midrash-compilations.[4] In most of the Midrash-compilations of the Oral Torah it is the simple fact that sages read from the whole to the parts, from the Written part of the Torah outward to the Oral part, as we shall observe in a moment. That explains why nothing arbitrary or merely occasional, nothing ad hoc or episodic or notional characterized sages reading of Scripture, but a theology, formed whole in response to the whole. That explains why the sages did not think they imputed to Scripture meanings not actually there, and this account of their theology proves that they are right.

Sages read Scripture as a letter written that morning to them in particular about the world they encountered. That is because for them the past was forever integral to the present. So they looked into the Written part of the Torah to construct the picture of reality that is explained by world-view set forth in the Oral part of the Torah. They found their questions in Scripture; they identified the answers to those questions in Scripture; and they then organized and interpreted the contemporary situation of holy Israel in light of those questions and answers. To that process the narrow focus of atomistic exegesis proves monumentally irrelevant, indeed, even incongruous. For the very category, proof-text, reduces that elegant theology of the here and now to the trivialities of grammar or spelling or other nonsense-details. It demeans sages' intellectual honesty, such as, on every page of the Talmud of Babylonia among many documents, is affirmed and attested by the very character of discourse. And it misses the fact that Scripture's corpus of facts, like nature's, was deemed to transcend the bonds of time. That explains why sages found in Scripture the main lines of structure and system that formed the architecture of their theology.

---

[4]To give a single example, I point to *Judaism and Scripture: The Evidence of Leviticus Rabbah*. Chicago, 1986: The University of Chicago Press. I have dealt systematically with the atomistic reading of the Midrash-compilations in *The Documentary Foundation of Rabbinic Culture. Mopping Up after Debates with Gerald L. Bruns, S. J. D. Cohen, Arnold Maria Goldberg, Susan Handelman, Christine Hayes, James Kugel, Peter Schaefer, Eliezer Segal, E. P. Sanders, and Lawrence H. Schiffman.* Atlanta, 1995: Scholars Press for South Florida Studies in the History of Judaism.

And it accounts for the fact that, in the heavenly academy to which corner of Eden imagination carried them, the great sages could amiably conduct arguments with God and with Moses. Not only so, but they engage in on-going dialogue with the prophets and psalmists and the other saints of the written Torah as well as with those of their masters and teachers in the oral tradition who reached Eden earlier (much as entire legions of participants in the Oral Torah in recent centuries aspire to spend an afternoon in Eden with Moses Maimonides). A common language joined them all, for in their entire engagement with the written part of the Torah, sages mastered every line, every word, every letter, sorting matters of the day out in response to what they learned in the written tradition.

That explains why we may justifiably say that on every page of the writings of the Oral Torah we encounter the sages' encompassing judgment of, response to, the heritage of ancient Israel's Scripture. There they met God, there they found God's plan for the world of perfect justice, the flawless, eternal world in stasis, and there in detail they learned what became of that teaching in ancient times and in their own day, everything seen in the same way. The result is spread out in the pages of this book: sages' account of the Torah revealed by God to Moses at Sinai and handed on in tradition through the ages. So if we ask, what if, in the timeless world of the Torah studied in the same heavenly academy, Moses and the prophets, sages, and scribes of Scripture were to take up the results of oral tradition produced by their heirs and successors in the oral part of the Torah? the answer is clear. They would have found themselves hearing familiar words, their own words, used by honest, faithful men, in familiar, wholly legitimate ways. When, for example, Moses heard in the tradition of the Oral Torah that a given law was a law revealed by God to Moses at Sinai, he may have kept his peace, though puzzled, or he may have remembered that, indeed, that is how it was, just so. In very concrete, explicit language the sages themselves laid their claim to possess the Torah of Moses.

So it is entirely within the imaginative capacity of the Oral Torah to raise the question: what came before in relationship to what we have in hand? To state the matter more directly, are the rabbis of the Oral Torah right in maintaining that they have provided the originally-oral part of the one whole Torah of Moses our rabbi? To answer that question in the affirmative, sages would have only to point to their theology in the setting of Scripture's as they grasped it. As I said at the very outset of the first lecture, the theology of the Oral Torah tells a simple, sublime story.

[1] God created a perfect, just world and in it made man in his image, equal to God in the power of will.

[2] Man in his arrogance sinned and was expelled from the perfect world and given over to death. God gave man the Torah to purify his heart of sin.

[3] Man educated by the Torah in humility can repent, accepting God's will of his own free will. When he does, man will be restored to Eden and eternal life.

In our terms, we should call it a story with a beginning, middle, and end. In sages' framework, we realize, the story embodies an enduring and timeless paradigm of humanity in the encounter with God: man's powerful will, God's powerful word, in conflict, and the resolution thereof.

But if about the written Torah I claim sages were right, then what about the hermeneutics of others? If the sages claimed fully to spell out the message of the written Torah, as they do explicitly in nearly every document and on nearly every page of the Oral Torah, so too did others. And those others, who, like the sages, added to the received Scripture other writings of a (to-them) authoritative character, set forth not only the story of the fall from grace that occupied sages but, in addition, different stories from those the sages told. They drew different consequences from the heritage of ancient Israel. Sages' critics will find their account not implausible but incomplete, a truncated reading of Scripture. They will wonder about leaving out nearly the entire apocalyptic tradition.[5] But, in the balance, sages' critics err. For no one can reasonably doubt that sages' reading of Scripture recovers, in proportion and accurate stress and balance, the main lines of Scripture's principal story, the one about creation, the fall of man and God's salvation of man through Israel and the Torah. In familiar, though somewhat gauche, language, "Judaism" really is what common opinion thinks it is, which is, "the religion of the Old Testament." That common characterization, profoundly wrong, is absolutely on target and affirms precisely what the sages alleged in behalf of their law and theology. If, as our generation's greatest theologian and scholar of Scripture, Brevard Childs, states, "The evangelists read from the New [Testament] backward to the Old,"[6] we may say very simply: *the sages read from the written Torah forward to the oral one.* When I say, the sages were right, this is what I claim to have shown in the Hiram College Lectures for 1999.

---

[5]That is with two exceptions, for, so far as that tradition can be naturalized into the framework established by sages' structure and system, sages do so, as in the case of Daniel. Second, they take over as fact and accept apocalyptic expectations, as with the war of Gog and Magog.

[6]*Biblical Theology of the Old and New Testaments*, p. 720.

OTHER ESSAYS

4

What Is "A Judaism"?
Seeing the Dead Sea Library as the Statement of a Coherent Judaic Religious System
A Programmatic Statement

Jacob Neusner
University of South Florida and Bard College

I

When the earliest documents of the Qumran library surfaced, people found a place for them within what they called "Judaism." This they did by classifying the writings among the known sects: Pharisees, Sadducees, Essenes. That is to say, they worked within the model of a single, unitary, normative Judaism, which encompassed also sects; they took for granted the library did not belong to the normative Judaism, so they attempted to situate it among the known sects, thus a sectarian Judaism, to be seen in comparison and contrast to the normative kind. Evidence to link the unknown to the known served to sustain every position and its opposite, though, for some decades, a consensus developed around "the Essene library of Qumran." During those same decades study of the writings from historical and philological perspectives achieved formidable progress, while the religious study of the same documents found itself paralyzed.

Two sources sustained the status quo of an obviously jerry-built construction. First, people were used to thinking in terms of a single, encompassing and normative Judaism, which defined the context in which all religious writing deriving from Jews, except for that of Jewish followers of Jesus, found a place. That other writing attested to yet another unitary and normative religion, Christianity. Second, the model of church and sect governed, with the result that the principal taxonomy directed writings to the taxon of church or the taxa of sects, the latter read in relationship to the former. The norm, the writings of the church, dictated the readings of sectarian documents: like or unlike the norm. The two givens joined to deprive the Dead Sea Writings of a systemic reading.

That is to say, in the main journals of Qumran studies and in the principal systematic statements on the library, we find ample attention to problems of a literary character. Sophisticated and ambitious historical readings of the whole library have placed the compositions within a particular time and place, and a consensus has taken shape around principal allegations as to concrete historical fact made by the writings. The debate on the standing and character of the library viewed whole has generated a variety of well-crafted positions. But we look in vain for a thorough and sustained examination of the library within the model of a textual community,[1] one that preserved in written form a coherent religious structure. While details of a religious character, e.g., the figure of the Messiah, the hermeneutics and exegetics of the commentaries on the Hebrew Scriptures, receive ample attention in the canon of Qumran learning, few have attempted to form of the details a single account: what is the religious system (a term defined in the shank of this chapter) that encompassed the whole of the writings, and what imparts to the details that governing world view that animated the life of the community and pervaded its inner life?

It was probably inevitable that questions that required seeing the library as a whole and within the model of a self-sustaining, self-validating religious community should be postponed two generations. If people took for granted that the library attested to an existing group, then established givens would dictate the reading of the parts and further lend coherence supplied from without to the links between and among those parts. And, further, if the paramount hermeneutics derived from historical and philological but not religious study, people were unlikely to ask questions of to perceive how the whole of the writings as evidence of a coherent world view distinctive to the community that produced much, and valued all, of the writings and therefore preserved them. When it came to the study of Judaism in particular, moreover, the theory of a single, unitary, harmonious, and continuous "tradition"

---

[1] A term invented by Brian Stock, *Implications of Literacy* (Princeton, 19 ?? Princeton University Press).

predominated. So long as elements of the Qumran writings taken out of their own context found a place within that tradition, e.g., as the missing link between Scripture's and the Mishnah's law, no one was apt to see matters in their own terms and framework at all.

But the prevailing hermeneutics of the Dead Sea library, with its heavy emphasis upon history and philology, met little competition from the side of the study of religion so far as Judaism was concerned. For not until the 1970s was the position, first outlined by Erwin R. Goodenough in his *Jewish Symbols in the Greco-Roman Period*[2] that antiquity knew more than one "Judaism," systematically explored. Others also recognize the diversity of evidence concerning "Judaism," and in the 1950s in the USA (but nowhere else) people began to try to explain, rather than merely explain away, the blatant indications that "Judaism" in ideal and reality could not be described simply by looking up pertinent passages in the Mishnah, Midrash, and Talmuds, that is, in the writings then, in the USA and the English-speaking world influenced by American scholarship, deemed normative for Judaism.

But like others Goodenough found himself constrained by George F. Moore's notion of "normative Judaism," with the result that he posited a Judaism portrayed by the literary sources, on the one side, and a Judaism set forth in the archaeological evidence, on the other. That essentially confirmed the status quo. And for another entire generation, until the mid-1970s, the notion of holistic description of a single body of evidence, viewed as a coherent statement, suffered neglect. That is because another way of seeing things than the prevalent one simply was not explored. Until the appearance of E. P. Sanders, *Paul and Palestinian Judaism*,[3] no one had ever shown what a coherent picture of several distinct Judaisms, each examined in its own terms, would look like.

So far as I know, Sanders was the first to portray as sustained and crafted religious systems, without attempting to harmonize, or correlate, or explain away differences among them, the Judaism of the Dead Sea community, the Judaism of the rabbis, and the Judaism of Paul. The work exhibited profound flaws, since it was undertaken on a narrowly-historical base and therefore required that all of the Judaisms flourish on the same plane of time. The advantages of the comparative study of religions applied to the study of different system of the same genus of religions (here: Judaism) were lost in a morass of historical confusion. And, alas, Sanders himself repudiated the entire approach in his *Judaism*, published two decades later.[4] But in his first, and single most

---

[2](Princeton, 19??: Princeton University Press for Bollingen), Volume IV Part 1.
[3]Philadelphia, 19??: Fortress Press.
[4]Philadelphia, 19??: Trinity Press International.

important work on Judaism, Sanders opened up an entirely new approach to the study of ancient Judaism, and in systematically differentiating between and among the formations of a single religion, he provoked thought on an entirely fresh set of questions.

Sanders' formulation in 1977 of the diversity of Judaism, within a few years prompted me to add two small details. These were revisions in the spelling of generative categories, [1] an "s" to Judaism, thus "Judaisms," and [2] an "f" in place of the n of normative, hence, formative Judaism. To speak of "Judaisms" instead of "Judaism" underscored the autonomy of a coherent body of data and sidestepped the problem of how to define a single "Judaism" out of all the diverse data deemed to attest to that one Judaism. That problem could be dealt with in its own, theological context; it need no longer intervene in the work of description, analysis, and interpretation of the data of a given religious community. The notion of "Judaisms" further responded to the fact that earliest Christians thought of themselves as "Israel" and (appealing now to our categories, not theirs) their religious system as Judaism.

How and why a single unitary Judaism and a uniform and whole Christianity parted company from one another no longer represented an urgent problem of historical description (though it would endure as a principal problem of theology of Christianity and therefore also of Judaism within the Judaeo-Christian ambiance). And concomitantly, speaking of formative, not normative Judaism made ample space for the diverse Judaisms, each represented by its own writings, that flourished in the centuries in which the paramount religions to emerge from the ancient world, catholic, orthodox Christianity and Rabbinic Judaism, were taking shape. Differentiating distinct and coherent bodies of data instead of trying to harmonize them would then represent a challenge to another generation's powers of analysis and imagination.

II

What required imagination was the answer to this question: given this detail, how would I conceive the whole of which the detail forms a part? Am I able to extrapolate a whole from a detail, to formulate a system that holds together all of the available parts? And that is the question – the question of systemic analysis – that we need to address to details of the Dead Sea library. That is not to suggest the Dead Sea writings constitute a single, systemic statement and stand for a uniform and unitary community of the faithful, one that differentiated itself from all others and set forth what in my language I call "a Judaism." That, as a matter of historical fact, remains moot. What we have take as postulate

What Is "A Judaism"?

is that the writings not only portray each its own picture but all together a coherent account of a Judaism: a world view, a way of life, and a theory of who and what is "Israel," terms spelled out in due course presently. It is time to engage in a collective act of imagination: what if? can I extrapolate a whole from a part, the whole from my particular component?

For such an exercise we postulate constitutes a coherent system, a complete Judaism (in whatever context the contributors think appropriate, whether a single continuous Judaism or multiple Judaisms, makes no difference here). Only for the purpose of speculation, we need to hypothesize that in the Qumran writings we hold in hand the components of a Judaism seen as a coherent system of thought and practice, a religious theory of a Judaic social order that probably produced and certainly valued these writings. Within that reading of the writings, we ask these questions: within the topic at hand, what is that theory, that system? We wonder, how does this group of people represented in the subject on which you write conceive of itself to be "Israel" in the tradition of Scripture? What way of life have they devised for themselves to express their relationship with God as the holy community, Israel? What world view accounts for, explains, that way of life, that sense of being "Israel"?

We ask, above all, are we able to propose a theory of the unifying question that the system identifies as critical, and what is the self-evident answer to that question that the system seen whole puts forth and then realizes in the way of life and world view that recapitulate the whole? The premise of systemic analysis is, the details recapitulate the system as a whole, so we work within that premise by reading details as though they recapitulate a system as a whole and speculating on what you conceive that system, viewed whole, to look like. This is an assignment in scholarly imagination, something scholars are not frequently asked to undertake. But when it comes to the study of religion, it is an assignment not to be avoided or dismissed.

In each case, the assignment is to address the questions that history and philology have neglected or ignore altogether: what world view, way of life, and theory of what and who is "Israel" animates the system, the component of which is treated in my chapter? Take the case of worship and divine service by way of illustration: here are people who framed prayers to God and otherwise worshipped God. Then how do they conceive God, how do they understand the act of prayer, what is the shape of their piety and the embodiment of their relationship – and, above all, how do we identify, within those facts that you will briefly summarize, the nourishing piety, the sustaining vision of God with us, that animated this community? If we look at the details set forth within what I postulate to represent the Pharisaic Judaism, we see a fully articulated religious system that focuses on issues of sanctification, and the critical question is, how are we to relate to the sanctification of the Temple, how does holy Israel attain sanctification not in the cult but in the model of the cult?

Accordingly, the program proposed in this essay raises this questions: What are the counterpart preoccupations of the group assembled at Qumran, represented by the documents? Can I see them whole, and can I show how the part for which I am responsible states (its contribution to) the whole? Among the many books on the Qumran library, none asks the question formulated here, broadly characterized as the question of *the religious study of religion*.

III

All systemic analysis of a religion begins with the social question: for whom do these data speak, and what social world do they represent. That foundation of systemic analysis makes the Qumran library an ideal setting for study, for what makes this collection of writings into an ideal setting for the description of a Judaic religious system is the given of all else. It is the simple fact, upon which most Qumran scholarship concurs, that the writings form a library and so tell us that a community of Jews valued and preserved the these writings. Within the hypothesis at hand, that suffices to allow us to postulate a social foundation, a communal context for the writings, seen not as a random collection of this and that but as a sustained account, in written permanent form, of ideas deemed authoritative by a community, an "Israel." A religious system, a Judaism, is not the same thing as a book or even a collection of books; it is what we find at the confluence of literary (and, where available, archaeological) evidence and (a theory of) the community for whom, and to whom, that evidence speaks. So we build on the premise, then, that the writings speak for those who chose them.

But I have gotten ahead of my story. Let me begin at the beginning. Systemic analysis aims to describe, analyze, and interpret the data of a single cogent origin, e.g., a library as at Qumran, or a canon (so determined perhaps late in the formation thereof), as with the dual Torah of Rabbinic Judaism. Systemic analysis takes up one Judaism at a time, and then aims at a later stage to compare one Judaic system with some other, so as to uncover the principles of selection and the logic operative within each. So systemic analysis seeks to locate the logic or the rationality of a given system and to relate that logic to the context of the system. Systemic analysis aims to interpret data seen whole. Now, if we wish to ask questions of interpretation, we have systematically to

What Is "A Judaism"?

describe, analyze, and then interpret. We need to know what it is that we wish to describe, how we shall analyze – that is, through systemic comparison and contrast – and what questions we ask in the quest for meaning we call interpretation.

JUDAISM AND A JUDAISM: While people commonly speak of "Judaism," in fact across time we find not one Judaism but many. The gap between one set of data, produced by a given group, in a determinate time and place, and another set of data, must impress anyone who stops to peer into the abyss that separates one group of Jews from some other. It is not a merely diachronic gap, in that "Judaism" in the time of Ezra is obviously different from "Judaism" in the time of the Essenes and "Judaism" as formulated by Maimonides. The synchronic problem is still more acute. The varieties of ways of life and worldviews exhibited by people who stoutly claimed for themselves the title, "Israel," must impress us not only in our own day but through history. The diversity of Judaisms generally characterizes not only the diachronic continuum but also the synchronic frame, which sets bounds around the data deemed definitive of, and appropriate to, (any) "Judaism." All solutions to the problem of difference and disharmony among Judaic data constitute statements of a theological (or ideological) judgment and bear no relevance to the requirements of description, analysis, and interpretation that dictate humanistic study.[5] That is why my method requires that we speak not of "Judaism" as a single, encompassing religion, but rather *a Judaism*, that is, a particular religious system, with its own traits and definitions.

WHAT IS A JUDAISM: A Judaism is a religious system comprising a theory of the social entity, the "Israel," constituted by the group of Jews who sustain that Judaism; a way of life characteristic of, perhaps distinctive to, that group of Jews; and a worldview that accounts for the group's forming a distinctive social entity and explains those indicative traits that define the entity. Within this definition, I see the formation of a religious system, e.g., a Judaism, in three aspects:

[1] a worldview, which by reference to the intersection of the supernatural and the natural worlds accounts for how things are and puts them together into a cogent and harmonious picture;

[2] a way of life, which expresses in concrete actions the worldview and which is explained by that worldview;

---

[5]I spell this out at some length in "Alike and Not Alike," in J. Neusner, ed., *Take Judaism for Example. Studies toward the Comparison of Religions* (Chicago: University of Chicago Press, 1983), pp. 227-236.

[3] and a social group, for which the worldview accounts, which is defined in concrete terms by the way of life, and therefore which gives expression in the everyday world to the worldview and is defined as an entity by that way of life.

That context finds definition in the encompassing society, by contrast to which the distinctive social entity sees itself as different. The encompassing world constitutes the framework within which a given Judaism takes shape. The social entity in the case of a Judaism always appeals to "Israel" and calls itself (an) "Israel. No Judaic system can omit a clear picture of the meaning and sense of the category, Israel. Without an *Israel*, a social entity in fact and not only in doctrine, we have not a system but a book. And a book is not a Judaism, it is only a book. This book is not about books that theologians, philosophers, or visionaries wrote. It is about Judaisms that Jews have created and that have sustained the lives of Jews. So let me repeat with emphasis, for all that follows, my choices of what to treat and what to bypass, rests upon this principle of the definition of a religious system: *a book is not a Judaism and a Judaism is not a book* – except after the fact.[6]

IV

In systemic analysis, we deal then with a religious theory of the social order. A theory of the social order need not appeal to religion or be characterized as a religious system of the social order, in the way in which I describe a Judaism. What makes a theory of the social order into a religious one? A religious system is one that appeals to God as the principal power, and a Judaic system is a religious system that identifies the Hebrew Scriptures or "Old Testament" as a principal component of its canon. A Judaism, then, comprises not merely a theory – a book – distinct from social reality but an explanation for the group (again: "Israel") that gives social form to the system and an account of the

---

[6]The importance of this principle of selection cannot be missed. Let me explain by way of example. I do not see the writings of Philo as a Judaism, though they may represent a Judaism. We have distinctive books that represent social groups, for instance the apocalyptic writings of the Second Temple period, but our knowledge of those social groups – their way of life, their worldview, their identification of themselves as Israel – is imperfect. Consequently we cannot relate the contents of a system to its context or account for the substance of a system by appeal to its circumstance. We therefore know the answers provided by a system – that is, the contents of the book – but have not got a clear picture of the questions that the answers take up, or, still more important, the political or social forces that made those questions urgent and inescapable, in just that place, in just that time. In my work I always select those Judaisms that do allow for reasonably complete description, therefore also analysis and interpretation.

distinctive way of life of that group. A Judaism is not a book, and no social group took shape because people read a book and agreed that God had revealed what the book said they should do. Let me state with emphasis: *a Judaic system derives from and focuses upon a social entity, a group of Jews who (in their minds at least) constitute not an Israel but Israel.* As we shall see in these pages, the Qumran library tells us about a community of Jews who saw themselves as Israel and the rest of the Jews as not-Israel.

Defined simply, a religion confronts urgent questions, such as who are we and why do we do the things we do, and presents compelling and self-evidently correct answers to those questions. A religious system for its part constitutes the statement of a social world constructed by a social entity through appeal to God as the foundation of the entity's shared society. Such a system comprises an intellectual construction that appeals to social facts and proposes to explain those facts. The facts encompass, first, the existence of the social entity, and, second, the indicative traits of that entity. The intellectual construction, then, accounts for the existence of the social entity and makes sense of the traits of that entity. Accordingly, to review, a religious system is made up of [1] a worldview – the intellectual construction just now noted; [2] a way of life, the indicative traits of the social entity; and [3] a social entity, to which the worldview refers and which embodies a distinctive and definitive way of life.

What – in theory at least – holds the whole together and makes of the parts a single coherent statement? Ideally, the details of the system recapitulate its main point, and that point constitutes a self-evidently valid answer to an urgent question confronting the social entity. In general, a Judaism takes shape, or comes into being, in answer to a particular problem. If that problem persists, then because of the very persistence of a chronic and generative problem, adequately answered by that Judaism, the Judaism that solves that problem – or more commonly, makes it bearable – endures and enjoys success among those Jews who find that problem and its solution the centerpiece of their shared and public existence. When, therefore, I approach the study of a religious system – in this case, Judaic systems, described, analyzed, interpreted – I ask a set of social and also political questions. My particular interest in religion is in the relationship between the ideas people hold and the world in which they live – and with which they have to cope. This concern for the interplay of setting and substance, of the circumstance and contents of a religious system, in a broad sense falls into the category of the study of the ecology of religion as an approach to the comparison of religious systems.

In framing the systemic analysis of religious systems, then, my focus of interest, therefore, is upon how humanity in society responds to challenge and change, mediates between the received tradition of politics and social life and the crisis of the age and circumstance. I propose to treat the social side of religion, viewing religion as something people do together. In my view religion is not trivial, not private, not individual, not mainly a matter of the heart. Religion is public, political, social, economic. My premise about the nature of religion is simple. No single object of study forms so public and social – indeed, so measurable – a presence as religion,. Nothing humanity has made constitutes a less personal, a less private, a less trivial fact of human life than religion.

We ask how we may know one Judaism from some other. When we identify Judaisms in one period after another, we begin by trying to locate, in the larger group of Jews, those social entities that see themselves and are seen by others as distinct and bounded, and that further present to themselves a clear account of who they are and what they do and why they do what they do: the rules and their explanations, their Judaism. This book rests on the simple premise that religion always is social, and therefore also political, a matter of what people do together, not just what they believe in the privacy of their hearts. And a Judaism for its part addresses a social group, an Israel, with the claim that that group is not merely an Israel but Israel, Israel *in nuce*, Israel in its ideal form, Israel's saving remnant, the State of Israel, the natural next step in the linear, continuous history ("progress") of Israel, everything, anything – but always Israel. So a Judaism, or a Judaic system, constitutes a clear and precise account of a social group, the way of life and worldview of a group of Jews, however defined.

What I have said requires the immediate specification of that single paradigmatic experience to which all Judaisms, everywhere and under all conditions, refer. As a matter of simple fact, we may identify that generative and definitive moment precisely as all Judaisms have done, that is, by looking into that same Scripture. All Judaisms identify (and privilege) the Torah or the Five Books of Moses as the written down statement of God's will for Israel, the Jewish people (which, as a matter of fact, every Judaism also identifies as its own social group). I suppose that on the surface, we should specify that formative and definitive moment, recapitulated by all Judaisms, with the story of Creation down to Abraham and the beginning of his family, the children of Abraham, Isaac and Jacob. Or perhaps we are advised to make our way to Sinai and hold that that original point of definition descends from heaven.

But allowing ourselves merely to retell the story deprives us of the required insight. Recapitulating the story of the religion does not help us understand the religion. Identifying the point of origin of the story, by contrast, does. For the story tells not what happened on the occasion to which the story refers (the creation of the world, for instance) but how (long afterward and for their own reasons) people want to portray themselves. The tale therefore recapitulates that resentment, that obsessive and troubling point of origin, that the group wishes to explain, transcend, transform.[7]

V

How, then, to explain what is systemic analysis? Systemic analysis in the case of a religious system aims at allowing us to see whole, complete, and as a cogent statement, a system comprising a way of life, a worldview, and the social entity that give reality to both way of life and worldview. These we see in all their coherence and cogency, each by itself. But that means to see systems one by one, as a single and singular statement, each as distinct and distinctive. The alternative is to see as a single group – one Judaism – what are in fact a elements of diverse systems or Judaisms. Then we combine systems that originally stood on their own, each facing its society. If we reflect for a moment on how one symbolic system excludes all others and conflicts with all others, we realize what is at stake in insisting that a Judaism make its own distinctive statement, in its context, for its purpose, addressing its social entity, answering the urgent question that it has identified as critical.

In describing a system, we see it whole and complete, but also all by itself. What we examine is as follows:

[1] the setting, hence the urgent questions,

[2] the evidence out of which to reconstruct the system, hence the scriptures and material artifacts, and

[3] the system that is at hand. The simplest facts of history define the setting of a system.

We look only at obvious things, events everyone had to have known, facts of social existence every person must acknowledge. So when we propose the facts that constitute the definitive setting, we look for simple

---

[7] I refer to my *Self-Fulfilling Prophecy: Exile and Return in the History of Judaism.* Boston, 1987: Beacon Press. Second printing: Atlanta, 1990: Scholars Press for South Florida Studies in the History of Judaism. With a new introduction. But there is a rather considerable problem to be addressed. Since all Christianities share the same books, the Torah, that for Judaisms portray the paradigmatic experience of exile and return, we have to wonder how the paradigm of resentment recapitulated makes its mark on the other family of biblical religious systems. When the comparative study of religions comes into being, that will be an interesting question for reflection.

things. Each system defines its evidence for us – whether the books of the dual Torah or the art of the synagogue walls. A system specifies the type of holy object, whether a book or a building, and then tells us which particular example of that type matters: the holy building, e.g., the Temple in Jerusalem, the holy books, e.g., the official and authoritative writings of the canon of the system, or the holy works of art and the sacred objects and the symbols that these stand for, e.g., the zodiac. All these in their settings respectively constitute, in a broad sense the "scripture," the definitive canon of the system. As to describing the system, we have the simple task of finding the questions and defining the answers. A system seen as it flourished – even for a brief span of time – served its society. Let me state with heavy emphasis: *At that moment, it had no past and defined its own future.*

At that moment that system stood not in linear relationship to a past and as part of an incremental process leading beyond itself. Rather, it constituted, on its own, one complete, whole, entirely sufficient Judaism: worldview, way of life, for (an) Israel, a social group. No system recapitulates any other. That is to say, none in the mind of its participants covered the same ground as some other. Each was unique: the truth. But all systems confronted the same social situation that characterized the Jews as a group. Every system had to answer essentially the same questions, though each did so in its own way. All systems sorted out those same facts of ecology – the natural, that is to say, the political situation of the Jewish people.

Now to move a step forward, toward one principal theoretical component of my argument, the conception of an ecology of religion. A religious system provides self-evidently true answers to questions people must ask. Those questions, those matters of concern or profound resentment, derive from the social world in which a group makes its life. So when we study a religious system, we want in particular to know about the relationship between two things, and here is where the notion of ecology of religion enters in:

[1] (a) the ideas people hold and (b) the way of life that expresses and is explained by those ideas as these address (c) the social entity that the people at hand are conceived to constitute, and

[2] the world in which that group makes its life.

We want to know about the interplay – the exegesis, in intellectual terms – between society and scripture. By scripture I mean, the written down ideas and prescriptions for everyday life. I want to know, along these same lines, about what happens in the encounter of system and setting,

What Is "A Judaism"? 77

the context of a group and the contents of that group's religious system. In asking that question, we turn to the perspective of ecology.

VI

Initial principles of systemic analysis come next. Let me then set forth what we may call the propositions or generalizations or "laws" of the systemic description, analysis, and interpretation, of a Judaism (or any religion):

[1] No religious system recapitulates any other.

[2] All religious systems within a given social and political setting recapitulate the same resentments.

The first of the two rules simply says that – for the purpose of systemic analysis – each system stands on its own and therefore has to be examined ecologically, that is to say, as a complete and cogent response to a particular setting. That means, for the purpose of systemic analysis we do not undertake to show how one Judaism relates to another, how, for example, the halakhah of Qumran stands in relationship to the halakhah of Elephantine or of the Priestly Code or of the Mishnah.[8]

How a system got going, where, when, and why people made it up or discovered it – these questions cannot be answered on the basis of the evidence we have, and they also are the wrong questions. That fact does not relieve us from trying to frame and answer those wrong questions. Nonetheless, in systemic description, what matters is not where a system came from but how it works when it works. That is the center of the problem of describing a system and making sense of it, that is, of interpretation. So in its moment of self-evidence – however brief – a system has no past and contemplates no future. At that moment a system does not derive from some other, nor does it stand behind one to come: it recapitulates no other system.

The second of the two rules spells out what links a family of systems, that is, a set of Judaisms, and makes of the species, Judaisms, one genus,

---

[8]That is not to suggest that the halakhah of Qumran stands entirely out of relationship with the halakhah of other Judaisms. After all, the halakhah of Scripture, read one way or another, functions as authoritative for all Judaisms, and that is by definition! So the notion of a single, unitary halakhah is not precluded by systemic analysis, though within the study of the history of Judaism, the debate must go forward on the very conception of a continuous tradition and a uniform, unitary Judaism. Systemic analysis contributes to the history of Judaism, but it does not address issues of continuity and uniformity ("normativity") such as occupy studies in the history of Judaism (or, titled otherwise, the histories of Judaisms and their common morphology, such as I should prefer).

Judaism. When we know those everyday questions that demanded answers – questions of politics, of social standing and status – we discover that any Judaism had to take up a certain few questions. But each Judaism framed its own answers to those questions, answers that proved self-evidently true, that is to say, appropriate and beyond all argument for the group at hand. To analyze a set of Judaic systems, then, we should compare and contrast the list of urgent questions asked by them all and the program of self-evidently valid answers – expressed in belief and behavior – proposed by each. This comparison of systems, of Judaisms, such as others undertake in the later chapters of this book, then forms the a critical step in the larger comparison of religions – religious systems, in our terminology – that allows us to reach a level of generalization about the nature of not religions but religion. When we attain that elevation from which we may see the landscape – the ecology not of religions but of religion – we shall find out what the serpent meant and whether or not the serpent was right about humanity: creators of worlds indeed!

Let me now specify the rules of procedure, to be followed in the description of each Judaism among the Judaisms of any age under study. These, it is clear, require attention to the following, in sequence:

[1] setting,

[2] scripture in the sense of pertinent literary evidence, as well as the counterpart facts of material culture, made available by the study of art and archaeology, and

[3] consequent system and its definition of urgent questions and self-evidently true answers.

In terms just now worked out, we want to know

[1] what particular "resentment," urgent question, captured the social imagination of a particular group, and how, described

[2] through the evidence now in our hand,

[3] the group's Judaic system responded to that inescapable question.

If this mode of description serves, then others should be able to construct their own theory of the description, analysis, and interpretation of a Judaism, *or of any other religious system*, by the procedures I have tried to work out.

VII

Systemic analysis then aims at show the relationship of the parts to the whole. It proposes to show how the parts speak for the whole, how the system as a whole selects its data and imparts to them the shape and structure that deliver its controlling message. How are the discrete data supposed to attest to the character of the system that produces them? The problem is in two parts. We have first of all to account for the way in which the data are selected and laid forth, that is, the principle of selection and, if follows, the mode by which data are put forth as description. We must, second, apply that principle of selection and show how, in interpreting the data which have been laid forth, that principle leads to results of sense and worth, that is, how it yields meaning. For example, from the way in which the ancient document before us treats women, we are able to make some sense of the way in which that same document selects and treats its other principal themes and topics.

Facts by themselves mean little. It is when they are brought into relationship with other facts to form a *context* that they begin to make those statements of meaning which the system as a whole wants to express. Merely knowing, for example, that a woman receives a marriage-contract when she is betrothed and wed, and that she receives a writ of divorce when she is sent away, tells us very little. These are the sorts of things which, "common sense" tells us, women in general will have to receive in these circumstances. But what if we ask whether a principle of selection is to be discerned? Then, in seeking that principle, we ask fresh and fructifying questions. We want, for instance, to understand why it is that one given system wishes to talk, in particular, about the documentation of the transfer of women while some other system wants to speak about the prohibitions of consanguinity, the behavior of mothers in relationship to children, or the sexual activities of women when they are at diverse points in relationship to men.

Then, I think, we begin to find something worth knowing. For what leads us into the center of a worldview, of a religious worldview in the case of an ancient Israelite document such as this one, is the capacity to discern and explain the principles of selection or inclusion, on the one side, and of disinterest or exclusion on the other. Why this topic and not some other? These seem to me the questions of the most fundamental, and therefore most revealing, character. For the answers to them lay out before our eyes the principles of selection and permit us to understand, by contrasting one set of principles with some other, the taxonomy of systems, both within a given cultural framework and across frontiers of space and time.

Systemic description, by contrast, aims at making sense of facts by reference to the context in which they occur and only then, if then, asking about the relationship of one fully articulated system, in its context, to some other, in its setting. Once a context has been defined and its perimeters carefully delineated and justified, the work of description involves placing into that context all data, without regard to theme, drawn out of that context. That is to say, we have to make sense of the parts in the context of the whole, and of the whole (that is, facts about many themes and topics) by reference to the parts. The principal intellectual challenge is to find out how rules about one matter may express a viewpoint, a detail of a harmonious and comprehensive and cogent worldview, shared and expressed in some other, indeed in many other, rules and details about other matters. But then the principal point of concern is not the data pertinent to a given theme but the systemic interrelationships of data on many themes.

Comparison, when it comes, is not among materials drawn from diverse contexts and relevant to a single theme, e.g., woman, or, more concretely, the character of divorce-documents and rules. Comparison is between one system and some other system. The appropriate task, in a taxonomy of systems compared to one another, will be to uncover the principles of selection, on the one side, and the relationships between those principles of selection and the encompassing ecological framework (using the word ecology in a social and historical sense) among the several systems under study, on the other.

External to its context, no fact bears on its own exegesis. But it is the context – and that alone – which supplies the exegesis. I do not conceive that within a given theme or topic is to be located a logic so compelling as to supply for thematic description and analysis the cogency and internal structure which context does for systemic description and analysis. I cannot imagine what it is that the theme of "women" or of "the writ of divorce" tells me, so that, out of context, I may bring together, in the work of hermeneutics, diverse facts about that theme. There is no structure but in context. But context, too, is not structure. For mere definition of context also is insufficient for the work of interpretation. The meaning of what we find is to be perceived within the system located and constructed in context. Context is not *a priori*, but merely prior to the work of interpretation.

What is to be said, then, about showing the coherence of the detail to the entire system? In the case at hand, I deal with women in the larger system set forth by the Mishnah, the foundation-document of Rabbinic Judaism. About woman as wife the Mishnah has little to say; about woman as mother, I cannot think of ten relevant lines in the Mishnah's division of Women[!]. For these are not the topics to which the Mishnah will devote itself. The Mishnah's system addresses and means to create an ordered and well-regulated world. The Mishnah states that which is the order and regulation for such a world. The division of Purities spells out the balance and wholeness of the system of cleanness, defining what is a source of uncleanness, a focus affected by uncleanness, and a mode of effecting cleanness or restoring the balance and the wholeness of the system in stasis. It is the most complete statement of that wholeness and regulation which are at every point besought and realized. The division of Holy Things addresses a different sort of message, speaking, as the division of Purities does not, to a real world. But it is the message which is unreal, for in A.D. 200 there is no cult. Holy Things provides a map for a world which is both no more and not yet, for a Temple which was and will be. The stasis attained therein, it must follow, is to portray how things truly are, at a moment at which they are not that way at all. By contrast to Purities, which conceives of a sequence of states in a reality out there and tells the regulations for each of those states, Holy Things speaks of how things are in mind, at a moment at which mind is all there is.

When we come to the division of Women, therefore, we find ourselves confronted by a familiar problem, expressed through (merely) unfamiliar facts. The familiar problem is an anomalous fact. An anomaly is for this system a situation requiring human intervention so that affairs may be brought into stasis, that is, made to conform with the Heavenly projections of the created world. That quest for stasis, order and regulation, which constitute wholeness and completeness, in the division of Women takes up yet another circumstance of uncertainty. This it confronts at its most uncertain. The system subjects the anomaly of women to the capacity for ordering and regulating, which is the gift and skill of priests and scribes.

The anomaly of woman therefore is addressed at its most anomalous, that is, disorderly and dangerous, moment, the point at which women move from one setting and status to another. The very essence of the anomaly, woman's sexuality, is scarcely mentioned. But it always is just beneath the surface. For what defines the woman's status – what is rarely made explicit in the division of Women – is not whether or not she may have sexual relations, but with whom she may have them and with what consequence. It is assumed that, from long before the advent of puberty, a girl may be married and in any event is a candidate for sexuality. From puberty onward she will be married. But what is selected for intense and continuing concern is with whom she may legitimately do so, and with what economic and social effect. There is no sexual deed without public consequence; and only rarely will a sexual deed not yield economic results, in the aspect of the transfer of property from one hand to another. So what is anomalous is the woman's sexuality, which is treated in a way wholly different from man's. And the goal and purpose of the Mishnah's division of Women are to bring under control and force into stasis all of the wild and unruly potentialities of sexuality, with their dreadful threat of uncontrolled shifts in personal status and material possession alike.

The Mishnah invokes Heaven's interest in this most critical moment for individual and society alike. Its conception is that what is rightly done on earth is confirmed in Heaven. A married woman who has sexual relations with any man but her husband has not merely committed a crime on earth. She has sinned against Heaven. It follows that when a married woman receives a writ of divorce and so is free to enter into relationships with any man of her choosing, the perceptions of that woman are affected in Heaven just as much as are those of man on earth. What was beforehand a crime and a sin afterward is holy, not subject to punishment at all. The woman may contract anew marriage on earth which Heaven, for its part, will oversee and sanctify. What is stated in these simple propositions is that those crucial and critical turnings at which a woman changes hands product concern and response in Heaven above as much as on earth below. And the reason is that Heaven is invoked specifically at those times, and in those circumstances, in which the Mishnah confronts a situation of anomaly or disorder and proposes to effect suitable regulation and besought order.

To conclude: It is to a situation which is so fraught with danger as to threaten the order and regularity of the stable, sacred society in its perfection and at its point of stasis that the Mishnah will devote its principal cognitive and legislative efforts. For that situation, the Mishnah will invoke Heaven and express its most vivid concern for sanctification. What breaks established routine or what is broken out of established routine is what is subject to the fully articulated and extensive reflections of a whole division of the Mishnah, or, in Hebrew, a *seder*, an order, of the whole. The Mishnah, as usual, provides its own most reliable exegesis in calling each one of its six principal divisions a *seder*, an order. The anomaly of woman is worked out – that is, held in stasis – by assigning her to man's domain. It follows that the stasis is disturbed at the point when she changes hands.

Then – to return to the relationship of the part to the whole of a system – the Mishnah's instincts for regulating and thereby restoring the balance and order of the world are aroused. So from the recognition of the anomalous character of women, we find ourselves moving toward the most profound and fundamental affirmations of the Mishnah about the works of sanctification: the foci and the means. Women are sanctified through the deeds of men. So, too, are earth and time, the fruit of the herd and of the field, the bed,[9] chair, table, and hearth – but, in the

---

[9] I do not make reference to the menstrual taboo because Mishnah's *system* of Women does not deal with it. Menstrual laws are a subdivision, or tractate, of

nature of things, women most of all. In a well-crafted system, every detail should serve equally well to point us toward the systemic center.

IX

Seeing the system whole requires that we ask how the details fit together, how each part recapitulates the entirety of the system. And we seek our answers in the social order that the system wishes to bring into being and for which the system wishes to account – which is to say, as I noted earlier, we are asking in the study of religion questions more familiar in the study of the world of nature, that is, ecological questions. Ecology is a branch of science concerned with the interrelationships of organisms and their environments. By "ecology of..." I mean the study of the interrelationship between a particular, religious way of viewing the world and living life, and the historical, social, and especially political situation of the people who view the world and live life in accord with the teachings of their religion. The Jewish people form a very small group, spread over many countries. One fact of Jews' natural environment is that they form a distinct group in diverse societies. A second is that they constitute solely a community of fate and, for many, of faith, but that alone, in that they have few shared social or cultural traits. A third is that the do not form a single political entity. A fourth is that they look back upon a very long and in some way exceptionally painful history.

A Judaism here defines the focus of discussion, so let us speak of the ecology of that family of closely related religious systems. A worldview suited to Jews' social ecology must make sense of their unimportance and explain their importance. It must explain the continuing life of the group, which in important ways marks the group as different from others, and persuade people that their forming a distinct and distinctive community is important and worth carrying on. The interplay between the political, social, and historical life of the Jews and their conceptions of themselves in this world and the next – that is, their worldview, contained in their canon, their way of life, explained by the teleology of the system, and the symbolic structure that encompasses the two and stands for the whole all at once and all together – these define the focus for the inquiry into the ecology of the religion at hand, that is, the ecology of a Judaism, here, the Judaism of Qumran.

---

the system of Purities. That is a systemic choice that speaks for itself – and argues powerfully against the notion that a theme as such makes much difference in the structure and proportions of a system. The system makes its own choices, to which a theme is subordinate. By "the system" of course, I mean "system-builders," who do their work long before the system comes to expression and affords us access to its traits.

The stress on the hermeneutical priority of systemic description and analysis over thematic description and analysis, the description of how facts fit into their own context rather than relate to thematically relevant facts drawn out of some other context, surely does not begin here, except for the Qumran library and the system that, we think, sustains it. For one example, Mary Boyce says precisely the same thing in connection with Zoroaster's eschatology:

> Zoroaster's eschatological teachings, with the individual judgment, the resurrection of the body, the Last Judgment, and life everlasting, became profoundly familiar, through borrowings, to Jews, Christians, and Muslims, and have exerted enormous influence on the lives and thoughts of men in many lands. *Yet it was in the framework of his own faith that they attained their fullest logical coherence.*[10]

At this point in the analysis of the Qumran's whole system, we cannot make a similar statement of what it is that defines that systemic conviction, expressed equally in all the parts. We do not know reveals the full, logical coherence of the whole and the meaning of these parts. But in the proposed project we take the first, somewhat uncertain steps, toward finding out.

---

[10]Neusner, *A History of the Mishnah Law of Purities* (Leiden: E. J. Brill, 1977), 22:13.

5

Religious Belief and Economic Behavior

How Religions Renew the Social Order

Jacob Neusner
University of South Florida and Bard College
University College, Worcester, May 14, 1998

I

Religions accomplish their this-worldly goals not by compromise with this world but by confronting the world as it is and demanding total reconstruction. That is because religions impose their vision upon the world, they do not derive their vision from it. They take shape within their own rationality, they undertake to make sense of all things by appeal to their own, cogent and uniform theory of matters. Take the case of monotheism, for example. Monotheism by nature explains many things in a single way. One God rules. Life is meant to be fair, and just rules are supposed to describe what is ordinary, all in the name of that one and only God. So in monotheism a simple logic governs to limit ways of making sense of things. But that logic contains its own dialectics. If one true God has done everything, then, since he is God all-powerful and omniscient, all things are credited to, and blamed on, him. In that case he can be either good or bad, just or unjust – but not both. Within that dialectic, monotheism systematically shows the rationality of all being, all becoming.

In less theological language, I can make the same point very simply. Religions undertake to explain other factors in the social order, they are not long and not successfully explained by other factors. In the language of social science, religion is an independent, not a dependent, variable: it takes the measure of things, it is not measured by things. What do I mean by explaining other factors or being explained by them? My answer is simple: in the century of struggle between atheistic Marxism and religion, it is the Pope that explains the demise of Communism, not the Party Secretary that delivers the eulogy for Christianity. So in our own century religion has been explained away by Marxism as a means of social control and exploitation and by Freudianism as wish-fulfillment. Stalin is gone, the Pope speaks to a billion Christians. The matter of Freudianism proves more subtle, since no dramatic political event marks the ultimate shift from one world to another. Freud's theory of matters competes, ever less successfully, with psychological theories based on physical, not narrative, considerations.

Religious reform rarely works, while prophets who advocate fundamental religious renewal count their successes, if they are so minded. Contrast, in the case of Christianity in the USA evangelical and Bible-believing Christians, who fill churches and make new ones, with the so-called mainstream denominations – dwindling to a trickle, gurgling within banks set by secular politics. Compare the various Orthodox Judaisms, those that segregate and those that integrate themselves, and their power to redefine the givens of Jewish existence away from ethnicity and toward religiosity, with the reformist Judaisms, Reform, Conservative, and Reconstructionist. The former fill synagogues and change lives, the latter feed from gimmicks and catalogue their losses. And, finally, for good or ill, what they call "Islamist" Muslims undertake a massive cultural and political struggle for the soul of the Muslim world, prepared to die or to kill for their cause.

Why do revolutionary religions prosper while reformist ones wane? Religion by its nature proposes to define the social order, not to be defined by it. Religion defines the social entity to which it speaks, dictating who belongs and who does not. Religion determines the way of life of that social entity, identifying the indicator-issues, be they food or sex or clothing or mode of earning a living or model of human relationships. Religion – and this is familiar to us all – formulates the world view, the self-evidently valid answers to the obviously-urgent questions, that shows the inner logic, the rationality, the coherence and proportion, of the way of life and the definition of the social entity formed by the faithful. So while religions comment on this and that, it is when they define the social order, determine who is in and who is out, describe the indicative traits of those that belong, and guide deliberation on the meaning and end of it all – it is when religions define the entirety of this world that they accomplish their other-worldly ends.

Three obvious cases supplied by the founders of the great monotheisms illustrate what I mean. Jesus finds himself represented as a reformer, but reforms do not break up families and call into question the very foundations of the social order, as he did. Muhammed failed at compromise but succeeded at the revolution God wrought (in Islamic faith) through the Quran. Moses made no compromises in Egypt, nor any, for that matter, at Sinai. He did not polish the golden calf, made of the gold of Egypt, he pulverized it and made the people drink the dirt with bitter water. Nor do contemporary religions lack for cases of the success of revolutionaries and the failure of synthesizers and compromisers. Joseph Smith brought a vision of the restored Gospel realized in Zion and his followers trod a bloody road from Ohio to Missouri to Illinois, before under Brigham Young's continuator-leadership, they broke with the USA altogether and escaped to the wilderness, there to build what must be the single most successful religious community begun in the nineteenth century. But (to revert to the American scene) the religious vigor of Reform and Conservative Judaism seems to have run its course, and what for the virtuosi is an instrument of reform and renewal for the ordinary folk has become a vehicle to be used and traded in as the season requires. That is not to suggest that the visionaries and radicals win all their wars, as Jim Jones in Jonestown and David Koresh in Waco illustrate. But note: within the framework of their religious system of the social order, they accomplished all of their goals. It is only the world that would not wait on them.

And these observations bring me to Bishop Peter Selby's *Grace and Mortgage, The Language of Faith and the Debt of the World*, which, bravely and perhaps quixotically, argues the case against interest as we know it. Credit and debt define what is wrong with the world order, he maintains, and at the root of things is interest, which makes money a profitable commodity and a powerful medium of social control. Debt has the power to enslave, he argues, and he advocates "the rehabilitation and control of the economy of debt: to bring it within the bounds of mutuality, equality and concern for its effects." "...what is taking place at the moment...is a progressive enslavement to an economy of credit and debt which is itself reducing the poorest nations and the poor of our own society to destitution." The final solution lies in the abolition of usury, and usury, prohibited in Islam, Judaism, and Christianity in their classical statements, constituted nothing other than interest. In the language of the law of Judaism, usury is "any payment for waiting on the return of a loan," and that is to say, interest in any and all forms.

Now as I read Bishop Selby's dense and rich and difficult book, I asked myself (as I ask myself when I read anything, starting with my own writing), what can be wrong with this? What would constitute a critique of fundamentals, not mere details, such as would precipitate reflection of another order altogether? I speak not of plausibility or practicality, for here is a man who says in the language of our own times, "Sell all you have and follow me." And yet, if Bishop Selby were to ask me, what book should I write next, and how do you advise me to translate advocacy into public policy, what advice ought I to give? In the context defined by his quest, how am I to relate religious belief to economic behavior?

As a scholar in the history of Judaism in particular, what wisdom do I have to offer, out of the history, theology, and law of Judaism, to someone who wishes to change the world? As I look back upon the history of Judaism for answers to these questions, I find a striking instance comparable to the case at hand. Let me tell you the story of how one set of sages of the Torah proposed a massive reform in economics, and how their heirs and successors transformed reform into revolution and renewal by transcending economics altogether. In those two verbs, transform and transcend, I mean to capture the contrast between reform and revolution. And when I have spelled out what I mean by "revolution," I shall have given to those in the Church of England and other Christian communions the gift that my particular learning has to offer, which is to say, the gift of perspective, through comparison and contrast.

The story that I have to tell divides into two chapters, one about sages intent on filling out and realizing Scripture's prohibition of usury, the next about sages implacably opposed to the this-worldly reading of issues of economics altogether, the one, as I said, reformers, the other, revolutionaries: system-builders. We begin with Scripture, which declares (at Lev. 25:35ff.), "And if your brother becomes poor and cannot maintain himself with you, you shall maintain him...Take no interest from him or increase, but fear your God, that your brother may live beside you. You shall not lend him your money at interest nor give him your good for profit, I am the Lord your God who brought you forth out of the land of Egypt to give you the land of Canaan and to be your God." Now, within that framework, the sages of the Mishnah understood that all money-borrowing represented a response to need, and they absolutely prohibited interest in all forms.

II

The framers of the Judaic religious system set forth in the aftermath of the destruction of the Second Temple and the catastrophic defeat of Bar Kokhba, defined a way of life, world view, and theory of the social order fully exposed in the Mishnah (ca. 200) and related documents. In that system they incorporated doctrines that are to be classified as economics, narrowly defined. Their doctrine of the rational disposition of scarce resources was utilized in order to set forth a systemic statement of fundamental importance. So far as a well-crafted theory of a social entity knows how and why scarce resources are assigned to, or end up in the hands of, one person or institution or class or other social organization, rather than some other, that system, in designing the social order, has worked out an economics for itself.[1] The Mishnah's system – absolutely alone among all of the Judaic (and Christian) systems of late antiquity – set forth as part of its systemic composition a fully-articulated economics. In its indicative traits, moreover, that system was entirely

---

[1] But not all systems work out an economics or require one. A system will address the rationality required for the disposition of scarce resources when, and only when, a systemic message may be set forth through the exemplification (or even specification) of that rationality. No Christianity developed an economics of systemic consequence prior to the medieval Christian encounter with Aristotle. And one of the marks of the Aristotelian character of the Mishnah's economics is its forthright utilization of economics in the formation and expression of its systemic message, and in the point-by-point replication of Aristotle's particular doctrines in the composition of that economics. I think the basic reason, as with politics, is that the Mishnah's framers took for granted their "Israel" formed not merely an ethnic group or a religious community (our terms, not theirs) but a nation living on its land; the enlandisement of their system necessitated address to the rational disposition of scarce resources, defined, as a matter of fact, as real estate; and the givenness of the nationhood of their system's social entity led them to reflect on the legitimate uses of violence. They took for granted theirs was an empowered social entity. Only in the diaspora do Judaic systems bypass economics and politics as media for the making of the system's larger statement, even though episodic sayings on economic action (e.g., in ethics) or on politics (in a supernatural context ordinarily) do make their appearance here and there. The fundamental criterion for sorting out Judaisms must be, then, enlandised and empowered or not; all systems must fall on one side or another of that line. If the hypothesis just now suggested is sound, then no diaspora-Judaism should resort to economics or politics as principal systemic components. The shift we shall trace in Part II then is not so odd, because while located in the Land of Israel, the framers had entered a period in which their Israel no longer governed within the Land, let alone overseas, and furthermore progressively was losing command of the real estate of what they called the Land of Israel to Christians, who called the same territory Palestine. The successor-system's utter reversal of the conventional meanings of politics and economics forms a response, of a kind, to that worldly transformation of the Jews' economic and political circumstances. The really interesting question lies elsewhere: the Talmud of Babylonia and related writings and whether and how the system to which they attest yields the stigmata of disenlandisement and disempowerment. If it does not, then the criterion of provenance in the Land of Israel does not serve so decisively as, at the present, it seems to me to.

congruent with the philosophical economics of Aristotle, answering questions concerning the definition of wealth, property, production and the means of production, ownership and control of the means of production, the determination of price and value and the like. The Mishnah's economics, in general in the theory of the rational disposition of scarce resources and of the management and increase thereof, and specifically in its definitions of wealth and ownership, production and consumption, point by point, corresponds to that of Aristotle.

Sayings relevant to an economics may take shape within a religion or a philosophy, without that religion's or philosophy's setting forth an economics at all. For unsystematic opinions on this and that, for instance, episodic sayings about mercy to the poor, recommendations of right action, fairness, honesty, and the like do not by themselves add up to an economics. Indeed, one of the marks of a system's lacking an economics is the presence of merely occasional and ad hoc remarks about matters of wealth or poverty that, all together, attest to complete indifference to the systemic importance of a theory of the rational disposition of scarce resources, their preservation and increase. By contrast, when issues of the rational disposition of scarce resources are treated in a sustained and systematic, internally coherent theory that over all and in an encompassing way explains why this, not that, and defines market in relationship to ownership of the means of production, then we have a systematic account, an economics. Not only so, but, as in the case of Aristotle's economics, the economics will prove to serve the interests of the system of which it is part when it makes a statement in behalf of that larger system. Through economics, the Mishnah's system makes a critical part of its systemic statement, and this authorship found economics, and only economics, the appropriate medium for making that part of its statement.

The general point in common between Aristotle's and the Mishnah's economics comes first: for both systems economics formed a chapter in a larger theory of the social order. The power of economics as framed by Aristotle, the only economic theorist of antiquity worthy of the name, was to develop the relationship between the economy to society as a whole.[2] And the framers of the Mishnah did precisely that when they incorporated issues of economics at a profound theoretical level into the system of society as a whole that they proposed to construct . The points in common lead us directly to the issue of interest, the definition of money, the conception of true value, and a variety of other principles of

---

[2]Polanyi, "Aristotle Discovers the Economy," in Polanyi, Karl , Conrad M. Arensberg, and Harry W. Pearson, *Trade and Market in the Early Empires. Economies in History and Theory* (Glencoe, 1957: Free Press), p. 79.

distributive economics. The theory of money characteristic of Aristotle (but not of Plato) and of the Mishnah for instance conforms to that required by distributive economics; exchange takes place through barter, not through the abstract price-setting mechanism represented by money. Both Aristotle and the authorship of the Mishnah formed the conception of "true value," which maintained that something – an object, a piece of land – possessed a value extrinsic to the market and intrinsic to itself, such that, if a transaction varied from that imputed true value by (in the case of the Mishnah) 18%, the exchange was null. Not only so, but the sole definition of wealth for both Aristotle's and the Mishnah's economics was real estate, only land however small. Since land does not contract or expand, of course, the conception of an increase in value through other than a steady-state exchange of real value, "true value," between parties to a transaction lay outside of the theory of economics. Therefore all profit, classified as usury, was illegitimate and must be prevented.

Now, in elaborating Scripture's prohibition of usury, the sages of the Mishnah made their contribution, as they often do, by extending and deepening the received notion. They not only prohibited the payment of money as interest. They also prohibited interest in kind. Encompassed by the prohibition against usury or interest is any sort of profit-sharing arrangement in which the capitalist does not compensate the partner for his labor, that is, in which the capitalist gets the labor of the partner for no compensation whatever. This yields a prohibition against partnerships of capital and labor, on the one side, and against factoring on the other.

> A. They do not set up a storekeeper for half the profit,
> B. nor may one give him money to purchase merchandise [for sale] at [the return of the capital plus] half the profit,
> C. unless one [in addition] pay him a wage as a worker.
>
> Mishnah-tractate Baba Mesia 5:4

The conception before us involves interest in the form of personal service, which also is prohibited. The case has a man commission a tradesman to sell goods in his shop and take half of the profits. But the condition is that, if the goods are lost or destroyed, the tradesman has to bear responsibility for half of the loss. Even if the stock depreciates, the tradesman makes it up at full value. Half of the commission, therefore, is in fact nothing but a loan in kind, for which the tradesman bears full responsibility. It follows that his personal service in selling the owner's half of the stock, if not compensated, in fact is a kind of interest in labor on that loan.

Now what we have seen in the Mishnah is simple: the sages have adopted prevailing conceptions of economics and adapted them for their own system. They did not innovate, they reformed; they did not make their own statement, set forth their own system, lay claim to their own rationality. They formed Aristotle's economics into a component of their essentially-Aristotelian philosophical statement. But the Mishnah is not the final statement of Judaism.

III

So much for religion as adaptation and reform, exemplified by the Mishnah-sages and their reworking of Aristotle's economics. The revolution in the very definition of scarce resources and the rational disposition thereof was yet to come. The Talmud is, or rather, the two Talmuds and associated sources of Scriptural exegesis carried out that revolution and set forth the last word on the subject.. That is to say, Judaism as we know it in its normative form, inclusive of the Judaisms of modern times that have continued normative Judaism with reform and revision, appeals to the Mishnah as read by the Talmuds, Scripture as read by the Midrash-compilations. The ancient sages' writings exhibit a remarkable shift in character, even while persisting through time in a coherent system. The earlier ones, represented by the Mishnah, a law code of ca. 200 C.E., pursued issues critical to Middle Platonism, that is to say, joining Aristotelian methods of hierarchical classification to Platonic issues of the relationship of the many to the one and the one to the many. The Aristotelian program extended to systematic thinking about economics within the framework of political economy, and so does that of the Mishnah. The result was a philosophical economics.. We have now to ask, what, happened then?

The heirs of the Mishnah, from the third through the seventh century, did two things. They systematically explained and amplified the statements of the Mishnah, one by one. They dismantled the systematic statement of the Mishnah and examined the parts, without paying much mind to the whole. At the same time, they constructed on their own, outside the framework of Mishnah-commentary, a successor system, one as profoundly religious as the Mishnah's was deeply philosophical. If by philosophical I mean, conducting thought in the manner that conventional philosophers will have found familiar, what can I possibly mean by "religious"? The answer is particular to the present inquiry, since everyone understands that standard qualities of religiosity – in the context of any Judaism, belief in God who created the world and revealed the Torah and whose providence governs the fate of holy Israel within the framework of all of human history – those qualities characterized all Judaisms. By "religious" in this context I mean, "religious by contrast with philosophical." That special usage will rapidly become clear in three simple contrasts. Philosophers such as Aristotle pursued inquiry by a systematic sifting of data, classifying in hierarchical structure by appeal to the traits of things. They set forth their results in free-standing essays, arguing from premise to proposition, evidence, and argument. And they subjected their propositions to systematic, reasoned criticism, in the conviction that contradictory positions cannot both be right, so truth transcends contradiction, not harmonizing it. Religious thought contrasts at all three points. The religious thinker in this context composes not a free-standing, autonomous inquiry but rather relies on tradition received by revelation. He gives his results in the form of a commentary upon a received text. And he takes as his exegetical task the harmonization of conflicting views, not the demonstration that one is right, the other wrong. In the present context, the indicative traits of the Rabbinic writings that succeeded the closure of the Mishnah must be characterized as religious and not philosophical: relying for truth upon revelation, the results set forth in the form of commentary, and the exegetical task finding its dynamic in dialectics and harmonization.

What happened, in the transformation of Rabbinic Judaism, the shift in its successive writings from the philosophical to the religious traits briefly outlined just now? We address only the matter of the Mishnah's philosophical economics, or, really, political economics. The transformation of economics involved the redefinition of scarce and valued resources in so radical a manner that the concept of value, while remaining material in consequence and character, nonetheless took on a quite different sense altogether. The category, "rational disposition of scarce resources," which serves as the working definition of economics, persisted only in one way, the formation of what functioned as a counterpart category. That is to say, the questions addressed in the Mishnah by philosophical economics persisted, but in the successor system represented by the documents that came to closure beyond the Mishnah and its companions, those questions radically changed in character.

Specifically, the counterpart category of the successor-system, represented by the authorships responsible for the final composition of the Yerushalmi, Genesis Rabbah, Leviticus Rabbah, and Pesiqta deRab Kahana, concerned themselves with the same questions as did the conventional economics, presenting an economics in function and structure, but one that concerned things of value other than those identified by the initial system. So indeed we deal with an economics, an economics of something other than real estate, to which philosophical economics appealed as the definition of wealth, the starting point of all else.

But it was an economics just as profoundly embedded in the social order, just as deeply a political economics, just as pervasively a systemic economics, as the economics of the Mishnah and of Aristotle. Why so? Because issues such as the definition of wealth, the means of production and the meaning of control thereof, the disposition of wealth through distributive or other media, theory of money, reward for labor, and the like – all these issues found their answers in the counterpart-category of economics, as much as in the received and conventional philosophical economics. The new "scarce resource" accomplished what the old did, but it was a different resource, a new currency. At stake in the category meant to address the issues of the way of life of the social entity, therefore, were precisely the same considerations as confront economics in its (to us) conventional and commonplace, philosophical sense. But since the definition of wealth changes, as we shall see, from land to Torah, much else would be transformed on that account.

That explains why, in the formation of the counterpart-category of value other than real value but in function and in social meaning value nonetheless, we witness the transformation of a system from philosophy to religion. We err profoundly if we suppose that in contrasting land to Torah and affirming that true value lies in Torah, the framers of the successor-system have formulated an essentially spiritual or otherwise immaterial conception for themselves, that is, a surrogate for economics in the conventional sense. That is not what happened. What we have is an economics that answers the questions economics answers, but that has chosen a different value from real value – real estate – as its definition of that scarce resource that requires a rational policy for preservation and enhancement. Land produced a living; so did Torah. Land formed the foundation of the social entity, so did Torah.

The transvaluation of value was such that an economics concerning the rational management and increase of scarce resources worked itself out in such a way as to answer, for quite different things of value from real property or from capital such as we know as value, precisely the same questions that the received economics addressed in connection with wealth of a real character: land and its produce. Systemic transformation comes to the surface in articulated symbolic change. The utter transvaluation of value finds expression in a jarring juxtaposition, an utter shift of rationality, specifically, the substitution of Torah for real estate. We recall how in a successor-document (but in none prior to the fifth century compilations) Tarfon thought wealth took the form of land, while Aqiba explained to him that wealth takes the form of Torah-learning. That the sense is material and concrete is explicit: land for

Torah, Torah for land. The following passage, from a document that reached closure in the fifth century, two hundred fifty years after the Mishnah, expresses the shift from real estate to "Torah" and does so in so many words:

Leviticus Rabbah XXXIV:XVI

1. B.   R. Tarfon gave to R. Aqiba six silver centenarii, saying to him, "Go, buy us a piece of land, so we can get a living from it and labor in the study of Torah together."
    C.   He took the money and handed it over to scribes, Mishnah-teachers, and those who study Torah.
    D.   After some time R. Tarfon met him and said to him, "Did you buy the land that I mentioned to you?"
    E.   He said to him, "Yes."
    F.   He said to him, "Is it any good?"
    G.   He said to him, "Yes."
    H.   He said to him, "And do you not want to show it to me?"
    I.   He took him and showed him the scribes, Mishnah teachers, and people who were studying Torah, and the Torah that they had acquired.
    J.   He said to him, "Is there anyone who works for nothing? Where is the deed covering the field?"
    K.   He said to him, "It is with King David, concerning whom it is written, 'He has scattered, he has given to the poor, his righteousness endures forever' (Ps. 112:9)."

The successor-system has its own definitions not only for learning, symbolized by the word Torah but also for wealth, expressed in the same symbol. Accordingly, the category-formation for worldview, Torah in place of philosophy, dictates, as a matter of fact, a still more striking category-reformation, in which the entire matter of scarce resources is reconsidered, and a counterpart-category set forth. When "Torah" substitutes for real estate, what, exactly, does the successor-system know as scarce resources, and how is the counterpart-category constructed?

Let us begin with a simple definition of "value." While bearing a variety of inchoate meanings, associated with belief, conviction, ideal, moral preference, and the like, the word to begin with bears an entirely concrete sense. Value means that which people value, under ordinary circumstances, what they hold to be of concrete, tangible, material worth. What is "of value" conventionally is what provides a life of comfort and sustenance and material position. In commonplace language, "value" (as distinct, therefore, from the vague term, "values") refers to those scarce resources to the rational management and increase of which economics devotes its attention: real wealth in the conventional sense This means, in our contemporary context, capital, and in the context of Aristotle's and the Mishnah's economics, real estate. Then when I speak of the transvaluation of value, I mean that the material and concrete things of worth were redefined – even while subjected to an economics functioning in the system as the counterpart to the initial economics of the Mishnah and of Aristotle. In the successor-writings ownership of land, even in the Land of Israel, contrasts with wealth in another form altogether, and the contrast that was drawn was material and concrete, not merely symbolic and spiritual. It was material and tangible and palpable because it produced this-worldly gains, e.g., a life of security, comfort, ease, as these, too, found definition in the systemic context of the here and the now.

It follows that, while in the successor system's theory of the component of the social order represented by the way of life, we find an economics, it is an economics of scarce resources defined as something other than particular real estate. Why do I insist that these questions remain economic in character? It is because they deal with the rules or theory of the rational management of scarce resources, their preservation and increase, and do so in commonplace terms of philosophical economics, e.g., the control of the means of production, the definition of money and of value, the distribution of valued goods and services, whether by appeal to the market or to a theory of distributive economics, the theory of the value of labor and the like.

But while the structure remained the same, the contents radically would differ, hence the transvaluation of value. It was as if a new currency were issued to replace the old, then declared of no value, capable of purchasing nothing worth having. In such an economics, there is far more than a currency-reform, but rather a complete economic revolution, a new beginning, as much as a shift from socialism to capitalism. But the transvaluation, in our case, was more thoroughgoing still, since involved was the very reconsideration of the scarcity of scarce resources. Both elements then underwent transvaluation: the definition of resources of value, the rationality involved in the management of scarcity. In a word, while real estate cannot increase and by definition must always prove scarce, the value represented by Torah could expand without limit. Value could then increase indefinitely, resources that were desired and scarce be made ever more abundant, in the transformed economics of the successor-system.

While responding to the same questions of that same part of the social order with which the received category concerned itself, the economics that emerged in no way proves discontinuous with the received economics. Why not just another economics than the philosophical one we have considered? The reason is that so abrupt and fundamental a reworking will be seen to have taken place that the category – way of life – *while yet an economics* – nonetheless is now a

Religious Belief and Economic Behavior

wholly-other economics, one completely without relationship to the inherited definition of way of life (manner of earning a living) as to both structure and system.

For at stake is not merely the spiritualization of wealth, that is to say, the re-presentation of what "wealth" *really* consists of in other-than-material terms. That would represent not an economics but a theology. For example, the familiar saying in tractate Abot, "Who is rich? One who is happy in his lot," simply does not constitute a statement of economics at all. Like sayings in the Gospels that denigrate wealth, this one tells nothing about the rational management (e.g., increase) of scarce resources, it merely tells about appropriate moral attitudes of a virtuous order: how life is worth living, not answering an economic question at all. On the other hand, the tale that contrasts wealth in the form of land and its produce with wealth in the form of Torah (whatever is meant by "Torah") does constitute a statement of economics. The reason is that the story-teller invokes precisely the category of wealth – real property – that conventional economics defines as wealth. If I have land, I have wealth, and I can support myself; if I have Torah, I have wealth, and I can support myself. Those form the two components of the contrastive equation before us. But then wealth is disenlandised, and the Torah substituted for real property of all kinds. That forms not a theology, nor an economics in any conventional sense, bur, rather, an anti-economics.

What we find in the Talmuds and associated Midrash-compilations is the formation of a new rationality, one that takes the place of the philosophical rationality of the Mishnah. The shift in the definition of value from real estate to Torah-learning is shown, among many ways. But the most important is the conception that sages' wealth in learning also provides this-worldly nourishment. That is, wealth in the conventional sense is shifted to Torah, but then Torah-learning is treated as the new wealth, the equivalent of real estate. There are passages that are quite explicit: land is wealth, or Torah is wealth, but not both; owning land is power and studying Torah permits (re)gaining power. To take the first of the two propositions in its most explicit formulation:

Leviticus Rabbah XXX:I.4

A. R. Yohanan was going up from Tiberias to Sepphoris. R. Hiyya bar Abba was supporting him. They came to a field. He said, "This field once belonged to me, but I sold it in order to acquire merit in the Torah."

B. They came to a vineyard, and he said, "This vineyard once belonged to me, but I sold it in order to acquire merit in the Torah."

C. They came to an olive grove, and he said, "This olive grove once belonged to me, but I sold it in order to acquire merit in the Torah."

D. R. Hiyya began to cry.

E. Said R. Yohanan, "Why are you crying?"
F. He said to him, "It is because you left nothing over to support you in your old age."
G. He said to him, "Hiyya, my disciple, is what I did such a light thing in your view? I sold something which was given in a spell of six days [of creation] and in exchange I acquired something which was given in a spell of forty days [of revelation].
H. "The entire world and everything in it was created in only six days, as it is written, 'For in six days the Lord made heaven and earth' [Ex. 20:11].
I. "But the Torah was given over a period of forty days, as it was said, 'And he was there with the Lord for forty days and forty nights' [Ex. 34:28].
J. "And it is written, 'And I remained on the mountain for forty days and forty nights'" (Deut. 9:9).

The sale of land for the acquisition of "merit in the Torah" introduces two principal systemic components, merit and Torah. For our purpose, the importance of the statement lies in the second of the two, which deems land the counterpart – and clearly the opposite – of the Torah.

Now one can sell a field and acquire "Torah," meaning, in the context established by the exchange between Tarfon and Aqiba, the opportunity to gain leisure to (acquire the merit gained by) the study of the Torah. That the sage has left himself nothing for his support in old age makes explicit the material meaning of the statement, and the comparison of the value of land, created in six days, and the Torah, created in forty days, is equally explicit. The comparison of knowledge of Torah to the merchandise of the merchant simply repeats the same point, but in a lower register. So, too, does the this-worldly power of study of the Torah make explicit in another framework the conviction that study of the Torah yields material and concrete benefit, not just spiritual renewal. Thus R. Huna states, "All of the exiles will be gathered together only on account of the study of Mishnah-teachings."[3]

No wonder then that sages protect cities. So it is claimed that sages are the guardians of cities, and later on that would yield the further allegation that sages do not have to pay taxes to build walls around cities, since their Torah-study protects the cities:

Pesiqta deRab Kahana XV:V.1

2. A. Rabbi sent R. Yosé and R. Ammi to go and survey the towns of the Land of Israel. They would go into a town and say to the people, "Bring me the guardians of the town."
   B. The people would bring out the head of the police and the local guard.

---

[3]Pesiqta deRab Kahana VI:III.3.B.

	C.	[The sages] would say, "These are not the guardians of the town, they are those who destroy the town. Who are the guardians of the town? They are the teachers of children and Mishnah-teachers, who keep watch by day and by night, in line with the verse, 'And you shall meditate in it day and night' (Josh. 1:8)."
	D.	And so Scripture says, "If the Lord does not build the house, in vain the builders labor" (Ps. 127:1).
7.	A.	Said R. Abba bar Kahana, "No philosophers in the world ever arose of the quality of Balaam ben Beor and Abdymos of Gadara. The nations of the world came to Abnymos of Gadara. They said to him, 'Do you maintain that we can make war against this nation?'
	B.	"He said to them, 'Go and make the rounds of their synagogues and their study houses. So long as there are there children chirping out loud in their voices [and studying the Torah], then you cannot overcome them. If not, then you can conquer them, for so did their father promise them: 'The voice is Jacob's voice' (Gen. 27:22), meaning that when Jacob's voice chirps in synagogues and study houses, The hands are not the hands of Esau [so Esau has no power].
	C.	"'So long as there are no children chirping out loud in their voices [and studying the Torah] in synagogues and study houses, 'The hands are the hands of Esau [so Esau has power].'"

The reference to Esau, that is, Rome, of course links the whole to the contemporary context and alleges that if the Israelites will support those who study the Torah and teach it, then their cities will be safe, and, still more, the rule of Esau/Rome will come to an end; then the Messiah will come, so the stakes are not trivial.

The disenlandisement of economics, the transvaluation of value so that Torah replaced land as the supreme measure of value and also, as a matter of fact, of social worth – these form (an) economics. It is, moreover, one that is fully the counterpart of the philosophical economics based upon real estate as true value that Aristotle and the framers of the Mishnah constructed, each party for its own systemic purpose. If we have not reviewed the components of the economics of the Torah – the theory of means of production and who controls the operative unit of production of value, the consideration of whether we deal with a market- or a distributive economics, the reason is that we have not had to. It is perfectly obvious that the sage controlled the means of production and fully mastered the power to govern them; the sage distributed valued resources – supernatural or material, as the case required – and the conception of a market was as alien to that economics as it was to the priestly economics revised and replicated by the Mishnah's system. Enough has been said, therefore, to establish beyond reasonable doubt the claim that in the Torah we deal with the system's counterpart category, its economics.

IV

Now we return to the point I made at the outset, that religions accomplish their goals not by reform but by effecting a categorical revolution. What we have seen is that economics deals with scarce resources, and the disenlandisement of economics in the successor-Judaism has turned upon its head the very focus of economics: scarcity and the rational confrontation with scarcity. To land rigid limits are set by nature, to the Holy Land, still more narrow ones apply. But to knowledge of the Torah no limits pertain. So we find ourselves dealing with an economics that concern not the rational utilization of scarce resources, but the very opposite: the rational utilization of what can and ought to be the opposite of scarce. In identifying knowledge and teaching of the Torah as the ultimate value, the successor-system has not simply constructed a new economics in place of an old one, finding of value something other than had earlier been valued; it has redefined economics altogether. It has done so, as a matter of fact, in a manner that is entirely familiar, by setting forth in place of an economics of scarcity an economics of abundant productivity.

Disenlandising value thus transvalues value by insisting upon its (potential) increase as the definition of what is rational economic action. The task is not preservation of power over land but increase of power over the Torah, because one can only preserve land, but one can increase one's knowledge of the Torah. So, to revert to the theoretical point that in context seemed so excessive, the economics of the initial system concerns the rational disposition of the scarce resource comprised by particular real property; the rational increase of the potentially-abundant resource comprised by Torah-learning is – serves and functions as – the economics of the successor-system. That is what I mean, then, by the transvaluation of value, in the most literal sense.

Which Judaism – the Mishnah's, or the Talmud's – prevailed? The answer is self-evident to all who know the history of Judaism. The Talmud's definition of wealth set the norm. Interest, usury, the commodization of gold – these foundations of the economics of both Aristotle and the Mishnah lost currency, when the new rationality took over, the new, theological definition of scarce resources replaced the old philosophical one. True, Israelites would not charge or pay interest among themselves; but the framing of matters in terms of broad and philosophical issues, pertaining to humanity in general, had given way to another set of values altogether, to which usury and interest were peripheral in interest. With what result? On the one hand, in the transformation of Judaism from a philosophical to a religious system, the religion, Judaism, came to sanctify and enchant transactions and activities that others deemed matters of indifference to God. Now true wealth would find its definition in learning in the revealed Torah, true virtue in gifts of the spirit. But, on the other hand, other-worldly aspirations crowded out this-worldly realities. Sustained reflection on Torah-teachings obscured the doughty, feisty wisdom of Aristotle, with his insistence on the integral relationships of politics and economics, the social order and its material arrangements. Eyes fixed on heaven, sages prohibited interest in all forms, usury in all the possible subterfuges – within holy Israel. But that prohibition ended at the outer limits of holy Israel, as Islam and Christendom concurred that the outside might lend at interest to the insider, or the insider to the outsider.

Now, since borrowing was understood as response to need, money-lending would and did carry out a social task of considerable weight. All three monotheisms thereby relieved themselves of much (though not all) responsibility for the poor by depending upon outsiders – the Jew in Christendom being the catastrophic case – to support the poor in crisis and then taxing the usury for the support of the state. Probably the single most regressive form of taxation ever invented and the cruelest for all concerned, usury and the attendant confiscatory taxes impoverished the poor and ruined Israel in the sight of its neighbors, rendering the money-lender, already an outsider, into villain and demon. I need not rehearse the ultimate consequence. But I do owe the reflection that, had the philosophical system of the Mishnah prevailed, with its capacity to speak in terms of a general theory covering all of the facts, without differentiation, sages would have taken another path than the one they followed. I mean to say, if usury were forbidden on grounds of a political economics comparable in breadth of rationality and insistence on generalization to that of Aristotle, then, guided by that rationality, sages would have had grounds to prohibit Israel from engaging in usury away, not only at home. The practice of usury, whether among Israel or among gentiles, would have presented no option to Israel. But, their minds fixed on other matters altogether, sages saw things differently, and conditions were created to make inevitable the European catastrophe. When I said at the outset, religion revolutionizes, it does not reform, I did not promise a prescription for saving the world. All I mean to offer is a theory on what it takes for religion to do its work.

6

The Theological Anthropology of Classical Judaism

Jacob Neusner
University of South Florida and Bard College

In Classical Judaism man not only complements God, he also corresponds to, is like, God. When sages read in the Torah that man is created in God's image, they understood that to mean, God and man correspond, bearing comparable traits. The theological anthropology of the Oral Torah defined correspondence between God and man in three ways: [1] intellectually, sharing a common rationality; [2] emotionally, sharing common sentiments and attitudes, and [3] physically, sharing common features.. That is why to begin with God and Israel relate. They think alike. They feel the same sentiments. And they look alike. Like God, man is in command of, and responsible for, his own will and intentionality and consequent conduct. The very fact that God reveals himself through the Torah, which man is able to understand, there to be portrayed in terms and categories that man grasps, shows how the characteristics of God and man prove comparable. The difference between man and God is that God is God.

We begin with that theological anthropology that sees man in God's image in a concrete way. Correspondence encompasses not only intangible, but material qualities. How do God and man compare in physical presence? Because theology in its philosophical mode has long insisted on the incorporeality of God, let us begin with the Oral Torah's explicit claim that God and man look exactly alike, being distinguished only by actions performed by the one but not the other:

Genesis Rabbah VIII:X.1

A. Said R. Hoshayya, "When the Holy One, blessed be he, came to create the first man, the ministering angels mistook him [for God, since man was in God's image,] and wanted to say before him, 'Holy, [holy, holy is the Lord of hosts].'

B. "To what may the matter be compared? To the case of a king and a governor who were set in a chariot, and the provincials wanted to greet the king, "Sovereign!' But they did not know which one of them was which. What did the king do? He turned the governor out and put him away from the chariot, so that people would know who was king.

C. "So too when the Holy One, blessed be he, created the first man, the angels mistook him [for God]. What did the Holy One, blessed be he, do? He put him to sleep, so everyone knew that he was a mere man.

D. "That is in line with the following verse of Scripture: 'Cease you from man, in whose nostrils is a breath, for how little is he to be accounted' (Isa. 2:22)."

Man – Adam – is in God's image, interpreted in a physical way, so the angels did not know man from God. Only that man sleeps distinguishes him from God. The theme derives from the verse that states, "...in our image, after our likeness" (Gen., 1:26). While this passage is not cited in the present construction, Genesis Rabbah VIII:X simply carries forward the concluding entry of Genesis Rabbah VIII:IX, examined at the end of Chapter Eight, in which the relevant verse is cited. Accordingly, "In our image" yields two views, first, that the complete image of man is attained in a divine union between humanity – man and woman – and, further, that what makes man different from God is that man sleeps, and God does not sleep. But was that face man and God have in common understood in a physical way, and to God are other human, physical characteristics ascribed? An affirmative answer emerges entirely clearly in the following:

Bavli-tractate Berakhot 7A, LVI

A. "And he said, 'You cannot see my face'" (Ex. 33:20).

B. It was taught on Tannaite authority in the name of R. Joshua b. Qorha, "This is what the Holy One, blessed be he, said to Moses:

C. "'When I wanted [you to see my face], you did not want to, now that you want to see my face, I do not want you to.'"

D. This differs from what R. Samuel bar Nahmani said R. Jonathan said.

E. For R. Samuel bar Nahmani said R. Jonathan said, "As a reward for three things he received the merit of three things.

F. "As a reward for: 'And Moses hid his face,' (Ex. 3:6), he had the merit of having a glistening face.

G. "As a reward for: 'Because he was afraid to' (Ex. 3:6), he had the merit that 'They were afraid to come near him' (Ex. 34:30).

The Theological Anthropology of Classical Judaism

H. "As a reward for: 'To look upon God' (Ex. 3:6), he had the merit: 'The similitude of the Lord does he behold' (Num. 12:8)."

A. "And I shall remove my hand and you shall see my back" (Ex. 33:23)

B. Said R. Hana bar Bizna said R. Simeon the Pious, "This teaches that the Holy One, blessed be he, showed Moses [how to tie] the knot of the phylacteries."

That God is able to tie the knot indicates that (in the present context at least) God has fingers and other physical gifts. God furthermore is portrayed as wearing phylacteries as well. It follows that God has an arm and a forehead. There is no element of a figurative reading of the indicated traits, no defense or apology for invoking a mere metaphor. Quite the opposite, in passage after passage, without the slightest trace of embarrassment or reservation, the correspondence of God and man yields a variety of physical traits. Indeed, the entirety of the Song of Songs is read as an account of God's love for Israel, and Israel's for God, and for the sages the most suitable way of expressing that account required the physicalization of God and of Israel alike.

Second, God and man intellectually correspond in the common logic and reason that they share. That is in two aspects. First, like Abraham at Sodom, sages simply took for granted that the same rationality governs. God is compelled by arguments man finds persuasive, appeals to which man responds: "Will not the Judge of all the world...." Second, meeting God through the study of the record of God's self-revelation, the Torah, sages worked out their conviction that man's mind corresponded to God's, which is why man can receive the Torah to begin with. That man can study the Torah proves that man has the capacity to know God intellectually.

Through their critical, analytical inquiry into the Torah and its law, sages thought to gain access to the modes of thought that guided the formation of the Torah. This involved, for instance, dialectical argument concerning comparison and contrast in this way, not in that, identification of categories in one manner, not in another. Since those were the modes of thought that, in sages' conception, dictated the structure of intellect upon which the Torah rested. It is that sages could meet God in the Torah. That is to say, in their analysis of the deepest structures of intellect of the Torah, sages supposed to enter into the mind of God, showing how God's mind worked when God formed the Torah. And there, in the intellect of God, in their judgment man gained access to God. But in discerning how God's mind worked, sages claimed for themselves a place in that very process of thought that had given birth to the Torah.

God not only follows and joins in the argument of the laws of the Torah conducted by sages. God is party to the argument and subjects himself to the ruling formed by the consensus of sages – and says so. God not only participates in the debate but takes pride when his children win the argument over him. The miracles of nature convey his vote. He is outweighed by reason, which man exercises, and which takes priority in the reading of the Torah's laws even over God's judgment! In the following story, we find an explicit affirmation of the priority of reasoned argument over all other forms of discovery of truth:

Bavli-tractate Baba Mesia 59A-B

A. There we have learned: If one cut [a clay oven] into parts [so denying it its normal form as an oven] but put sand between the parts [so permitting it to function as an oven]

B. Eliezer declares the oven [broken-down and therefore] insusceptible to uncleanness. [A utensil that is broken and loses the form in which it is useful is deemed null, and so it cannot receive the uncleanness that pertains to whole and useful objects.]

C. And sages declare it susceptible [because while it is formally broken it is functionally useful, and therefore retains the status of an ordinary utensil].

D. And this is what is meant by the oven of Akhenai [Mishnah-tractate Kelim 5:10].

E. Why [is it called] the oven of Akhenai?

F. Said R. Judah said Samuel, "It is because they surrounded it with argument as with a snake and proved it was insusceptible to uncleanness."

G. It has been taught on Tannaite authority:

H. On that day R. Eliezer produced all of the arguments in the world, but they did not accept them from him. So he said to them, "If the law accords with my position, this carob tree will prove it."

I. The carob was uprooted from its place by a hundred cubits – and some say, four hundred cubits.

J. They said to him, "There is no proof from a carob tree."

K. So he went and said to them, "If the law accords with my position, let the stream of water prove it."

L. The stream of water reversed flow.

M. They said to him, "There is no proof from a stream of water."

N. So he went and said to them, "If the law accords with my position, let the walls of the school house prove it."

O. The walls of the school house tilted toward falling.

P. Joshua rebuked them, saying to them, "If disciples of sages are contending with one another in matters of law, what business do you have?"

Q. They did not fall on account of the honor owing to R. Joshua, but they also did not straighten up on account of the honor owing to R. Eliezer, and to this day they are still tilted.

R. So he went and said to them, "If the law accords with my position, let the Heaven prove it!"

S. An echo came forth, saying, "What business have you with R. Eliezer, for the law accords with his position under all circumstances!"
T. Joshua stood up on his feet and said, "'It is not in heaven' (Deut. 30:12)."
U. What is the sense of, "'It is not in heaven' (Deut. 30:12)"?
V. Said R. Jeremiah, "[The sense of Joshua's statement is this:] For the Torah has already been given from Mount Sinai, so we do not pay attention to echoes, since you have already written in the Torah at Mount Sinai, 'After the majority you are to incline' (Ex. 23:2)."
W. Nathan came upon Elijah and said to him, "What did the Holy One, blessed be he, do at that moment?"
X. He said to him, "He laughed and said, 'My children have overcome me, my children have overcome me!'"

Here man is not only like God but, in context, equal to God because subject to the same logic. God is bound by the same rules of logical argument, of relevant evidence, of principled exchange, as is man. So man can argue with the mere declaration of fact or opinion – even God's, beyond the Torah, must be measured against God's own reason, set forth, we see, within the written part of the Torah. That is why the (mere) declaration of matters by Heaven is dismissed. Why? Because God is bound by the rules of rationality that govern in human discourse, and because humanity in the person of the sage thinks like God, as God does; so right is right, and nature has no call to intervene, nor even God to reverse the course of rational argument.

Third comes the matter of how God and man are alike in their attitudes and emotions. What moves God, and moves God to action, are emotions that man too feels, attitudes that guide man's actions as much as God's. Uncoerced love matched by an act of grace – that transaction above all tells us what really matters, and it is precisely there that the correspondence of man and God extends to emotional or attitudinal traits. God emerges in the Oral Torah as a fully-exposed personality. The common character of divinity and humanity, therefore, encompassed God's virtue, the specific traits of character and personality that God exhibited above and here below. Above all, humility, the virtue sages most often asked of themselves, characterized the divinity. God wanted people to be humble, and God therefore showed humility.

Bavli-tractate Shabbat 89a

A. Said R. Joshua b. Levi, "When Moses came down from before the Holy One, blessed be he, Satan came and asked [God], "'Lord of the world, Where is the Torah?'"
B. "He said to him, 'I have given it to the earth...' [Satan ultimately was told by God to look for the Torah by finding the son of Amram.]

C. "He went to Moses and asked him, 'Where is the Torah which the Holy One, blessed be he, gave you?'
D. "He said to him, 'Who am I that the Holy One, blessed be he, should give me the Torah?'
E. "Said the Holy One, blessed be he, to Moses, 'Moses, you are a liar!'
F. "He said to him, 'Lord of the world, you have a treasure in store which you have enjoyed every day. Shall I keep it to myself?'
G. "He said to him, 'Moses, since you have acted with humility, it will bear your name: "Remember the Torah of Moses, my servant" (Mal. 3:22).'"

God here is represented as favoring humility and rewarding the humble with honor. What is important is that God does not here cite Scripture or merely paraphrase it; the conversation is an exchange between two vivid personalities. True enough, Moses, not God, is the hero. But the personality of God emerges in a vivid way. Arrogance – the opposite – is treated as denial of God, humility, the imitation of God. When we take up the cause of sin, which disrupts the world order, we shall see why the opposite of humility, which is arrogance, takes so critical a role. It is because sin forms the action of which arrogance is the attitude, and catastrophe for man, on the one side, and for Israel, on the other, the result. So what provokes the calamitous transaction that is the story of mankind to begin with originates in the attitude of arrogance. This, quite naturally, links itself to idolatry, the supreme act of arrogance, the quintessential sin:

Bavli-tractate Sotah 5b, XVI

P. And R. Yohanan said in the name of R. Simeon b. Yohai, "Whoever is arrogant is as if he worships idolatry.
Q. "Here it is written, 'Everyone who is arrogant in heart is an abomination to the Lord," (Prov. 16:5), and elsewhere it is written, 'You will not bring an abomination into your house' (Deut. 7:26)."
R. And R. Yohanan on his own account said, "He is as if he denied the very Principle [of the world],
S. "as it is said, 'Your heart will be lifted up and you will forget the Lord your God' (Deut. 8:14)."
T. R. Hama bar Hanina said, "He is as if he had sexual relations with all of those women forbidden to him on the laws of incest.
U. "Here it is written, 'Everyone who is arrogant in heart is an abomination to the Lord' (Prov. 16:5), and elsewhere it is written, 'For all these abominations...' (Lev. 18:27)."
V. Ulla said, "It is as if he built a high place,
W. "as it is said, 'Cease you from man, whose breath is in his nostrils, for wherein is he to be accounted of' (Isa. 2:22).
X. "Do not read, 'wherein,' but rather, 'high place.'"

God hates idolatry as an act of arrogance and rebellion against him, so God is capable of hatred, so too, God is made angry by idolatry, so God possesses the quality of anger. These and other traits of emotion in God then find their correspondence in man, who is to learn from God's emotions and attitudes and imitate them.

God enters into transactions with human beings and accords with the rules that govern those relationships. So God exhibits precisely the social attributes that human beings do. A number of stories, rather protracted and detailed, tell the story of God as a social being, living among and doing business with mortals. These stories provide extended portraits of God's relationships, in particular arguments, with important figures, such as angelic figures, as well as Moses, David, and Hosea. In them as does man, God negotiates, persuades, teaches, argues, exchanges reasons. God will engage in arguments with men and angels, and so enters into the existence of ordinary people. These disputes, negotiations, transactions yield a portrait of God who is reasonable and capable of give and take, as in the following:

Bavli-tractate Arakhin 15A-B

F. Rabbah bar Mari said, "What is the meaning of this verse: 'But they were rebellious at the sea, even at the Red Sea; nonetheless he saved them for his name's sake' (Ps. 106:7)?

G. "This teaches that the Israelites were rebellious at that time, saying, 'Just as we will go up on this side, so the Egyptians will go up on the other side.' Said the Holy One, blessed be he, to the angelic prince who reigns over the sea, 'Cast them [the Israelites] out on dry land.'

H. "He said before him, 'Lord of the world, is there any case of a slave [namely, myself] to whom his master [you] gives a gift [the Israelites], and then the master goes and takes [the gift] away again? [You gave me the Israelites, now you want to take them away and place them on dry land.]'

I. He said to him, 'I'll give you one and a half times their number.'

J. "He said before him, 'Lord of the world, is there a possibility that a slave can claim anything against his master? [How do I know that you will really do it?]'

K. "He said to him, 'The Kishon brook will be my pledge [that I shall carry out my word. Nine hundred chariots at the brook were sunk, (Jud. 3:23) while Pharaoh at the sea had only six hundred, thus a pledge one and a half times greater than the sum at issue.]'

L. "Forthwith [the angelic prince of the sea] spit them out onto dry land, for it is written, 'And the Israelites saw the Egyptians dead on the sea shore' (Ex. 14:30)."

God is willing to give a pledge to guarantee his word. He furthermore sees the right claim of the counterpart actor in the story. Hence we see how God obeys precisely the same social laws of exchange and reason that govern other incarnate beings.

Still more interesting is the picture of God's argument with Abraham. God is represented as accepting accountability, by the standards of humanity, for what he does.

Bavli-tractate Menahot 53b

A. Said R. Isaac, "When the temple was destroyed, the Holy One, blessed be he, found Abraham standing in the Temple. He said to him, 'What is my beloved doing in my house?'

B. "He said to him, 'I have come because of what is going on with my children.'

C. "He said to him, 'Your children sinned and have been sent into exile.'"

D. "He said to him, 'But wasn't it by mistake that they sinned?'

E. "He said to him, 'She has wrought lewdness' (Jer. 11:15).

F. "He said to him, 'But wasn't it just a minority of them that did it?'

G. "He said to him, 'It was a majority' (Jer. 11:15).

H. "He said to him, 'You should at least have taken account of the covenant of circumcision [which should have secured forgiveness despite their sin]!'

I. "He said to him, 'The holy flesh is passed from you' (Jer. 11:15).

J. "And if you had waited for them, they might have repented!'

K. "He said to him, 'When you do evil, then you are happy' (Jer. 11:15).

L. "He said to him, 'He put his hands on his head, crying out and weeping, saying to them, 'God forbid! Perhaps they have no remedy at all!'

M. "A heavenly voice came forth and said, 'The Lord called you "a leafy olive tree, fair with excellent fruit"' (Jer. 11:16).

N. "'Just as in the case of an olive tree, its future comes only at the end [that is, it is only after a long while that it attains its best fruit], so in the case of Israel, their future comes at the end of their time.'"

God relates to Abraham as to an equal. That is shown by God's implicit agreement that he is answerable to Abraham for what has taken place with the destruction of the Temple. God does not impose on Abraham silence, saying that that is a decree not to be contested but only accepted. God as a social being accepts that he must provide sound reasons for his actions, as must any other reasonable person in a world governed by rules applicable to everyone. Abraham is a fine choice for the protagonist, since he engaged in the argument concerning Sodom. His complaint is expressed at B: God is now called to explain himself. At each point then Abraham offers arguments in behalf of sinning Israel, and God responds, item by item. The climax of course has God promising Israel a future worth having. God emerges as both just and merciful, reasonable but sympathetic. The transaction attests to God's conformity to rules of reasoned transactions in a coherent society.

Among the available models for the comparing man to God – warrior, teacher, young man – the one that predominated entailed representation of God as sage. That is because the sage in the Oral Torah embodied the teachings of the Oral Torah, did the deeds that the Torah required, such as Torah-study, and so conformed to God's image of man as set forth in the Torah. We already realize that that representation of the correspondence of God and the sage takes a subordinate position behind the representation of the correspondence of God's emotions and man's to the opportunity of grace. But an important chapter in any picture of correspondences encompasses the one between God and the sage. In this connection we recall that God is represented as a school master: "He sits and teaches school children, as it is said, 'Whom shall one teach knowledge, and whom shall one make to understand the message? Those who are weaned from milk' (Isa. 28:9)" (Bavli-tractate Abodah Zarah 3b) But this is not the same thing as God as a master-sage teaching mature disciples, that is, God as rabbi and sage.

God's personality merged throughout with personality of the ideal master or sage. That representation proves detailed and specific. A sage's life – Torah first learned through discipleship in the chain extending backward to Sinai, then taught, through discipleship – encompassed both the correct modes of discourse and ritual argument, on the one side, and the recasting of all relationships in accord with received convention of courtesy and subservience. God then is represented in both dimensions, as a master requiring correct conduct of his disciples, and as a teacher able to hold his own in arguments conducted in accord with the prevailing ritual. For one example, a master had the right to demand an appropriate greeting, and God, not receiving that greeting, asked why:

Bavli-tractate Shabbat 89a

A. Said R. Joshua b. Levi, "When Moses came up on high, he found the Holy One, blessed be he, tying crowns onto the letters of the Torah. He said to him, 'Moses, don't people say hello in your town?'
B. "He said to him, 'Does a servant greet his master [first]?'
C. "He said to him, 'You should have helped me [at least by greeting me and wishing me success].'
D. "He said to him, '"Now I pray you let the power of the Lord be great, just as you have said" (Num. 14:17).'"

Moses here plays the role of disciple to God the teacher, a persistent pattern throughout. Not having offered the appropriate greeting, the hapless disciple is instructed on the matter. Part of the ritual of "being a sage" thus comes to expression.

The Oral Torah deems humanity to be divided into two parts, Israel with the Torah, the nations with idolatry. We may hardly find surprising that, while God corresponds to man in general, the relationship of correspondence, shading over into intimacy and union, takes place with Israel in particular. Where there is love, there is true identification, such as takes place in Song of Songs Rabbah, so frequently cited in these pages. But for the most part, in the Oral Torah's representation of matters God's person forms the counterpart to Israel's person, and the two are complementary but not one. The two, when equally hypostatized, are deemed counterparts, forming a relationship of deep love for one another. God indeed attains person-hood in relationship to Israel, God's twin:

Pesiqta deRab Kahana V:VI.2

A. Said R. Hiyya bar Abba, "How do we know that the Holy One is called 'the heart of Israel'?

B. "On the basis of this verse: Rock of my heart and my portion is God forever (Ps. 73:26)."

The amplification of the foregoing yields the picture of God as Israel's kin and lover, so both parties – the abstraction, "Israel," along with the abstraction, divinity, takes on the traits of personhood, personality in particular:

Pesiqta deRab Kahana V:VI.3

A. "...My beloved is knocking" refers to Moses: "And Moses said, Thus said the Lord, At about midnight I shall go out in the midst of Egypt" (Ex. 11:4).

B. "Open to me:" said R. Yosé, "Said the Holy One, blessed be he, 'Open to me [a hole] as small as the eye of a needle, and I shall open to you a gate so large that troops and siege-engines can go through it.'"

C. "...my sister:" [God speaks:] "My sister – in Egypt, for they became my kin through two religious duties, the blood of the Passover-offering and the blood of circumcision."

D. "...my dearest" – at the sea, for they showed their love for me at the sea, "And they said, the Lord will reign forever and ever" (Ex. 15:19).

E. "...my dove" – my dove at Marah, where through receiving commandments they become distinguished for me like a dove.

F. "...my perfect one" – My perfect one at Sinai, for they became pure at Sinai: "And they said, all that the Lord has spoken we shall do and we shall hear" (Ex. 24:7)."

G. R. Yannai said, "My twin, for I am not greater than they, nor they than I."

H. R. Joshua of Sikhnin said in the name of R. Levi, "Just as in the case of twins, if one of them gets a headache, the other one feels it, so said the Holy One, blessed be he, 'I am with him in trouble' (Ps. 91:15)."

I. "...for my head is drenched with dew." "The heavens dropped dew" (Judges 5:4).

J. "...my locks with the moisture of the night:" "Yes, the clouds dropped water" (Judges 5:4).

The Theological Anthropology of Classical Judaism

K. When is this the case? In this month: "This month is for you the first of the months" (Ex. 12:2).

The notion of God and Israel as twins, the one formed as the counterpart of the other, thus involves the hypostatization of both parties to the transaction.

Accordingly, the final focus of correspondence between God and man concerns Israel, unique among nations and holy to God. How do God and, within humanity, Israel correspond? It is, first, that Israel forms on earth a society that corresponds to the retinue and court of God in heaven. No surprise, then, that, just as Israel glorifies God, so God responds and celebrates Israel. Here correspondence of man and God, now Israel and God, in physical, emotional, and social traits, comes to expression. God wears phylacteries, as does Israel, but while Israel's phylacteries contain verses of Scripture in praise of God, God's choice of Scripture praises Israel. God further forms the correct attitude toward Israel, which is one of love, an indication of an attitude on the part of divinity corresponding to right attitudes on the part of human beings. Finally, to close the circle, just as there is a "you" to whom humanity prays, so God too says prayers – to himself, to God, and the point of these prayers is that God should elicit from himself forgiveness for Israel. If there is sublimity in the Oral Torah, this is where it is:

Bavli-tractate Berakhot 6a-b XXXIX

A. Said R. Nahman bar Isaac to R. Hiyya bar Abin, "As to the phylacteries of the Lord of the world, what is written in them?"
B. He said to him, "'And who is like your people Israel, a singular nation on earth' (1 Chr. 17:21)."
C. "And does the Holy One, blessed be he, sing praises for Israel?"
D. "Yes, for it is written, 'You have avouched the Lord this day... and the Lord has avouched you this day' (Deut. 26:17, 18).
E. "Said the Holy One, blessed be he, to Israel, 'You have made me a singular entity in the world, and I shall make you a singular entity in the world.
F. "'You have made me a singular entity in the world,' as it is said, 'Hear O Israel, the Lord, our God, the Lord is one' (Deut. 6:4).
G. "'And I shall make you a singular entity in the world,' as it is said, 'And who is like your people, Israel, a singular nation in the earth' (1 Chr. 17:21)."
H. Said R. Aha, son of Raba to R. Ashi, "That takes care of one of the four subdivisions of the phylactery. What is written in the others?"
I. He said to him, "'For what great nation is there... And what great nation is there...' (Deut. 4:7, 8), 'Happy are you, O Israel...' (Deut. 33:29), 'Or has God tried...,' (Deut. 4:34). And 'To make you high above all nations' (Deut. 26:19)."
J. "If so, there are too many boxes!
K. "But the verses, 'For what great nation is there' and 'And what great nation is there,' which are equivalent, are in one box, and

'Happy are you, O Israel' and 'Who is like your people Israel' are in one box, and 'Or has God tried...,' in one box, and 'To make you high' in one box.

L. "And all of them are written in the phylactery that is on the arm."

We proceed to God's saying prayers, as does man, and the contents of those prayers:

Bavli-tractate Berakhot 7A. XLIX

A. Said R. Yohanan in the name of R. Yosé, "How do we know that the Holy One, blessed be he, says prayers?

B. "Since it is said, 'Even them will I bring to my holy mountain and make them joyful in my house of prayer' (Isa. 56:7).

C. "'Their house of prayer' is not stated, but rather, 'my house of prayer.'

D. "On the basis of that usage we see that the Holy One, blessed be he, says prayers."

E. What prayers does he say?

F. Said R. Zutra bar Tobiah said Rab, "'May it be my will that my mercy overcome my anger, and that my mercy prevail over my attributes, so that I may treat my children in accord with the trait of mercy and in their regard go beyond the strict measure of the law.'"

God seeks the blessing of the sage as well:

Bavli-tractate Berakhot 7a, L

A. It has been taught on Tannaite authority:

B. Said R. Ishmael b. Elisha, "One time I went in to offer up incense on the innermost altar, and I saw the crown of the Lord, enthroned on the highest throne, and he said to me, 'Ishmael, my son, bless me.'

C. "I said to him, 'May it be your will that your mercy overcome your anger, and that your mercy prevail over your attributes, so that you treat your children in accord with the trait of mercy and in their regard go beyond the strict measure of the law.'

D. "And he nodded his head to me."

E. And from that story we learn that the blessing of a common person should not be negligible in your view.

God's wearing phylacteries treats him as physically comparable to man; but the consubstantial traits of attitude and feeling – just as humanity feels joy, so does God, just as humanity celebrates God, so does God celebrate Israel – are the more urgent. Just as Israel declares God to be unique, so God declares Israel to be unique. And just as Israel prays to God, so God says prayers. What God asks of himself is that he transcend himself – which is what, in prayer, humanity asks for as well. It would be difficult to find more ample evidence of a theological system that deems God and man to share a great many traits.

Among these, however, as in the Written Torah, the point of correspondence of greatest consequence concerns attitudes, feelings, and emotions. Tractate Abot presents the single most comprehensive account of religious affections. These turn out to pertain to God's as much as to man's feelings. The reason is that, in that document above all, how we feel defines a critical aspect of virtue. A simple catalogue of permissible feelings comprises humility, generosity, self-abnegation, love, a spirit of conciliation of the other, and eagerness to please. A list of impermissible emotions is made up of envy, ambition, jealousy, arrogance, sticking to one's opinion, self-centeredness, a grudging spirit, vengefulness, and the like. People should aim at eliciting from others acceptance and good will and should avoid confrontation, rejection, and humiliation of the other. This they do through conciliation and giving up their own claims and rights. So both catalogues form a harmonious and uniform whole, aiming at the cultivation of the humble and malleable person, one who accepts everything and resents nothing. And, time and again, the compilation underscores, one who conciliates others is favored by God, who respects and honors those who, as in the stores that convey the transaction that generates *zekhut*, give up what no one can demand:

Tractate Abot

2:4   A.   He would say, "Make his wishes into your own wishes, so that he will make your wishes into his wishes.

        B.   "Put aside your wishes on account of his wishes, so that he will put aside the wishes of other people in favor of your wishes."

If a man makes God's wishes his own, he will make the man's wishes his, and if one gives way to others, God will protect the man from the ill-will of others. God further favors those who seek to please others:

3:10   A.   He would say, "Anyone from whom people take pleasure – the Omnipresent takes pleasure.

        B.   "And anyone from whom people do not take pleasure, the Omnipresent does not take pleasure."

Along these same lines, Mishnah-tractate Abot 3:10 advises that God is pleased by those who try to please others: "Anyone from whom people take pleasure – the Omnipresent takes pleasure. Aqiba at T. Berakhot 3:3 goes over the same ground: "One in whom mankind delights, God delights. One in whom mankind does not delight, God does not delight. One who is content with his own portion, it is a good sign for him. One who is not content with his own portion, it is a bad sign for him."

A sequence of paradoxes – strength is marked by weakness, wisdom by the capacity to learn, wealth by making do, honor by the power to honor others – yields the picture of traits that man should cultivate, to which God will respond:

4:1   A.   Ben Zoma says, "Who is a sage? He who learns from everybody,

	B.	"as it is said, From all my teachers I have gotten understanding (Ps. 119:99).
	C.	"Who is strong? He who overcomes his desire,
	D.	"as it is said, He who is slow to anger is better than the mighty, and he who rules his spirit than he who takes a city (Prov. 16:32).
	E.	"Who is rich? He who is happy in what he has,
	F.	"as it is said, When you eat the labor of your hands, happy will you be, and it will go well with you (Ps. 128:2) .
	G.	("Happy will you be in this world, and it will go well with you in the world to come.")
	H.	"Who is honored? He who honors everybody,
	I.	"as it is said, 'For those who honor me I shall honor, and they who despise me will be treated as of no account' (I Sam. 2:30)."
4:18	A.	R. Simeon b. Eleazar says, "(1) Do not try to make amends with your fellow when he is angry,
	B.	"or (2) comfort him when the corpse of his beloved is lying before him,
	C.	"or (3) seek to find absolution for him at the moment at which he takes a vow,
	D.	"or (4) attempt to see him when he is humiliated."
4:19	A.	Samuel the Small says, "Rejoice not when your enemy falls, and let not your heart be glad when he is overthrown, lest the Lord see it and it displease him, and he turn away his wrath from him (Prov. 24:17)."

True, these virtues, in this tractate as in the system as a whole, derive from knowledge of what really counts, which is what God wants. But God favors those who – like God – aspire to please others. The point of correspondence then is clear: virtues appreciated by human beings prove identical to the ones to which God responds as well. And what single virtue of the heart encompasses the rest? Restraint, the source of self-abnegation, humility, serves as the antidote for ambition, vengefulness, and, above all, for arrogance. It is restraint of our own interest that enables us to deal generously with others, humility about ourselves that generates a liberal spirit towards others.

So the emotions prescribed in tractate Abot turn out to provide variations of a single feeling, which is the sentiment of the disciplined heart, whatever affective form it may take. And where does the heart learn its lessons, if not in relationship to God? So: "Make his wishes yours, so that he will make your wishes his" (Abot 2:4). Applied to the relationships between human beings, this inner discipline of the emotional life will yield exactly those virtues of conciliation and self-abnegation, humility and generosity of spirit, that the framers of tractate Abot spell out in one example after another. Imputing to Heaven exactly those responses felt on earth, e.g., "Anyone from whom people take pleasure, God takes pleasure" (Abot 3:10), makes the point at the most general level.

Do sages mean that man and God correspond, or do we deal with some sort of figurative or poetic representing relationships of a less tangible character than I have suggested? I should claim that the entire system of theology, with its account of world order based on God's pervasive justice and rationality, means to portray exactly how things actually are – or can be made to be, with man's correct engagement. For sages we deal with the true reality that this world's corruption obscures. What we see is an application of a large-scale, encompassing exercise in analogical thinking – something is like something else, stands for, evokes, or symbolizes that which is quite outside itself. It may be the opposite of something else, in which case it conforms to the exact opposite of the rules that govern that something else. The reasoning is analogical or it is contrastive, and the fundamental logic is taxonomic. The taxonomy rests on those comparisons and contrasts we should call parabolic. In that case what lies on the surface misleads, just as we saw how sages deem superficial the challenges to God's justice that private lives set forth. Conceding the depth of human suffering, sages also pointed out that sometimes, suffering conveys its own blessing. And so throughout, what lies beneath or beyond the surface – there is the true reality. People who see things this way constitute the opposite of ones who call a thing as it is. Self-evidently, they have become accustomed to perceiving more – or less – than is at hand.

God and man corresponded in the call to each for forbearance, patience, humiliation, self-abnegation. God, disappointed with creation, challenged by the gentiles with their idolatry, corresponded with Israel, defeated and subjugated, challenged by the worldly dominance of those who rejected the Torah. Both, sages maintained, dealt with failure, and both had to survive the condition of defeat. To turn survival into endurance, pariah-status, for Israel, into an exercise in Godly living, the glory lavished on idols into an occasion for forbearance and restraint on God's part, the sages' affective program served full well. Israel would see power in submission, wealth in the gift to be grateful, wisdom in the confession of ignorance. For God as for Israel, ultimate degradation was made to stand for ultimate power. Israel in exile served God through suffering.

True, the condition of Israel then would represent a scandal to the nations and foolishness too. That is why man and God corresponded at just that present failure that, for the here and now so concretely understood by sages, both parties to the cosmos shared. That is why from both God and Israel was demanded humility as a mark of strength, feelings of conciliation, restraint, and conformity as a mark of ultimate dignity. God and Israelite man corresponded at heart. The heart would serve as the best defense, inner affections as the police who are always there when needed, the tamed attitude as the ultimate arbiter of what would come about in the future.

7

Comparing Sources: Mishnah/Tosefta and Gospel

Jacob Neusner
University of South Florida and Bard College

The Mishnah, a philosophical law code that came to closure at ca. 200 C.E., along with the Tosefta, a compilation of correlative laws, some clarifying the Mishnah's, others going their own way, that may have reached something like its present form in ca. 300 C.E., share with the Gospels a single striking characteristic. Just as for Catholic, Orthodox Christianity, the Gospels form the starting point and foundation-stone for all else, so for normative Judaism, the Mishnah and its associated traditions in the Tosefta serve the same function. When we align the two foundation-documents side by side, we establish a point of comparison and contrast for the religious systems that begin with each one, Rabbinic Judaism and Catholic, Orthodox Christianity, respectively.

Not only so, but the two documents further intersect in the Hebrew Scriptures of ancient Israel, which both religious systems claim for their own, the one as the Written part of the one whole Torah of our rabbi, Moses, the other as the Old Testament, prefiguring the new. And both compilations concur that the Hebrew Scriptures set forth authoritative teachings, but need not be emulated. Neither pretends to recapitulate the traits of Scripture. The Mishnah's laws are given no revelation-myth ("the Lord spoke to Moses say, Speak to the children of Israel and say to them"), and the Gospel's accounts of the life and teachings of Jesus draw upon – but do not copy – any of the Israelite Scripture's lives. Each document, then, pays profound respect to that Scripture while going its own way. The acutely logical organization of the Mishnah, the Passion Narrative at the climax of the Gospels – neither imitates any prior

Israelite writing, whether Scripture or otherwise, and both inaugurate a length and vital tradition, each of its own character and quality.

And, it further follows, the two foundation-writings – the Mishnah and the Gospels – share a common aspiration: to make an autonomous statement, free-standing and not exegetical in form. Rather than setting forth a statement in exegetical form – citing a verse of the Hebrew Scriptures and commenting on it in such a way as to make a fresh point – displaying such ideas as the framers wished to lay out, both the Mishnah and the Gospels define their own organizing structures, even while utilizing exegetical forms here and there, at Matthew 2-3, Mishnah-tractate Sotah chapter eight, for instance.

Viewed as foundation-documents for the religious community to which each is addressed – each a group claiming to embody the "Israel" of Scripture they part company from one another, but predictably so. The Mishnah bears a social message, aiming at a restorationist vision of the heart of the Torah's vision of humanity – how Adam and Eve will regain Eden in the embodiment of Israel restoring the Land of Israel to perfection. Necessarily, therefore, its authorship (those responsible for the document as we now know it) chooses the form of a systematic law code, laying out whatever theological ideas it wishes to present in the form of detailed rules. The Gospels, representing their "Israel" in the embodiment of God, through Christ as the Last Adam, the model of humanity in God's image, after God's likeness ("God incarnate") frame their messages around the biography of the principal figure of the faith. But Rabbinic Judaism makes its principal statements through describing the norms of the Israelite social order, and the Gospels, theirs through appealing to the figure and the model of Jesus Christ, whom the faithful are to emulate. So matters of virtue, theological convictions, formulations of the holy, in the Mishnah find their place in a large legal system, and in the Gospels, in a counterpart biographical structure.

A. Dating, Provenience, and Purpose of the Literature

The canonical Gospels had reached closure a century before the Mishnah was concluded, the former around 100 at the latest, the latter around 200 at the earliest. The provenience of the Gospels, all scholarship concurs, finds its location in the communities of Christians who treasured the remembered model of the earthly life of the risen Lord. The purpose of the Gospels was to set forth what it means for God to take the form of man, so providing the model for the Christian communities themselves to aspire to live Godly lives in the interim until Christ returns. These well-established readings of the Gospels underscore the social character of the Gospels, their power to make a systemic statement of the faith through their portrayal of the founder thereof.

The same aspiration to lay out the shape and structure of the holy community of the faithful characterizes the formation of the traditions attributed to oral tradition from Sinai that are recorded in the counterpart foundation documents of Rabbinic Judaism. The Mishnah, the Tosefta, and a third corpus of kindred traditions, external to the Mishnah and called by an Aramaic word meaning, "external traditions," baraitot, systematically cite authorities who flourished in the first and second centuries C.E. Some of these laws and teachings may well originate in the period in which the named authorities flourished. But the first documentary evidence we have of them is the Mishnah, the Tosefta, and for the corpus of baraitot, the two Talmuds, the Talmud of the Land of Israel of ca. 400 C.E., and the Talmud of Babylonia of ca. 600 C.E. Consequently, we cannot take for granted that the Mishnah, Tosefta, and baraita-literature informs us about the state of the law that sages put forth in first two centuries.

The compilations find a common provenience in the circles of masters and disciples who are described as links in the chain of oral tradition beginning with Moses at Sinai and concluding with named authorities who appear in the Mishnah itself. The upshot is, the Mishnah and related legal traditions are assigned a place in the on-going chain of oral tradition, commencing with God to Moses "our rabbi," and ultimately transcribed in the Mishnah, Tosefta, and the baraita-corpus of the Talmuds. That provenience is best described for us in the following account of how the Mishnah-traditions were formulated from ancient times onward to the Mishnah itself:

> A. Our rabbis have taught on Tannaite authority:
> B. What is the order of Mishnah teaching? Moses learned it from the mouth of the All-Powerful. Aaron came in, and Moses repeated his chapter to him and Aaron went forth and sat at the left hand of Moses. His sons came in and Moses repeated their chapter to them, and his sons went forth. Eleazar sat at the right of Moses, and Itamar at the left of Aaron.
> D. Then the elders entered, and Moses repeated for them their Mishnah chapter. The elders went out. Then the whole people came in, and Moses repeated for them their Mishnah chapter. So it came about that Aaron repeated the lesson four times, his sons three times, the elders two times, and all the people once.
> E. Then Moses went out, and Aaron repeated his chapter for them. Aaron went out. His sons repeated their chapter. His sons went out. The elders repeated their chapter. So it turned out that everybody repeated the same chapter four times.
>   Babylonian Talmud tractate
>   Erubin 5:1 I.43/54b

The Mishnah is represented, therefore, as a document that was orally formulated and orally transmitted in a process of memorization. The principle of imitating God here is embodied in the master-disciple relationship; for each master himself was a disciple, each a link backward in the chain of tradition to Moses, God's disciple on Sinai, so states tractate Abot, the Mishnah's first apologetic, of ca. 250 C.E.:

> A. Moses received Torah at Sinai and handed it on to Joshua, Joshua to elders, and elders to prophets. And prophets handed it on to the men of the great assembly.
> B. They said three things: (1) "Be prudent in judgment. (2) Raise up many disciples. (3) Make a fence for the Torah."
> Tractate Abot 1:1

Here we see two allegations, the first, oral tradition, the second, oral tradition is not the same as the tradition of the Written Torah; the three sayings are not citations of Scripture but statements of sages themselves. Each link in the chain of tradition, from God to Moses, from master to disciple, bears its own inscription, and every statement forms part of that same tradition, orally formulated and orally transmitted through human memory, of Sinai.

If the dating and provenience of the great foundation-code prove difficult to ascertain, the purpose is blatant. When we realize that the Mishnah took shape in the aftermath of the destruction of the Temple in 70 C.E. and the defeat of Bar Kokhba and the definitive closure of Jerusalem to Jewry in ca. 135 C.E., the topical program of the Mishnah attests to its purpose. The Mishnah covers these large subjects: agricultural laws, with special attention to the continuing sanctification of the Land of Israel and God's enduring possession of it; laws of appointed times and seasons and the Sabbath, with emphasis upon the permanent sanctification of the festivals and Sabbaths, within the household of Israel, even though the Temple rites were suspended; family law, with heavy stress upon the act of sanctification involved in the formation of the family-unit through the betrothal and marriage of a woman by a man; civil law, drawing extensively upon the law of the Hebrew Scriptures; Holy Things, the law governing the conduct of the Temple rites and the maintenance of the Temple structure; and Purities, the law pertaining to the protection of the Temple and its altar from the sources of uncleanness designated by the Written Torah and to the application to the household table of the same rules of cultic cleanness. So the Mishnah, and the entire legal code given its classical formulation in the Mishnah, forms a systematic, sustained essay on the sanctification of Israel, the people, in its enduring realization of God's rule in the Torah.

The Mishnah and related compilations make the opening statement of a large and coherent theological structure, which animates the entirety of the Rabbinic writings of late antiquity and imparts cogency to the message of each with the messages of all the others. No consideration of the provenience of the Mishnah in relationship to the Gospels can ignore the theology that is embodied in the law of the Mishnah as much as in the lore and exegesis of its counterpart documents, the Midrashim, treated elsewhere in this book. The theological system that is built upon the Mishnah, Tosefta, and baraita-corpus, rests on four propositions, all of them variations on the authorized history of Scripture from Genesis through Kings:

1. God formed creation in accord with a plan, which the Torah reveals. World order can be shown by the facts of nature and society set forth in that plan to conform to a pattern of reason based upon justice. Those who possess the Torah – Israel – know God and those who do not – the gentiles – reject him in favor of idols. What happens to each of the two sectors of humanity, respectively, responds to their relationship with God. Israel in the present age is subordinate to the nations, because God has designated the gentiles as the medium for penalizing Israel's rebellion, meaning through Israel's subordination and exile to provoke Israel to repent. Private life as much as the public order conforms to the principle that God rules justly in a creation of perfection and stasis .

2. The perfection of creation, realized in the rule of exact justice, is signified by the timelessness of the world of human affairs, their conformity to a few enduring paradigms that transcend change. Involved here is a theology of history, an account of how God works through what happens to man. No present, past, or future marks time, but only the recapitulation of those patterns. Perfection is further embodied in the unchanging relationships of the social commonwealth. What is required here is a theology of political economy, which assures that scarce resources, once allocated, remain in stasis. In that way the politics and economics of the social order will correspond to that perfection that was attained at Eden. A further indication of perfection lies in the complementarity of the components of creation, on the one side, and, finally, the correspondence between God and man, in God's image (theological anthropology), on the other. At stake here is an account of God's view of man, a systematic investigation of how God intended man to be.

3. Israel's condition, public and personal, marks flaws in creation. What disrupts perfection is the sole power capable of standing on its own against God's power, and that is man's will. What man controls and God cannot coerce is man's capacity to form intention and therefore choose either arrogantly to defy, or humbly to love, God. Because man defies God, the sin that results from man's rebellion flaws creation and disrupts world order. The paradigm of the rebellion of Adam in Eden governs, the act of arrogant rebellion

leading to exile from Eden thus accounting for the condition of humanity. But, as in the original transaction of alienation and consequent exile, God retains the power to encourage repentance through punishing man's arrogance. In mercy, moreover, God exercises the power to respond to repentance with forgiveness, that is, a change of attitude evoking a counterpart change. Since, commanding his own will, man also has the power to initiate the process of reconciliation with God, through repentance, an act of humility, man may restore the perfection of that order that through arrogance he has marred.

4. God ultimately will restore that perfection that embodied his plan for creation. In the work of restoration death that comes about by reason of sin will die, the dead will be raised and judged for their deeds in this life, and most of them, having been justified, will go on to eternal life in the world to come. In the paradigm of man restored to Eden is realized in Israel's return to the Land of Israel. In that world or age to come, however, that sector of humanity that through the Torah knows God will encompass all of humanity. Idolators will perish, and humanity that comprises Israel at the end will know the one, true God and spend eternity in his light.[1]

Now, recorded in this way, the story told by the Mishnah proves remarkably familiar, with its stress on God's justice (to which his mercy is integral), man's correspondence with God in his possession of the power of will, man's sin and God's response. But the Mishnah and the other halakhic compilations do not tell their story through narrative but through law. The story that the law means to translate into normative rules of conduct turns out to account for the condition of the world and also to adumbrate the restoration of humanity to Eden through the embodiment of Israel in the Land of Israel.

Sages call the Mishnah "the oral Torah," and it is therefore correct to ask, is the purpose of the literature congruent with the message of the Hebrew Scriptures, a.k.a., the Written Torah? If we translate into the narrative of Israel, from the beginning to the calamity of the destruction of the (first) Temple, what is set forth in both abstract and concrete ways in the Oral Torah, we turn out to state a reprise of the story laid out in Genesis through Kings and amplified by the principal prophets. Recorded in this way, the story told through law by the Mishnah and related writings proves remarkably familiar, with its stress on God's justice (to which his mercy is integral), man's correspondence with God in his possession of the power of will, man's sin and God's response.

These form the paramount motifs of the law, and they recapitulate the story of humanity. First comes Adam and Eve and their fall from

---

[1] I have shown that these four propositions encompass the entire system of Rabbinic Judaism in my *Theology of the Oral Torah: Revealing the Justice of God* (Kingston, 1998: McGill-Queens University Press).

Eden, then Israel and its fall from the Land of Israel. But Israel has what Adam lacked, which is the Torah, and by realizing its norms in the life of the community, Israel has the power to restore itself to the Land of Israel, and, standing for humanity, to bring Adam and Eve back to Eden. And Eden is represented by the law of the Mishnah as life eternal, Israel being defined there as those who will rise from the dead, stand in judgment, and enter into immortality:

> A. All Israelites have a share in the world to come, as it is said, "Your people also shall be all righteous, they shall inherit the land forever; the branch of my planting, the work of my hands, that I may be glorified" (Is. 60:21).
> B. And these are the ones who have no portion in the world to come:
> C. (1) He who says that the resurrection of the dead is a teaching which does not derive from the Torah, (2) or that the Torah does not come from Heaven; or (3) an Epicurean.
>
> Mishnah-tractate Sanhedrin 10:1

That well crafted system explains why each of the four parts of my account of the theology of the Mishnah within the encompassing Oral Torah – [1] the perfectly just character of world order,[2] indications of its perfection, [3] sources of its imperfection, [4] media for the restoration of world order and their results – belongs in its place and set in any other sequence the four units become incomprehensible.

Are the Mishnah's sages right about the written part of the Torah, meaning, is what they say the Written Torah says actually what the ancient Israelite Scriptures say? Will those who put forth the books of Genesis through Kings as a sustained narrative and those who in that same context selected and organized the writings of the prophets, Isaiah, Jeremiah, Ezekiel, and the twelve, in the aggregate have concurred in sages' structure and system? Certainly others who lay claim to these same Scriptures from the Gospels forward could not and did not concur. At the time the sages did their greatest theological work, in the fourth and fifth century C.E., their Christian counterparts, in the Latin, Greek and Syriac speaking sectors of Christianity alike, not only read Scripture in a very different way but also accused the rabbis of falsifying the Torah. How would the sages have responded to the charge? They would point to the fact that nearly every proposition they set forth, the main beams of the structure of faith they construct, all sets securely and symmetrically upon the written Torah. Proof-texts constantly reinforce the structure by showing its scriptural foundations. That is why sages speak of the one whole Torah, in two media, correlative and complementary. Second, sages' formulation of the Torah, the one whole Torah of Moses, our rabbi, defines holy Israel's relationship with God for all time to come. Accordingly – that is now sages' view – if we take up the Oral Torah and explore its theological structure and system, we meet Judaism, pure and simple. There we find its learning and its piety, what it knows about and hears from God, what it has to say to God. So much for the claim of theological apologetics.

The facts support that claim. Sages have hermeneutics on their side. In their reading of the written Torah whole, in canonical context, as a record of life with God, they are right to say their story goes over the written Torah's story. But in the Mishnah, they design the story of the restoration of Israel to the Land, of Adam to Eden. Start to finish, creation through Sinai to the fall of Jerusalem, all perceived in the light of the prophets' rebuke, consolation, and hope for restoration, Scripture's account is rehearsed in the Oral Torah. All is in proportion and balance. Viewed as a systematic hermeneutics, the sages' theology accurately sets forth the principal possibility of the theology that is implicit in the written part of the Torah – to be sure, in a more systematic and cogent manner than does Scripture. And that is with greater emphasis on the theme that the fulfillment of Scripture's promise can only be restoration. So it is entirely within the imaginative capacity of the Oral Torah to raise the question: what came before in relationship to what we have in hand? To state the matter more directly, are the rabbis of the Oral Torah right in maintaining that they have provided the originally oral part of the one whole Torah of Moses our rabbi? To answer that question in the affirmative, sages would have only to point to their theology in the setting of Scripture's as they grasped it. The theology of the Oral Torah embodied in the halakhah of the Mishnah and associated compilations tells a simple, sublime story.

[1] God created a perfect, just world and in it made man in his image, equal to God in the power of will.

[2] Man in his arrogance sinned and was expelled from the perfect world and given over to death. God gave man the Torah to purify his heart of sin.

[3] Man educated by the Torah in humility can repent, accepting God's will of his own free will. When he does, man will be restored to Eden and eternal life.

In our terms, we should call it a story with a beginning, middle, and end. In sages' framework, we realize, the story embodies an enduring and timeless paradigm of humanity in the encounter with God: man's powerful will, God's powerful word, in conflict, and the resolution thereof. The task of the law of the Mishnah and related writings was to spell out the requirements of that community that would restore Adam and Eve to Eden through Israel to the Land of Israel.

But if about the written Torah I claim sages were right, then what about the hermeneutics of others? If the sages claimed fully to spell out the message of the written Torah, as they do explicitly in nearly every document and on nearly every page of the Oral Torah, so, too, did others. And those others, who, like the sages, added to the received Scripture other writings of a (to-them) authoritative character, set forth not only the story of the fall from grace that occupied sages but, in addition, different stories from those the sages told. They drew different consequences from the heritage of ancient Israel. Sages' critics will find their account not implausible but incomplete, a truncated reading of Scripture. They will wonder about leaving out nearly the whole of the apocalyptic tradition. But, in the balance, sages' critics err. For no one can reasonably doubt that sages' restorationist reading of Scripture recovers, in proportion and accurate stress and balance, the main lines of Scripture's principal story, the one about creation, the fall of man and God's salvation of man through Israel and the Torah. If, as Brevard Childs states, "The evangelists read from the New [Testament] backward to the Old [Testament],"[2] we may say very simply, the sages read from the written Torah forward to the oral one, the Evangelists, from the New Testament to the Old. In this, the Gospels show that they are irreducibly eschatological, their telos is not restoration but transformation.

B. Questions in, and methods of, comparison with the Gospels

Now that we have dealt with the hermeneutics, we may reasonably translate the result into exegesis. The large-scale comparison of entire constructions and systems, such as is briefly adumbrated in the presentation of the theological provenience of the Mishnah, defines the work of comparison. Now what is required is comparison and contrast, not only of details at which the norms of the Gospels and those of the Mishnah intersect, but also of large-scale conceptions. Comparison of how major components of the Mishnah's law and doctrine address issues taken up by the Gospels' traditions of Jesus affords perspective on the systems that build through those components. And that perspective affords insight into two fundamental traits of Catholic, Orthodox Christianity and Rabbinic Judaism: how they sort out the heritage of a shared Scripture, where and why they part company in their respective systems for human salvation. It is time for the comparison of wholes:[3]

---

[2]*Biblical Theology of the Old and New Testaments*, p. 720.
[3]Until the appearance of E. P. Sanders, *Paul and Palestinian Judaism*, (Philadelphia, 1975: Fortress) no one had ever shown what a coherent picture of several distinct Judaisms, each examined in its own terms, would look like, either each on its own or all seen side by side. So far as I know, Sanders was the first to portray as sustained and crafted religious systems, without attempting to harmonize, or

large constructs of a systematic character concerning normative conviction and conduct, the one set forth in the Gospels, read not only discretely but also as a whole composite of Christian conviction, the other set forth in the counterpart construction of the Mishnah and associated legal traditions.

What is the alternative to the kind of holistic comparison of theological and even legal (normative) constructions characteristic of the Christianity and the Judaism represented by Gospels and Mishnah, respectively? A century of exegetical work leaves in obscurity few points of intersection at details. Everyone now knows that Jesus concurs with the House of Shammai as to grounds for divorce, that Hillel and Jesus agree on Lev. 19:18 as the center-piece of faith, and much else. If Jesus has been described as a Sadducee and also as a Pharisee, as a member of the House of Shammai and also as a member of the House of Hillel, as a rabbi who said especially well what rabbis were supposed to say and as an anti-rabbi whose authentic sayings can only be those not found in the Rabbinic corpus, then matters have pretty well run their course. But that is not only because a method that yields everything and its opposite provides flawed guidance in the study of the privileged documents, in the present instance, the Gospels and the figure of Jesus portrayed therein. It is also because nearly everybody in Gospels- and Rabbinics-scholarship today recognizes the problem of critical history: the Mishnah comes to closure a century after the Gospels. How then are we supposed to open the Mishnah for an account of "Jewish law" or "Pharisaic law" a century earlier?

The labor-saving response – "they must have had a tradition" – no longer compel broad credence. In fact, if we want to know the state of "Jewish law" in the first century, we begin not with the Mishnah and its attributions of sayings to first century figures – these are beyond all tests of verification or falsification – but with the Gospels' stories themselves.

---

correlate, or explain away differences among them, the Judaism of the Dead Sea community, the Judaism of the rabbis, and the Judaism of Paul. The work exhibited profound flaws, since it was undertaken on a narrowly-historical and historicistic base and therefore required that all of the Judaisms flourish on the same plane of time. The advantages of the comparative study of religions applied to the study of different systems of the same genus of religions (here: Judaism) were lost in a morass of historical confusion. And, unfortunately, Sanders himself repudiated the entire approach in his *Judaism,* published two decades later, which portrays a supposed unitary Judaism, encompassing all sources, whatever their systemic provenience. But in his first, and most important work on Judaism, Sanders opened up an entirely new approach to the study of ancient Judaism, and in systematically differentiating between and among the formations of a single religion, he provoked thought on an entirely fresh set of questions.

These stand far closer to the events of which they speak than the Mishnah's counterpart laws. Not only so, but until the Mishnah enjoys a privileged position in the shared enterprise of biblical studies concerning New Testament times, the Gospels will always define the governing agenda, dictating the points of inquiry. And, finally, the kind of history of Mishnaic law that the Mishnah (and the Tosefta) itself makes possible allows us to identify conceptions that, logically, must precede and precipitate subordinate conceptions; then we have a logical sequence, A must come before B, which can correspond to a temporal sequence, A was set forth, and then, confronted with the inner tensions contained by A, B was formulated.[4] That is to say, before we can conduct an argument on how to divide an apple, we have to affirm that we have an apple to divide. Before sages can debate secondary questions, they have to have in hand primary principles subject to refinement later on. All that the test at hand does is search out anachronism of an intellectual character, for instance, attributing to an early authority an opinion on a question that is systematically investigated only much after that authority flourished.

But these logical- and possibly-temporal-sequences hardly correspond to a social history of how the law actually was set forth and practiced. The upshot is, unless we accept at face value the attributions of sayings to named authorities, and further take as fact that the authorities really said what is attributed to them at that particular time, we cannot assume that the Mishnah and related documents tell us about the state of law or theology in the time in which Jesus lived, on the one side, or in the age in which the Evangelists wrote the Gospels, on the other.

The comparison of large-scale theological constructs yields insight into the theological structure set forth by the respective religious systems that afford a place for those constructs, for in comparison, we gain perspective on the traits of each system, on the choices its framers have made. Such a comparison means, then, to afford a deeper understanding not so much for detail pertinent to a given, one-time historical moment, but for the sustaining religious world-view and way of life embodied, also, in a given construct. The basis for comparison is, Catholic, Orthodox Christianity and Rabbinic Judaism appeal to the same Scriptures. Now, even though, commonly enough, they quote each its own repertoire of verses of Scripture, still, as my theological reprise indicates, they accept as the foundation for all else the Israelite

---

[4]I have systematically set forth the logical sequences of primary and subsidiary laws for the entirety of the Mishnah-Tosefta in my *History of the Mishnaic Law* (Leiden, 1974-1986: E. J. Brill) in forty-three volumes.

Scriptures' account of humanity and of Israel within humanity: Adam and the Last Adam, for Christianity, Adam and Eve and Israel, Eden and the Land of Israel, for Rabbinic Judaism. In the end we may conclude, the purpose of studying the Gospels and Rabbinic counterparts is to understand the religion that the Gospels and the Rabbinic writings, respectively, put forth. It is now time to undertake the religious study of the religions of Catholic, Orthodox Christianity, represented by the Gospels, and Rabbinic Judaism, represented by the Mishnah, the Tosefta, and the baraita-collections, not only severally but, by reason of their shared heritage, jointly as well.

C. Examples of Illuminating Comparisons

Take the case of Jesus's healing on the Sabbath, for instance. There we see how profound walls of incomprehension separate New Testament exegesis from the Rabbinic sources supposedly drawn upon to sustain that exegesis. What we see here is that the same topic, healing on the Sabbath, in the Gospels makes one point, in the halakhah of the Mishnah and the Tosefta makes an entirely different point, and treating the same subject the two bodies of tradition simply part company. But that fact affords striking insight into the issues that inhere in the whole of the two religious systems, respectively.

Matt. 12:9-14=Mark 3:1-6=Lk. 6:6-11 show Jesus challenged to heal on the Sabbath. Mark has, "Is it lawful on the Sabbath to do good or to do harm, to save life or to kill?" In Matthew he answers, "What man of you, if he has one sheep and it falls into a pit on the Sabbath, will not lay hold of it and lift it out? Of how much more value is a man than a sheep. So it is lawful to do good on the Sabbath." The premise throughout is, it is lawful on the Sabbath to save life, as indeed, the law of the Mishnah and the Tosefta and the exegetical readings of the pertinent passages in the Written Torah all concur is the fact. But saving life is not at issue in the story, only doing good. And that brings us to the specific premise in the version of Matthew, that one may lift a sheep out of a pit on the Sabbath. The Tosefta (among many documents) is explicit that one saves life on the Sabbath, and any show of piety is hypocrisy:

T. Shabbat 15:11

They remove debris for one whose life is in doubt on the Sabbath. And the one who is prompt in the matter, lo, this one is to be praised. And it is not necessary to get permission from a court. How so? [If] one fell into the ocean and cannot climb up, or [if] his ship is sinking in the sea, and he cannot climb up, they go down and pull him out of there. And it is not necessary to get permission from a court.

T. Shabbat 15:12

If he fell into a pit and cannot get out, they let down a chain to him and climb down and pull him out of there. And it is not necessary to get permission from a court. A baby who went into a house and cannot get out – they break down the doors of the house for him, even if they were of stone, and they get him out of there. And it is not necessary to get permission from a court. They put out a fire and make a barrier against a fire on the Sabbath [cf. M. Shab. Chap. 16]. And one who is prompt, lo, this one is to be praised. And it is not necessary to get permission from a court.

Tosefta-Tractate Shabbat 15:11-12

But what about the animal in a pit?

L. For a beast which fell into a pit they provide food in the place in which it has fallen, so that it not die, [and they pull it up after the Sabbath].

Tosefta-tractate Shabbat 14:3

The rule is given anonymously; it is not subject to dispute but is normative. But then how are we to understand the certainty with which Jesus asks, "What man of you, if he has one sheep and it falls into a pit on the Sabbath, will not lay hold of it and lift it out? Of how much more value is a man than a sheep. So it is lawful to do good on the Sabbath."

Clearly, for the Synoptic picture of Jesus deems the critical issue to concern whether or not it is lawful to do good on the Sabbath, and the answer is, it is indeed lawful to do good, and the Pharisees do not understand the law. But what if, to the framers of the Mishnah[5] the Sabbath involves other issues entirely, so that when they speak of the Sabbath, the use a theological language that simply does not intersect with the language of doing work on the Sabbath or doing good on the Sabbath? After all, even the parallelism, do good or do harm, save life or kill, hardly is commensurate; sages concur, one must save life, and everyone knows, one may never murder, not on a week day, not on the Sabbath. So the framing of the question, sensible in the setting of Jesus's teaching, proves disingenuous in the setting of the sages' system. But then in what context do sages consider healing on the Sabbath? It is not a matter of (excess) labor – and the story strikingly does not represent Jesus as having done an act of labor, for no labor is involved in the healing. Jesus tells the man, "Come here." He said to the man, "Stretch out your hand." He stretched it out, and his hand was restored. In fact, Jesus has done nothing; labor is not the issue.

---

[5]The role of Pharisees before 70 in the framing of Rabbinic Judaism afterward sets forth its own set of problems, which I have discussed in *Eliezer ben Hyrcanus. The Tradition and the Man.* Leiden, 1973: Brill, I-II.

Now with regard to the Sabbath, let me specify what as I examine the halakhah of the Mishnah and related writings I conceive to be the encompassing principles, the generative conceptions that the laws embody and that animate the law in its most sustained and ambitious statements. They concern three matters, [1] space, [2] time, and [3] activity, as the advent of the Sabbath affects all three. The advent of the Sabbath transforms creation, specifically reorganizing space and time and reordering the range of permissible activity. First comes the transformation of space that takes effect at sundown at the end of the sixth day and that ends at sundown of the Sabbath day. At that time, for holy Israel, the entire world is divided into public domain and private domain, and what is located in the one may not be transported into the other. What is located in public domain may be transported only four cubits, that is, within the space occupied by a person's body. What is in private domain may be transported within the entire demarcated space of that domain. All public domain is deemed a single spatial entity, so, too, all private domain, so one may transport objects from one private domain to another. The net effect of the transformation of space is to move nearly all permitted activity to private domain and to close off public domain for all but the most severely limited activities; people may not transport objects from one domain to the other, but they may transport objects within private domain, so the closure of public domain for most activity, and nearly all material or physical activity, comes in consequence of the division of space effected by sunset at the end of the sixth day of the week.

When it comes to space, the advent of the Sabbath divides into distinct domains for all practical purposes what in secular time is deemed divided only as to ownership, but united as to utilization. Sacred time then intensifies the arrangements of space as public and private, imparting enormous consequence to the status of what is private. There, and only there, on the Sabbath, is life to be lived. The Sabbath assigns to private domain the focus of life in holy time: the household is where things take place then. When, presently, we realize that the household (private domain) is deemed analogous to the Temple or tabernacle (God's household), forming a mirror image to the tabernacle, we shall understand the full meaning of the generative principle before us concerning space on the Sabbath. Second comes the matter of time and how the advent of sacred time registers. Since the consequence of the demarcation on the Sabbath of all space into private and public domain effects, in particular, transporting objects from one space to the other, how time is differentiated will present no surprise. The effects concern private domain, the household.   Specifically, what turns out to frame the halakhic issue is what objects may be handled or used, even in private domain, on the Sabbath. The advent of the Sabbath thus affects the organization of space and the utilization of tools and other objects, the furniture of the household within the designated territory of the household. The basic principle is simple. Objects may be handled only if they are designated in advance of the Sabbath for the purpose for which they will be utilized on the Sabbath. But if tools may be used for a purpose that is licit on the Sabbath, and if those tools are ordinarily used for that same purpose, they are deemed ready at hand and do not require reclassification; the accepted classification applies. What requires designation for Sabbath use in particular is any tool that may serve more than a single purpose, or that does not ordinarily serve the purpose for which it is wanted on the Sabbath. Designation for use on the Sabbath thus regularizes the irregular, but is not required for what is ordinarily used for the purpose for which it is wanted and is licitly utilized on the Sabbath.

The Sabbath then finds all useful tools and objects in their proper place. But what are the implications for practical behavior? That may mean, they may not be handled at all, since their ordinary function cannot be performed on the Sabbath. That is, useful tools are to be left alone. Or it may mean, they may be handled on the Sabbath exactly as they are handled every other day, the function being licit on the Sabbath. That is to say, since they may be used on the Sabbath, they may be used in the same way in which they are used on ordinary days. Or it may mean, they must be designated in advance of the Sabbath for licit utilization on the Sabbath. On Friday one must form the intention in his heart to utilize the utensil on the Sabbath. And that may mean, to use the utensil in a common manner. That third proviso covers utensils that serve more than a single function, or that do not ordinarily serve the function of licit utilization on the Sabbath that the householder wishes them to serve on this occasion. The advent of the Sabbath then requires that all tools and other things be regularized and ordered.

The rule extends even to utilization of space, within the household, that is not ordinarily used for a (licit) purpose for which, on the Sabbath, it is needed. If guests come, storage-space used for food may be cleared away to accommodate them, the space being conceived as suitable for sitting even when not ordinarily used for that purpose. But one may not clear out a store room for that purpose. One may also make a path in a store room so that one may move about there. One may handle objects that, in some way or another, can serve a licit purpose, in the theory that that purpose inheres. But what is not made ready for use may not be used on the Sabbath. So the advent of the Sabbath not only divides space into public and private, but also differentiates useful tools and objects into those that may or may not be handled within the household.

We come to the third generative problematic that is particular to the Sabbath. The influence upon activity that the advent of the Sabbath makes concerns constructive labor. I may state the generative problematic in a simple declarative sentence: Normally one may not carry out entirely on his own a completed act of constructive labor, which is to say, work that produces enduring results. That is what one is supposed to do in profane time. What is implicit in that simple statement proves profound and bears far-reaching implications. No prohibition impedes performing an act of labor in an other-than-normal way, e.g., in a way that is unusual and thus takes account of the differentiation of time. Labor in a natural, not in an unnatural, manner is prohibited. But that is not all. A person is not forbidden to carry out an act of destruction, or an act of labor that produces no lasting consequences. Nor is part of an act of labor, not brought to conclusion, prohibited. Nor is it forbidden to perform part of an act of labor in partnership with another person who carries out the other requisite part. Nor does one incur culpability for performing an act of labor in several distinct parts, e.g., over a protracted, differentiated period of time. The advent of the Sabbath prohibits activities carried out in ordinary time in a way deemed natural: acts that are complete, consequential, and in accord with their accepted character.

What is the upshot of this remarkable repertoire of fundamental considerations having to do with activity, in the household, on the holy day? The halakhah of Shabbat in the aggregate concerns itself with formulating a statement of how the advent of the Sabbath defines the kind of activity that may be done by specifying what may not be done. That is the meaning of repose, the cessation of activity, not the commencement of activity of a different order. To carry out the Sabbath, one does nothing, not something. And what is that "nothing" that one realizes through inactivity? One may not carry out an act analogous to one that sustains creation. An act or activity for which one bears responsibility, and one that sustains creation, is [1] an act analogous to one required in the building and maintenance of the tabernacle, [2] that is intentionally carried out [3] in its entirety, [4] by a single actor, [5] in the ordinary manner, [6] with a constructive and [7] consequential result – one worthy of consideration by accepted norms. These are the seven conditions that pertain, and that, in one way or another, together with counterpart considerations in connection with the transformation of space and time, generate most of the halakhah of Shabbat.

Like God at the completion of creation, so is Israel on the Sabbath: the halakhah of the Sabbath defines the Sabbath to mean to do no more, but instead to do nothing. At issue in Sabbath rest is not ceasing from labor but ceasing from labor of a very particular character, labor in the model of God's work in making the world. Then why the issues of space, time, and activity? Given the division of space into public domain, where nothing much can happen, and the private domain of the household, where nearly everything dealt with in the law at hand takes place, we realize that the Sabbath forms an occasion of the household in particular. There man takes up repose, leaving off the tools required to make the world, ceasing to perform the acts that sustain the world. The issue of the Sabbath is the restoration of Eden, the realization of Eden in the household of holy Israel.

To that issue, the matter of how much effort is involved in saving the beast proves monumentally irrelevant. Nor can sages have grasped what someone meant in saying, "The son of man is the Lord of the Sabbath." When set alongside the Gospels' framing of issues, we realize, the two pictures of the Sabbath and the issues that inhere therein scarcely intersect. But knowing that fact affords perspective on both the figure of Jesus and the Torah of the sages that seeing each on its own does not provide. Small details turn out to recapitulate large conceptions, and that, in the end, ought to define the hermeneutics, and the consequent exegesis, of the next phase of study of both the Gospels and the Mishnah.

8

Vow-Taking, the Nazirites and the Law: Does James's Advice to Paul Accord With the Halakhah

Jacob Neusner
University of South Florida and Bard College

> After this Paul stayed many days longer...at Cenchreae he cut his hair, for he had a vow.
> Acts 18:18

> They said to him, "You see, brother, how many thousands there are among the Jews of those who have believed; they are all zealous for the law...What then is to be done? They will certainly hear that you have come. Do therefore what we tell you. We have four men who are under a vow. Take these men and purify yourself along with them and pay their expenses so that they may shave their heads. Thus all will know that there is nothing in what they have been told about you, but that you yourself live in observance of the law"
> Acts 21:23-24

Pretty much everyone concurs that Paul's haircut had to do with a Nazirite vow, in line with the provisions of Numbers 6, and, further, James's party counseled Paul to show himself observant of the law by supplying the Nazirites with the offerings that they required to complete their Nazirite vows in the Temple rites specified at Numbers 6. The happenstance that Paul himself had taken such an oath, had completed the span of time subject to the Nazirite rule, and was expected to present the necessary offerings need not detain us. Within the halakhah of the Mishnah, one had the possibility of taking a vow to supply Nazirites with their offerings; a father might so commit himself to his son, or the son to the father, for instance. So the picture is clear: James deemed vow-taking in general, and the Nazirite vow in particular, to signify loyalty to law-observance in the framework of the Torah, and Paul concurred, having himself taken such an oath. Now, everyone knows, one significant figure in the same framework will have found such counsel puzzling, and that is Jesus himself, to whom the Sermon on the Mount attributes the explicit statement (Mt. 5:33), "You have heard that it was said to the men of old, 'You shall not swear falsely, but shall perform to the Lord what you have sword.' But I say to you, Do not swear at all, either by heaven...or by earth...or by Jerusalem...And do not swear by your heard, for you cannot make one hair white or black.'"

The statement on its own presents a puzzle. For the context of the statement carries us to swearing in two categories that are kept separate in the halakhah, "swearing" referring to an oath by God's name in court, and "vows," e.g., the Nazirite vow, such as would be represented by "swearing by your head," or "by the hairs of your head." But in treating the two matters together, the statement leaves no doubt of the intent. Hence James's advice to Paul certainly presents a puzzle. I propose to show that it may not the rabbis represented later on by the Mishnah and the other halakhic and aggadic documents also will have identified more eloquent media for the expression of piety than vowing and keeping vows in general, and the Nazirite vow in particular, and it is to make that point that I wish to spell out in an exposition of the halakhic sources on both issues. With the halakhah in hand, the truly jarring effects of James's advice will make their impact.

I. The Halakhah of Nedarim

A survey of the halakhah of vowing, in tractate Nedarim of the Mishnah, Tosefta, Yerushalmi, and Bavli, and the halakhah of the Nazirite vow in particular will show us how the sages, start to finish both expounded the topic and evaluated it. When, thereafter, we take up the religious statement that the halakhah makes and identify the corresponding position of the aggadic writings, we shall see a uniform judgment of the matter, start to finish. The halakhah set forth in the Mishnah, Tosefta, and two Talmuds deems language the mirror of the soul; the words we use expose man's heart, articulate and give effect to his intentionality. The key to the entire system comes to expression in the language of the halakhah, "An act of consecration done in error is not binding or consecrated." And from the viewpoint of the Torah's halakhah, what we intend makes all the difference: God responds to what we want, more than to what we do, as the distinction between murder and manslaughter shows in an obvious way. For the critical dialectics of the Torah embodies the conflict between God's and man's will. That focus upon the definitive, taxonomic power of intentionality explains, also, why if a man says to a woman, "Lo, you are consecrated...," and the woman acquiesces, the intentionalities matching, the woman is thereby sanctified to that man and forbidden to all others; the act of intention formulated in words bears the power of classification upon which the entire system builds. But – self-evidently – not all intentionality finds Heaven's approval, and that is so even though Heaven confirms and acquiesces therein. And that brings us to the vow, which realizes in words the intentionality of the person who takes the vow and imposes upon himself restrictions of various kinds. And, inseparable from the vow, in sequence comes the special vow of the Nazirite.

Stated simply, the sages' position, in the halakhah and the corresponding aggadah, rejects vow-taking as disreputable, for reasons I shall explain. Not only so, but the Nazirite vow in particular is singled out as an act of personal arrogance, not of piety at all. The dismissive judgment of the halakhah upon the vow is fully exposed in the rule, "He who says, 'As the vows of the suitable folk' has said nothing whatsoever. Such a statement does not constitute a euphemism for a vow. Why not? Because suitable folk (*keshérim*) do not take vows. And the rest follows. But most people do take vows, and in the exemplary language of the halakhah they are particularly common in the life of the household, meaning, in relationships between husband and wife. For the vow is the weapon of the weak, the way by which the lesser party to a transaction exercises power over the greater. If the wife says to the husband, "By a vow, I shall not derive benefit from you," or "What food you feed me is qorban," she removes from herself her husband's control, so too, the guest to the host. But the vow also stands for the release of discipline, it is an expletive and an outcry, an act of temper, and no wonder sages do not respect those that take vows. Now let us see matters in more general, theoretical terms.

The power of the word to change the status of persons and things defines and sustains the household above all, which rests in the last analysis upon the foundations of commitment, responsibility, and trust – all to begin with embodied in language. The sanctity of one's word forms a corollary of the proposition that the language we use bears the power of classification, and, in the present context, of therefore effecting sanctification. If, after all, by declaring a woman consecrated to a man, or an animal to the altar or a portion of the crop to the priesthood, one brings about the sanctification of the woman or the beast or the grain, then what limits to the power of language to affect the everyday world are to be set? In that same framework, after all, God communicates and is communicated with: in the present age, with the Temple in ruins, worship is through prayer, which takes the form of words whether spoken or not.

But why focus the discussion of vowing as a component of the law that pertains within the household (in the received organization of the Mishnah, within the division devoted to the family), when vows can take place in the larger framework of the Israelite social order? Scripture imposes its judgment on the point, within the social order, at which vows become pertinent when it presents the matter as a dimension of the life of wives with their husbands or daughters with their fathers. That fact emerges from the pertinent verses of Scripture at Numbers 30:1-16:

> Moses said to the heads of the tribes of the people of Israel, "This is what the Lord has commanded. When a man vows a vow to the Lord or swears an oath to bind himself by a pledge, he shall not break his word; he shall do according to all that proceeds out of his mouth.
>
> "Or when a woman vows a vow to the Lord and binds herself by a pledge, while within her father's house in her youth, and her father hears of her vow and of her pledge by which she has bound herself and says nothing to her, then all her vows shall stand, and every pledge by which she has bound herself shall stand. But if her father expresses disapproval to her on the day that he hears of it, no vow of hers, no pledge by which she has bound herself, shall stand; and the Lord will forgive her, because her father opposed her. And if she is married to a husband while under her vows or any thoughtless utterance of her lips by which she has bound herself, and her husband hears of it, and says nothing to her on the day that he hears, then her vows shall stand, and her pledges by which she has bound herself shall stand. But if, on the day that her husband comes to hear of it, he expresses disapproval, then he shall make void her vow which was on her and the thoughtless utterance of her lips, by which she bound herself; and the Lord will forgive her. But any vow of a widow or of a divorced woman, anything by which she has bound herself, shall stand against her.
>
> "And if she vowed in her husband's house or bound herself by a pledge with an oath, and her husband heard of it, and said nothing to her and did not oppose her, then all her vows shall stand, and every pledge by which she bound herself shall stand. But if her husband makes them null and void on the day that he hears them, then whatsoever proceeds out of her lips concerning her vows or concerning her pledge of herself shall not stand; her husband has made them void. But if her husband says nothing to her from day to day, then he establishes all her vows or all her pledges that are upon her; he has established them, because he said nothing to her on the day that he heard of them. But if he makes them null and void after he has heard of them, then he shall bear her iniquity."

> These are the statues that the Lord commanded Moses, as between a man and his wife, and between a father and his daughter, while in her youth, within her father's house.

The generalization, that a person is not to break his word but keep "all that proceeds out of his mouth," meaning, his vows, immediately finds its amplification in the framework of the household.

The halakhah of vows (drawing in its wake the halakhah of the special vow of the Nazirite) concerns matters of personal status: what may a person do or not do by reason of a self-imposed vow? The halakhah so reveals what it finds especially interesting in marriage, which is, relationships: shifts and changes in the relationship of the wife to the husband. That is consistent with the points pertinent to the status of a woman in relationship to a man at which the halakhah begins and ends: the creation of the marriage through Heavenly action (the halakhah of Yebamot) or human intervention (Qiddushin, Ketubot); the cessation of a marriage through Heavenly action (death) or through the writ of divorce (Gittin). Now we raise the question about the interplay between responsibilities to Heaven, on the one side, and to the husband, on the other, that the woman takes upon herself – the gray area in which the woman owes fealty to Heaven and to husband alike. Here we find ourselves in dialogue with the three pertinent chapters of the Written Torah that all together address the matter, Numbers Chapter Five for the woman investigated for faithfulness; Numbers Chapter Six for the Nazirite vow; and Numbers Chapter Thirty for the ordinary vow.

The most general statement of matters then invokes the matter of relationships with Heaven that affect relationships on earth, that is, the woman's vow to Heaven that affects her relationships with her husband and family. That is what is at stake in the halakhah of Qiddushin and Gittin as well – only now in the reverse. Acts of consecration involve declarations made on earth and confirmed in Heaven, e.g., consecration of a woman to a particular man. Here we address the effects of declarations made to Heaven that shape a woman's status and relationships on earth, and that means, in the nature of things, with her father before marriage and with her husband in marriage.

The presentation of the halakhah starts with the definition of a vow and proceed to consider the affects of a vow upon what a person may or may not do, mainly, eat. We conclude with close attention to how one may gain absolution from a vow, releasing its binding character by reason of diverse grounds or pretexts. That is the whole story, beginning, middle, and end, a structure that is simple and logical. That vows principally locate themselves within the household – the premise of the Scripture's statements and the halakhah's presentation throughout – guides the articulation of the details of the law. But the halakhah as the

Written Torah defines it and the formulation of the halakhah by the Oral Torah do not coincide in one fundamental way. Scripture treats the matter as principally one involving women – wives and daughters – while the halakhah of the Oral Torah presents it as a sex-neutral one, involving vows by man or woman alike. What is nearly the whole story of the topic in Numbers is handled in Nedarim as subordinate and secondary. Rather, the halakhah of the Oral part of the Torah wants to know about the language that makes the vow effective, the results of vows, the release of vows – topics implicit, but not explored, within the Scripture's account of the matter.

The halakhah spreads a broad net over the language people use, treating every sort of euphemism as effective in imposing the vow. The halakhah of definition yields no problematics I can discern, only a principle richly instantiated that any sort of language that resembles the language of a vow takes effect. The essay on language that the halakhah embodies proceeds to language that is null, or language used without adequate reflection, e.g., vows of incitement, on the one side, vows of exaggeration, on the other. In both cases the vow does not follow much thought. Or, more to the point, the intention behind the language is inappropriate. Vows of incitement – to purchase an object at a given price – embody inappropriate intentionality; they are meant to influence the other only. Vows made in error, like acts of consecration made in error, do not stand for the intentionality of the speaker, and so are null. Finally, vows broken under constraint are null. Along these same lines, one may intentionally take a false vow to save life or limb or to deceive the thief and the tax-collector (regarded as one and the same).

The second important problematics that provokes legal inquiry provides a systematic exercise in differentiating the genus from the species, embodied in the distinction between a vow against deriving benefit from the genus, which encompasses all the species of that genus (the genus, house, the species, upper chamber), and a vow against deriving benefit from a particular species, which leaves available the other species of the same genus (upper chamber, house). That exercise is worked out in vast detail, repeating the same point throughout. The difference between genus and species (wool, shearings) and between two distinct genera (clothing, sacking) accounts for a broad range of the issues dealt with here, and the matter of speciation covers much of the rest. Thus we differentiate cooking from roasting or seething. So too, language that is general is interpreted in minimal ways, "pickling" applying only to vegetables. In all, the exercise of speciation and its effects accounts for many of the concrete halakhic problems that are set forth, and a few generalizations, even given in abstract terms, would encompass much of the halakhah in its details.

Vow-Taking, the Nazirites and the Law

If speciation explains a broad range of rules, the matter of causation accounts for another. Specifically, the third type of problem addressed by the halakhah concerns the effects of vows, e.g., the result of general statements about deriving benefit for specific types of benefit. A vow against deriving benefit from his friend leaves the friend free to perform certain general actions, e.g., paying the man's half-sheqel tax to the Temple and restoring what he has lost. The distinction between forbidden and permitted benefit is subtle, and so far as I can see rests upon the difference between efficient cause and proximate cause, benefit deriving from actions in the category of efficient causes being forbidden, the other kind permitted.

That that distinction governs is shown, among other cases, by the rule that allows the fellow, forbidden by the man's vow to give him any benefit, to hire a storekeeper to give what the man cannot directly give himself. The rule is worth reviewing: The fellow goes to a storekeeper and says, "Mr. So-and-so is forbidden by vow from deriving benefit from me, and I don't know what I can do about it." And the storekeeper gives food to him who took the vow and then goes and collects from this one against whom the vow was taken. [If] he against whom the vow was taken had to build the house of the one prohibited by vow from deriving benefit, or to set up his fence, or to cut the grain in his field, the fellow goes to the workers and says to them, "Mr. So-and-so is forbidden by vow from deriving benefit from me, and I don't know what I can do about it." Then the workers do the work with him who took the vow and come and collect their salary from this one against whom the vow was taken. Clearly, the difference between direct and indirect action governs. But if we differentiate indirect from direct cause, we also focus upon direct cause in its own terms, e.g., fruit, what is exchanged for the fruit, what grows from the fruit. So from an exercise on the difference between genus and species we here proceed to one on the difference between direct and indirect causation.

Vows are remitted or lose effect when the conditions specified in them have been realized or proved null. They also are remitted when the purpose of the vow is shown spurious, e.g., "Did you not speak only to do me honor? But this [not taking your wheat and wine for my children] is what I deem to be honorable!" Further, vows cannot in the end take effect so as to bring about the violation of existing obligations or contracts. A vow against what is written in the Torah is null; one that violates the marriage-contract is ineffective; one that requires dishonoring parents is null. Vows that contradict the facts explicitly invoked in making them are null. The point is then obvious: language takes effect only when the facts embodied in the language to begin with are valid.

The power of the husband or the father, as the case may be, to annul the vows of the wife or the daughter presents no surprises. We deal with the familiar range of cases, e.g., the interstitial status of the betrothed girl, over which both father and husband enjoy power. Once the woman is on her own, it goes without saying, no man may nullify her vows. The husband may annul the vows of the wife once she comes into his domain. The action must take place on the spot, through the day in question; it cannot be done in advance. The halakhah clearly makes provision for the autonomous woman, not subject to father or husband, and treats as valid whatever vows she makes on her own account.

II. The Halakhah of Nazir

The special vow of the Nazirite, like the vow in general, draws in its wake consequences for the life of the family of which that individual that takes the vow is (by definition) a key member: the householder, his wife, children, and slaves. Not drinking wine, not shaving the head, not contracting corpse-uncleanness are matters that are personal and impinge upon the household; they do not pertain in any weighty way to public life, on the one side, or to relations between the people, Israel, and God, on the other. The Nazirite cannot attend to the deceased, cannot drink wine with the family, and subjects himself to his own rule when it comes to his appearance. As is the priest to the family of Israel, so is the Nazirite to the household of Israel, a particular classification of persons, distinguished in consequential and practical ways as to nourishment and comportment.

Nor should we miss the negative case. The vow does not encumber all Israel in relationship to God. It is not an obligatory act of service, as an offering is, but a votive one. And while other votive acts of service, e.g., the thank-offering or the peace-offerings, engage the priesthood in the Temple, the vow does not, and the Nazirite vow brings about offerings given to the priest at the door of the tent of meeting, in the manner of the offerings of the person afflicted with the skin ailment described in Leviticus Chapters 13 and 14; and there he stays.

Hence the special vow of the Nazirite forms an event at the door of the Temple courtyard but in the heart of the household. That is not all that explains why the tractate is situated, in the Mishnah, where it is, in the division on the family ("Women"), even though it bears upon men as much as upon women. The Nazirite vow forms a subdivision of the category, vows, and is treated as continuous with the exposition of that topic. That is because the right of the husband to annul his wife's vows extends to the Nazirite vow that she may take. That is surely the formal reason that justifies situating the tractate where it is. Scripture deals with two topics, the restrictions self-imposed by the vow, and the offerings required in connection therewith. The relevant verses of Scripture are at Num. 6:10-21. The exposition of the law set forth by Scripture, which preoccupies the halakhah of the Oral Torah in the present case, explicitly concerns husband-wife relationships at M. 4:4-7, the husband's annulling the vows of the wife, the affect upon the wife of the husband's sudden death without an act of nullification, and the like. Not only so, but the tractate commences with a formulation modeled upon that of Mishnah-tractate Nedarim. But the true continuities, which make the two tractates into a single, continuous statement, will impress us only when we have reviewed the halakhah of the Nazirite vow.

The Written Torah finds two points of interest in the present topic, the prohibitions upon the Nazirite, the offerings that come as the climax of the vow. The Nazirite then is comparable to a *kohen* or priest: subject to certain prohibitions and is assigned a particular position in the conduct of the Temple cult. The priest cannot serve if he is drunk or contaminated by a corpse or bald (a bald-headed man is invalid to serve as a priest, so M. Bekh. 7:2A). A single paradigm pertains, a single analogy governs. From the perspective of Scripture, once the Nazirite vow takes effect, prohibitions are invoked against wine, hair-cutting, and corpse-uncleanness; the other point of interest is the offerings that are required if the Nazirite is made unclean with corpse-uncleanness and when the Nazirite completes the vow in a state of cleanness. All this the halakhah both takes for granted and in the main simply ignores. What Scripture holds does not require detailed analysis, by contrast, is the process by which the woman or man becomes a Nazirite, that is to say, the vow itself. To that problem fully half of the halakhah as defined by the Mishnah with the Tosefta is devoted.[1] So while the triple taboo is merely restated by the halakhah of the Oral Torah, it is the exposition of the vow that defines the tough problems, generates interesting conundrums, and entails the rich exposition that the Tosefta and two Talmuds would ultimately provide.

But in the Oral Torah, the halakhah, for its part, characteristically ignores what is securely classified and instead takes up interstitial problems, generated by intersecting rules or classes of data. In the present case, the halakhah focuses upon not the black-and-white language that invokes the vow, but on euphemisms that may or may not

---

[1]As usual, the contribution of the Talmuds to the formulation of halakhah proves negligible. Their interest is in analysis, not legislation. The Yerushalmi's formulations show little augmentation of the law, much amplification; I give no indication of the speculative problems explored therein, which are as usual imaginative and rich, but add nothing to the halakhah in its classical formulation except refinements.

pertain, just as we saw with Nedarim. Language that is similar in sound or in sense takes effect. What about stipulations that might affect the vow, conditions under which the vow is or is not invoked, the taking of sequences of Nazirite-vows at a single moment? That is the next problem. The duration of the vow, undefined in Scripture, occupies attention. Then comes the intervention of the husband into the applicability of the vow his wife has taken. We turn, further, to designating the diverse animals that are to serve as the Nazirite's offerings at the end of the vow, with special attention to situations in which the animals are not used in accord with the original language of sanctification.

It is no surprise that the problematics of the halakhah, then, finds acute interest in the working of euphemisms. But that is not only because of the unclear status of euphemistic language – does it mean what it seems or not? Language, the halakhah recognizes, conveys sense and meaning in many ways. Language stands for what is intensely personal and private. But language also conveys meanings of general intelligibility. It is by definition a public act. With what result for the halakhah? What is private (mumbled, unintelligible, gibberish) bears no consequence, what is intelligible by a common-sense standard takes effect. That is how the halakhah sorts matters out. Thus, when it comes to euphemisms, all of them take effect; for what matters about language is not adherence to the governing formula, though it matters. What makes all the difference is the perceived and publicly comprehensible intent. If the intent conveyed by the language is clear and unmistakable, then the language has done its task of embodying intentionality. And then the language is affective. If the intentionality is not vividly conveyed, however indirectly, then the language is null. The power of language lies in its capacity to convey, to embody, inchoate intentionality, to realize in the shared world of public transactions the individual and private attitude or intentionality that motivates action. To that matter we shall return when we ask about the religious meaning of the halakhah.

And that accounts for the halakhah's recognition of the special status of a Samson-Nazirite: the language that is used signals the intentionality to accept the model of Samson, and hence fully exposes the will of the one who takes the special vow. Whether or not the Oral Torah has invented the category of the Samson-Nazirite to build upon the implications of its theory of the relationship of language to intentionality – the necessary connection between language and intention, public metaphor and private attitude and will – we cannot surmise. It is the simple fact that once the important questions pertinent to the topic at hand center upon the power of language to embody and realize, confirm and convey the attitude, the (mere) details of language will precipitate the formation of specificities of the halakhah. The main problem addressed by the halakhah pertaining to the language of the vow to be a Nazirite is how to standardize matters, so that private meanings and personal stipulations do not corrupt discourse. Then the prevailing solution is to identify what is general and intelligible and dismiss the rest. One example serves. That is why if someone specifies a detail as incumbent, then all the details of a Nazirite vow pertain to him. Nothing remains private, personal, idiosyncratic, once language serves. Even what affects the household in particular is framed for effect for all Israel.

The Tosefta's contribution to all this is, predictably, expansive: Just as euphemisms for Nazirite-vows are equivalent to Nazirite-vows, so euphemisms for Samson-vows are equivalent to Samson-vows. The vow applies in the Land and abroad, to hirsute and bald alike, and – it goes without saying – whether or not the Temple is standing. The intention is the key, not the limitations of circumstance. And that same governing principle accounts for the interpretation of the language, "I will be a Nazir like the hairs of my head" or "like the dust of the earth." That is taken to mean, for an unlimited period of time. The net effect of the halakhah is to generalize upon specific and idiosyncratic usages. Individual conditions are null, e.g., If one said, "Lo, I am a Nazir on condition that I shall drink wine and become unclean with corpse uncleanness," lo, this one is a Nazir. But he is prohibited to do all of these things that he has specified as conditional upon his vow. If he said, "I recognize that there is such a thing as Naziriteship, but I do not recognize that a Nazir is prohibited from drinking wine," lo, this one is bound by the Nazirite oath. But legitimate stipulations bear consequences, e.g., conditions that do not violate the law of the Torah: "...if my wife bears a son" or "a daughter."

Because the husband has the power to nullify the vows of the wife (or the father of the daughter), the halakhah attends to the case of nullification. But I see nothing of special interest in the laws, except that while the husband may nullify the wife's vow, he may not nullify his own. If his vow is contingent upon her vow, by contrast, neither is subject to the Nazirite rule. Limits are set upon intentionality; if one intended to violate the vow but in fact was not subject to the vow, there is no penalty: If her husband annulled the vow for her, but she did not know that her husband had annulled it for her and nonetheless continued to go around drinking wine and contracting corpse uncleanness, she does not receive forty stripes. So too, someone who violated the vow but had a sage annul it is not penalized; the vow never took effect. Here intention to violate the vow is insufficient to precipitate sanctions; the actualities intervene. Or, to put it otherwise, improper intention not confirmed by improper deed is null. Mere intention on its own is null – language and action decide everything, and, when it comes to the vow, the language constitutes the act.

When it comes to the offerings of the Nazirite, the halakhah – as at Pesahim and elsewhere – takes special interest in the interstitial case of the beast that has been consecrated but cannot be offered in fulfillment of the intent of the sacrifier: what to do with a beast designated for a given purpose that no longer is needed for that purpose? That involves the general rules that pertain. If a beast is designated as a burnt offering, it is presented in that designation; so too, a peace offering, differentiated from the Nazirite's peace-offering as to accompanying gifts. When it comes to the disposition of the coins that are designated for the purchase of an animal to be consecrated for the stated purpose, the rules follow the same lines. The upshot is, the language that is used to designate the animal or the coins takes effect, even though the purpose for which the animal or coins is required is nullified by circumstance. What is the stopping point? It is the tossing of the blood. At that point, the vow has been fully carried out and can no longer be annulled.

When it comes to the restrictions upon the Nazirite, which the Written Torah has defined, the Oral Torah devotes its halakhah to the familiar problem of differentiating among a sequence of actions of a single type, that is, the general theme of the many and the one, the one and the many, that preoccupies the halakhah in one topic after another. This routine problem comes to expression in the language, A Nazir who was drinking wine all day long is liable only on one count. If they said to him, "Don't drink it! Don't drink it!" and he continues drinking, he is liable on each and every count [of drinking. The problem is particular, the resolution and consequent rule not. So, too, the conundrum about the high priest and the Nazirite, both of them subject to the same restriction against corpse-uncleanness, who share the obligation to bury a neglected corpse requires us to hierarchize the sanctity of each in relationship to that of the other. This, too, represents a particular form of a general problem of the halakhah in its work of hierarchical classification, here of competing sanctities: who is holier than whom, and so what? For the same reason, we need not be detained by the halakhah covering cases of doubt. They merely illustrate prevailing principles on how cases of doubt are to be resolved; another tractate provides the systematic statement of governing principles of the matter, the present one, merely concrete problems for solution.

III. Religious Principles of Nedarim-Nazir

The halakhah of Nedarim-Nazir takes up the theme, the power of language to impose changes in status. That is a common theme of the halakhah, paramount in the halakhah of Israel's relationships with God as much as that of Israel within the household walls. In words a magic dwells. In relationship to God what is at issue is the designation of what belongs to God or God's surrogates. Here at stake is personal status. The former then concerns how language affects the tangible world of wine and grain and oil, the latter, the intangible but very real world of a person's standing in the sight of Heaven and Israel alike. By using certain language, a man or woman effects an alteration in his or her condition, e.g., in relationships with other people, or in food that may or may not be eaten, or situations that may or may not be entered into. In both realms of being words affect the world of tangible substances and real relationships. Here, as we noted earlier, by words a man declares himself analogous to a priest – and his actions confirm his intention, realized in language.

What the vow does is to call down Heaven's sanctity upon the benefit, material or otherwise, that the donor wishes to give over for the sake of Heaven. No wonder then, that in analyzing vows, we call upon the conceptions of the gift to Heaven that form the center of Holy Things. The intention of the farmer to consecrate the beast, expressed in the proper language, is confirmed: the beast enters the status of sanctification even before it is set on the altar and slaughtered, its blood tossed at the corners of the altar. "Qorban," "Nazir," and other effective language – these form a single classification, words that transform by reason of the intent with which they are spoken, which they realize because they are spoken.

To state matters in more general terms: at stake in the vow and in the special vow of the Nazirite is the realization of intention brought about through the use of language. But language used for vows, so sages portray matters, does not sanctify, it contaminates, that language ought to express reflected-upon intentionality – like the designation of an animal to expiate an inadvertent, newly-realized sin – but it conveys the outcome of temper and frustration. Designating a beast as consecrated realizes a noble, godly intention; designating benefit one receives from one's spouse as "qorban" uses language to embody a lowly and disreputable intention, one to humiliate and reject and disgrace the other. Sages' message registers that language is dangerous because it realizes intentionality, which had best, therefore, be expressed with probity and restraint. And these virtues form the opposite of the traits of mind and character of the vow-taking Israelite, wife or husband, host or guest, salesman or customer, as the exemplary cases of Nedarim have shown us.

All the consequences of the use of special language – the illustrative materials of both bodies of halakhah, Nedarim and Nazir – concern relations of husbands and wives, or parents and children, or the localized transactions of the household and the service-economy round-about (the shop-keeper for example), thus the household and the conduct of life therein. Only rarely does the language, e.g., of the vow or of the special vow of the Nazirite, spill over into the public affairs of Israel in general. Being private, the vow and the Nazirite vow have no consequences for the relationship of Israel to God in general; breaking the vow or failing to observe what is pledged concerns the individual and God, the community being a bystander to the transaction and bearing no stake therein. The category-formations involved in vows and Nazirite vows do not encompass transactions within the social order, never alluding to a Nazirite's cow that gored the cow of a woman, or a man subject to a vow who struck another and injured him; the compensation is unaffected by the status of the Nazirite or the person who has taken a vow, in the way in which compensation is shaped by the status, e.g., of the slave, the minor, or the idiot:

M. Baba Qamma 8:4
A. A deaf-mute, idiot, and minor – meeting up with them is a bad thing.
B. He who injures them is liable.
C. But they who injure other people are exempt.
D. A slave and a woman – meeting up with them is a bad thing.
E. He who injures them is liable.
F. And they who injure other people are exempt.

No such provision in public law ever takes account of the status of the Nazirite or the person subject to a vow; these do not define classifications of persons for which the social order publicly makes provision. The exemplary cases in Nedarim-Nazir reinforce the essentially private circumstance of matters, their restriction to the household or the village formed by households. The matter of accepting gifts or hospitality hardly registers as a social event. In two of the three dimensions of Israel's world order, its public relationship with God and the conduct of its social order, vows and special vows make no material difference.

But language on its own is a public event, not subject to private manipulation. Language matters because of what it represents and conveys, which is, the solemn intentionality of the one who uses the language, and that is the key to all else. Language makes public and attracts public attention to the intentionality of the private person, forms the point of intersection ("the interface") between the individual and the community. So the classification of the law at hand within the framework of the Israelite household, while appropriate, somewhat misleads. For when it comes to the theme and problem at hand – the interplay of intentionality and language – the halakhah uniformly explores the matter in its impact upon Israel's relationship with God, Israel's social order, and Israel's life within the household, all three. But sages' category-formation, setting Nedarim-Nazir in the framework of home and family, and mine, placing the halakhah within the walls of the household, find ample justification.

That is because, as one may see, also, with reference to Hullin, Qiddushin, Ketubot, and Nedarim, the halakhah of Nazir carries us deep into the recesses of Israel in its tents, within the walls (whether tangible or otherwise) of its households – there alone. Intentionality matters in many category-formations of the halakhah, but in connection with vows and the Nazirite vow in particular do sages localize their statement on the matter. Here they say, people bear direct, personal responsibility for what they say, and while statements made in error are null, those made in jest bear real consequences. That is why, as we have seen in the consideration of both bodies of halakhah, euphemisms form so central a concern. There is no fooling around with God, no language exempt from God's hearing. Accordingly, the halakhah of vows and the Nazirite vow finds an appropriate situation here because it is coherent in its generative problematics with the halakhah of the household in general. For what makes the Nazirite vow effective is language that an individual has used, and it is the power of language to bring about profound change in the status of a person that forms the one of the two centers of interest of the halakhah of life within the walls of the Israelite household – the focus of sanctification. That formal fact explains the topical pertinence.

The halakhah of Nedarim-Nazir investigates is the power of a person through invoking the name of Heaven to affect the classification in which he or she is situated and so his or her concrete and material relationships with other people. This is done by stating, "May what I eat of your food be prohibited to me as is a sacrifice prohibited to me," all conveyed in the word "Qorban." Having said that, the person may not eat the food of the other. The reason is that the other person's food has been declared by the individual who took the vow to be in the status of a sacrifice. We know that what makes an ordinary beast into a holy beast, subject to the laws of sacrilege and set aside for the alter, is a verbal designation as a sacrifice. Here, too, what makes ordinary food into food in the status of Holy Things, so far as the given individual is concerned, is the verbal designation of that ordinary food as Holy Things. The difference is that designating an animal as a beast for sacrifice is a public act, affecting society at large. No one then can make use of said animal. Declaring that a dish of oatmeal is in the status of a qorban by contrast, has no affect upon the cereal, except for the person who made that declaration.

That language confirms and conveys the intentionality to effect sanctification hardly presents a surprise at this point in our study; it is, after all, the governing principle of Qiddushin for the spoken word and Ketubot for the written word, the legal document. But what sages wish to say in the halakhah before us differs from their message concerning Qiddushin and Ketubot, even though all four tractates take up the power of language to bring about changes in status. Sages revere the language that brings about sanctification of a woman to a man, and they treat with great punctiliousness the language of the marriage-contract, which, indeed, they subject to the closest exegetical processes of reading and interpretation. If they wished to say, language bears its own power (for the reason stated earlier, its capacity to embody intentionality), they could have no superior choice of topic than the halakhah of Qiddushin and Ketubot (and Gittin).

IV. Sages' Evaluation of Vow-Taking and of the Nazirite Vow

But what if they wanted to say, language bears power even for purposes of which we (and Heaven) disapprove? And what if their intent was to warn, watch what you say, hold your tongue and keep your temper, because in expressing intentionality, your words give effect to your will, and you will be unable to retract? In other words, if sages wanted to make the point that people had best use in a wise and astute manner the power of language, how would they best say so? Within the framework of the halakhah, vows, inclusive of the special vow of the Nazirite, present the particular and appropriate medium for such a message. That is not only because sages want to tell people to watch their words and not pretend to joke when it comes to matters where intentionality makes a difference as to personal status. That is also because sages to begin with take a negative view of vowing. While of oaths taken in court with full deliberation, invoking the name of God, they approve, vows they despise. They are explicit on that matter: people who take vows show their weakness, not their strength. Vows represent the power of the weak and put-upon, the easy way to defend oneself against the importunities of the overbearing host, the grasping salesman, the tormenting husband or wife. But sages do not honor those who take the easy way, asking God to intervene in matters to which on our own we ought to be able to attend.

Sages do not treat respectfully the person who takes vows. Vow-takers yield to the undisciplined will, to emotion unguided by rational considerations. But intentionality must (ideally) take form out of both emotion and reflection. Vows explode, the fuel of emotion ignited by the heat of the occasion. "Qonam be any benefit I get from you" hardly forms a rational judgment of a stable relationship; it bespeaks a loss of temper, a response to provocation with provocation. Right at the outset the halakhah gives a powerful signal of its opinion of the whole: suitable folk to begin with do not take vows, only wicked people do. That explains in so many words why, if one says, something is subject to "the vows of suitable folk," he has said nothing. Suitable people – *keshérim* – make no vows at all, ever. A distaste for vowing and disdain for people who make vows then characterize the law. People who take vows are deemed irresponsible; they are adults who have classified themselves as children. They possess the power of intentionality but not the responsibility for its wise use. That is why they are given openings toward the unbinding of their vows; they are forced at the same time to take seriously what they have said. Vows are treated as a testing of Heaven, a trial of Heavenly patience and grace. Sanctification can affect a person or a mess of porridge, and there is a difference. Expletives, with which we deal here, make that difference; these are not admired.

But because the halakhah begins and ends with the conviction that language is power, the halakhah also takes account of the sanctifying effect of even language stupidly used. That is the message of the halakhah, and it is only through the halakhah at hand that sages could set forth the message they had in mind concerning the exploitation and abuse of the power of language. It is a disreputable use of the holy. And language is holy because language gives form and effect to intentionality – the very issue of the halakhah at hand! That is why we do admit intentionality – not foresight but intentionality as to honor – into the repertoire of reasons for nullifying vows, as we note in the halakhah of Nedarim:

> M. 9:1 In a matter which is between him and his mother or father, they unloose his vow by [reference to] the honor of his father or mother.

> M. 9:9 They unloose a vow for a man by reference to his own honor and by reference to the honor of his children. They say to him, "Had you known that the next day they would say about you, 'That's the way of So-and-so, going around divorcing his wives,' "and that about your daughters they'd be saying, 'They're daughters of a divorcée! What did their mother do to get herself divorced' [would you have taken a vow]?" And [if] he then said, "Had I known that things would be that way, I should never have taken such a vow," lo, this [vow] is not binding.

The normative law rejects unforeseen events as a routine excuse for nullifying a vow; foresight on its own ("had you known...would you have vowed?") plays a dubious role. But when it comes to the intentionality involving honor of parents or children, that forms a consideration of such overriding power as to nullify the vow.

So sages' statement through the halakhah of Nedarim-Nazir is clear. Vows are a means used on earth by weak or subordinated person to coerce the more powerful person by invoking the power of Heaven. They are taken under emotional duress and express impatience and frustration. They are not to be predicted. They do not follow a period of sober reflection. They take on importance principally in two relationships, [1] between friends (e.g., host and guest), [2] between husband and wife. They come into play at crucial, dangerous points, because they disrupt the crucial relationships that define life, particularly within the household: marriage, on the one side, friendly hospitality, on the other. They jar and explode. By admitting into human relationships the power of intentionality, they render the predictable – what is governed by regularities – into a source of uncertainty, for who in the end will penetrate what lies deep in the heart, as Jeremiah reflected, which is beyond fathoming? But language brings to the surface, in a statement of will best left unsaid, what lurks in the depths, and the result, Heaven's immediate engagement, is not to be gainsaid. That is why vows form a source of danger. What should be stable if life is to go on is made capricious. So far as marriage is concerned, vows rip open the fabric of sacred relationships.

Language represents power, then, and it is a power not to be exercised lightly. In the cases examined in Ketubot as those laid out here, the weaker side to the party is represented as taking a vow – whether the milquetoast husband, whether the abused wife. It is the wife against the husband, the harried guest against the insistent host, the seller against the buyer, the boastful story-teller against the dubious listener, the passive against the active party, that the vow is taken. The strong incites, the weak reacts, and the language of reaction, the vow, contains such power as is not to be lightly unleashed even against the one who gives and therefore dominates, whether in sex or food or entertainment. Vows then are the response: the mode of aggression exercised by the less powerful party to the relationship. The weak invoke Heaven, the strong do not have to. A vow will be spit out by a guest who has been importuned to take a fourth portion in a meal he does not want to eat. A wife will exclaim that she will derive no benefit whatsoever from her husband. A whole series of cases emerges from a vow taken by a person not to derive benefit from his friend, with the consequence that the friend, who wants to provide some sort of support for the dependent person, does so through a third party. The dependence then is less obtrusive. So, once more: who gives, dominates, and the vow is the instrument to escape earthly domination in the name of Heaven.

V.

The Aggadic Reading of the Halakhic Circumstance

As usual, what the halakhah states in its way, the aggadah expresses in its manner too. Here is the Bavli's topical composite on losing one's temper, which is deemed the basis for taking vows:

> B. Ned. 3:1 A-D I.14/22 A. Said R. Samuel bar Nahman said R. Yohanan, "Whoever loses his temper – all the torments of Hell rule over him: 'Therefore remove anger from your heart, thus will you put away evil from your flesh' (Qoh. 11:10), and the meaning of 'evil' is only Hell: 'The Lord has made all things for himself, yes, even the wicked for the day of evil' (Prov. 16:4). Moreover, he will get a belly ache: 'But the Lord shall give you there a trembling heart and failing of eyes and sorrow of mind' (Deut. 28:65). And what causes weak eyes and depression? Stomach aches."
>
> B. 3:1A-D I.16/22b Said Rabbah bar R. Huna, "Whoever loses his temper – even the Presence of God is not important to him: 'The wicked, through the pride of his countenance, will not seek God; God is not in all his thoughts' (Ps. 10:4)."
>
> B. 3:1A-D I.17/22b A. R. Jeremiah of Difti said, "[Whoever loses his temper] – he forgets what he has learned and increases foolishness: 'For anger rests in the heart of fools' (Qoh. 7:9), and 'But the fool lays open his folly' (Prov. 13:16)."
>
> B. R. Nahman bar Isaac said, "One may be sure that his sins outnumber his merits: 'And a furious man abounds in transgressions' (Prov. 29:22)."
>
> B. 3:1A-D I.18/22b Said R. Ada b. R. Hanina, "If the Israelites had not sinned, to them would have been given only the Five Books of the Torah and the book of Joshua alone, which involves the division of the Land of Israel. *How come?* 'For much wisdom proceeds from much anger' (Qoh. 1:18)." [Freedman, *Nedarim, ad loc.*: The anger of God caused him to send prophets with their wise teachings.]

Sages leave no doubt as to their view of matters, which they express with the usual explicit clarity.

The same negative view pertains to the Nazirite vow. It is a mark of arrogance. The special vow of the Nazirite arrogates to the person who takes it the special status of a holy man or woman, even though Heaven has not endowed him or her with that status by nature, by birth. The priest by birth cannot function drunk or subject to corpse-uncleanness. The Nazirite takes on himself the same prescriptions and beautifies himself with abundant hair, held by sages a mark of pride.

> T. Nazir 4:7 A. Said Simeon the Righteous, "In my entire life I ate a guilt-offering of a Nazir only one time.
>
> B. M'SH B: "A man came to me from the south, and I saw that he had beautiful eyes, a handsome face, and curly locks. I said to him, 'My son, on what account did you destroy this lovely hair?'
>
> C. "He said to me, 'I was a shepherd in my village, and I came to draw water from the river, and I looked at my reflection, and my bad impulse took hold of me and sought to drive me from the world.
>
> D. "'I said to him, 'Evil one! You should not have taken pride in something which does not belong to you, in something which is going to turn into dust, worms, and corruption. Lo, I take upon myself to shave you off for the sake of Heaven.'
>
> E. "I patted his head and kissed him and said to him, 'My son, may people like you become many, people who do the will of the Omnipresent in Israel. Through you is fulfilled this Scripture, as it is said, 'A man or a woman, when he will express a vow to be a Nazir, to abstain for the sake of the Lord'" (Num. 6:2).

But the Nazirite is one who lets his hair grow long, cutting it only at the end of the process, when the vow has been fulfilled. So the Nazirite has undertaken important restrictions incumbent on the priesthood and beautified himself with long hair. Only at the end does the Nazirite make himself praiseworthy, in line with Simeon's judgment, by cutting off all the hair. In line with this statement of matters, sages treat the Nazirite vow as they treat vows in general, as a mark of inferior character or conscience, here, of pride. Here is where James's advice registers: go, help Nazirites pay for their vows (and do your own), and so show your adherence to the Torah. But that does not change the fact that Simeon does not approve of the vow except in the most unusual case.

What is at stake, then, in the halakhah of Nedarim-Nazir? It is sages' interest in defining the source of the power of language. This they find in Heaven's confirmation of man's or woman's affirmation. By using formulary language man or woman invoke the response of Heaven more really by throwing up words toward Heaven and so provoking a response in Heaven. That is how patterns of behavior and relationship, such as are defined by the vow, the Nazirite-vow, the act of sanctification of a woman to a particular man or a marriage contract, are subjected to Heaven's concerned response. Relationships and deeds are subjected to Heaven's engagement by the statement of the right words. So the halakhah explores the effects of words, and it is in the halakhah of the Oral Torah – and not that of the Written Torah, with its powerful bias toward priestly concerns – that that exploration takes place.

VI. Does James's Advice to Paul Accord with the Halakhah

The halakhah of the Oral Torah answers the question, what can a man or a woman say so as to become obliged to do or not do a specified range of deeds? And the answers to that question respond to yet another, still more profound question. It is, how is Heaven mindful of man and woman on earth? The ornate essays into the trivialities of language and the use of language that we find in the halakhah of Qiddushin, Ketubot, Nedarim, Nazir, and Gittin respond to that question. The halakhah speaks large and simple truths in conveying a remarkable vision of humanity in God's image. Man and woman are so like God as to be able through what they say to provoke, and even encumber, God's caring and concern. That is because man and woman know how to say the ordinary words that make an extraordinary difference on earth and in Heaven. The message of the halakhah of the Oral Torah is, we are responsible for what we say – there is no such thing as "mere words" – because what we say brings to full articulation what we want, words bearing the burden of intentionality. After all, the first act of creation is contained in the statement, "And God said...."

When it comes to the Nazirite vow in particular, sages recognize the Nazirite and respect his obedience to the provisions of the law. But they take note that the Nazirite puts on airs, grows his hair long and imposes upon himself restrictions indicative (otherwise) of priestly status. So they take the view, "If you take the vow, carry it out," but they do not counsel the pious to show their piety by taking the vow. If James were to have advised Paul to take the vow and keep it for the requisite thirty days, he would have given poor advice. Telling Paul to complete the vow and help out others in the same position – that represents a mediating position. Advising Paul not to keep the vow at all would have marked the other extreme.

But so far as James had in mind for Paul to make a public affirmation of his adherence to the law of the Torah, the case at hand proves ambiguous, the advice bearing a measure of irony: if that's what you have done, then do it up and do it right. It accordingly is self-evident that James's advice on how to show oneself obedient to the law will not have scandalized the sages, but it also will not have found agreement among the rabbis of the Mishnah represented by the halakhah of the Mishnah, Tosefta, Yerushalmi, and Bavli. Whether or not their view of matters circulated – if not under their auspices, let alone in formulations later on cast by them into halakhic language – is not subject to doubt. Jesus said exactly the same thing in the Sermon on the Mount. But that carries us to the very crux of the issue that separated James from Paul.

CURRENT BOOK REVIEWS

9

Halbertal's *People of the Book*

Moshe Halbertal, *People of the Book. Canon, Meaning, and Authority.* Cambridge, 1997: Harvard University Press. 185 pp.

Halbertal, a professor of Jewish Thought and Philosophy at the Hebrew University, writes on "the canonical text and the text-centered community. In particular, I seek to understand the Jewish tradition as a text-centered tradition...as this centrality [sic!] affects life on earth...I have chosen to focus on the shared commitment to certain texts and their role in shaping many aspects of Jewish life and endowing the tradition with coherence." This, he claims, "takes the place of theological consistency." In this work of ignorance and self-indulgence, all he means is that various Judaic systems have diverse views: "These conceptions...have little in common and they are specifically Jewish only insofar as each is a genuine interpretation of Jewish canonical texts." But who is to determine what is a genuine interpretation and a wrong one? What we have is an exercise in theology in the form of description of how various documents have been read – that is to say, an abdication of intellectual responsibility. Halbertal meanders through this and that and in the end discovers nothing very special.

If the program of the work – Judaism through books – strikes readers as familiar, being the model that has governed intellectual history and theology from the formation of the Wissenschaft des Judenthums to the present, the execution will disappoint as well. The work is badly written, ignorant of most of the scholarship of the past half-century on many of the very writings treated here, and disorganized and free-associative – a mass of confusion and disconnection. The impoverished aspect of intellect finds its match in the poor quality of research.

Predictably, the book is sketchy and sustains no continuous account even of the announced subject. The work is organized "thematically," "different historical moments and...the various canons as they relate to the theme at hand." How much hard work Halbertal saves himself in the resort to "thematic" presentation of the topic (we can hardly say, the problem) he has chosen to address. He summarizes the work in this language:

> The first chapter discusses relationships between canon and meaning. The second treats tensions and competing ideas about the notion of authority of texts and interpreters, while the problem of the value of text and curriculum is discussed in the third chapter. Each chapter deals with a different canon within the Jewish tradition: the fist focuses on the canonization of the Bible [he means, Tanakh, he does not deal with the New Testament] and its effects on Jewish trends in its interpretation; the second analyzes the canonization of the Mishnah and subsequent codes in the Jewish tradition as they relate to the problem of authority and controversy; and the third deals with the struggle accompanying the rise of the Talmud as the main text in the Jewish curriculum from the Middle Ages onward. Although the intense production of different Jewish canons over such a long time does not receive a systematic historical treatment, the accumulated total does serve as a continuous resource for dealing with problems of canons in their relation to meaning, authority, and value within the Jewish tradition...

Anyone who has followed scholarship in the study of religions and their texts (not "canons"!) will find nothing surprising in an inquiry into how the continuous reading of authoritative writings over time provides a means of defining a religion in an other-than-theological way.

Covering so much ground, Halbertal depends upon secondary literature throughout, passing his opinion everywhere but contributing original scholarship nowhere. Then the value of the work – meaning, Halbertal's opinion on this and that – must rest in the end on the quality of research, and that is in two aspects.

First, does he bring fresh ideas or conduct stimulating analyses? No, he does not. What is truly remarkable in this book is how Halbertal solemnly and pretentiously states banalities and asks us to receive them as wonderful and new. Any standard religious studies textbook or encyclopaedia article (and Halbertal seems to know almost nothing of the study of religion) will greet this work with a huge ho-hum. For from square one ("Texts form a normative canon; they are obeyed and followed, as, for example, are Scriptures and legal codes") to the conclusion on "the Bible" instead of the Talmud in Israeli politics (the reversal of the curriculum from Talmud to Bible represents a major shift in political awareness and identity...."), what we have is an interminable parade of self-evident and (in context) vacuous observations, things that textbooks and encyclopaedias and handbooks have long recorded. What

Halbertal contributes is a turgid way of saying the obvious. In defense of Jerusalem scholarship I hasten to add – that conception of what scholarship requires cannot be imputed to Hebrew University professors alone.

Second, does he at least provide a reliable account of the state of the various questions he raises? No, he does not. Alas, while most professors conduct a dialogue with scholarship, I state flatly that, when it comes to his treatment of the Mishnah and of rabbinic literature, which I know, Halbertal presents himself as utterly ignorant; he simply has not read the scholarship outside of what he implicitly deems "canonical." But that marks Halbertal as a politician, not a scholar, for in scholarship the canon encompasses all learning, not only some of it. His narrow, selective reading of a vast corpus of work on the very subjects that he addresses marks the man as too ignorant of a vast range of scholarly discussion to deserve consideration. All we learn from Halbertal's second chapter is how things look to someone who does not choose to read the scholarship on his subject. (Not a specialist in the areas treated in the first and third chapters, I can only hope he does a better job there, but I doubt it.) The result is pseudo-scholarship of surpassing superficiality and sustained, conceptual confusion.

People of the Book surely does not represent what Jerusalem can and ought to expect of its professors. It may be safely discarded, with nothing lost but disheartening evidence of dismal standards where we rightly expect excellence and rigor. But no one thinks that Halbertal embodies the standards of his University.

Jacob Neusner
University of South Florida and Bard College

10

Nadler's *Faith of the Mithnagdim*

Allan Nadler, *The Faith of the Mithnagdim. Rabbinic Responses to Hasidic Rapture.* JOHNS HOPKINS JEWISH STUDIES, ed. by Sander Gilman and Steven T. Katz. Baltimore & London, 1997: The Johns Hopkins University Press. 254 pp.

The Hasidim these days enjoy a good press, the Mithnagdim – defined merely as critics of Hasidism – have none. And that is because the Hasidim have defined their opposition as much as the early Christians created "Judaism." In neither case does the consequent portrait aim at a fair account of an authentic alternative within religion. Within the Hasidic caricature of those identified merely as "the opposition," Hasidism represented encounter with God, Mithnagdism, formalism and ritualism; Hasidism afforded authentic spirituality, Mithnagdism, a mere imitation, a going-through-motions, a desiccated academicism. For the English-reading world, that picture now competes with another. For in an original and important account, Allan Nadler, of YIVO, delves deep into the difficult, arcane sources of the later eighteenth and early nineteenth century Judaisms of Eastern Europe and comes up with a plausible and compelling account of the authentically religious position of the Opposition to Hasidism. All we need now is an appropriate label for that Judaism that animates the yeshiva-world today: the normative Judaism of segregationist, academic Orthodoxy that flourishes throughout the world of Judaism.

In a masterful work of original scholarship, Nadler takes not only the principal Oppositionist-voices, the Vilna Gaon and Haim of Volozhin, but Phinehas of Polotsk, who represents a more articulate and accessible statement of matters than the better known figures. His survey then focuses upon issues as scholarship has defined matters. Hasidic thought is represented as immanentalist, Nadler shows, so is the thought of GRA and others. Hasidism nourished itself on Qabbalah – so did Mithnagdism. Hasidism poured energy into prayer, so did the opposition, and so too with asceticism and the other points at which the two Judaisms are supposed to have differed. If, therefore, Hasidism offered an authentic encounter with God, at every point Mithnagdism did too. Then where the true points of difference? They emerge from a basic philosophy of life, a theological anthropology.

Hasidism, true to the spirit of eighteenth century revivalism, thought that humanity was capable of transcendence, Mithnagdism took a more pessimistic view of humanity's possibilities. Hasidism thought that, in this world, we may meet God, Mithnagdism found in death the beginning of an authentic life with God. Nadler states it simply, "As far as the Mithnagdim were concerned, the attainment of Kabbalistic erudition or mystical union with God was possible, if at all, only in the world to come." Hasidism thought that ordinary folk could master difficult writings, Mithnagdism doubted it. Hasidism exalted prayer over Talmud Torah, Mithnagdism insisted upon the classic priority of learning over spiritualism. Mithnagdism held that "only the full and final obliteration from the created cosmos offered man complete salvation from a physical world so far removed from God and so saturated with the evil desire...for many of the Mithnagdim only physical death allowed man to attain that proximity to the Lord that is his final good." Above all, Mithnagdism affirmed the received definition of the religious leader in the Torah-world, while Hasidism framed a theory of the Zadik out of "a general theological monism and its mystical notions of cosmic harmony and restoration."

Above all, Mithnagdism preserved a more realistic, more pessimistic view of human potentiality. Nadler states the matter in this language:

> "In the process of attaining...communion with God, the Hasid inevitably departs from the traditional, restricted modes of organized religious and social behavior. He then appears to those who are faithful to the normative limits of social, legal, and religious protocol as at best eccentric or somewhat deranged and at the very worst fraudulent. This is precisely how the Mithnagdim perceived the adherents of Hasidism. ...they simply could not accept that such significant numbers from among the Jewish masses had legitimately reached the level of its attainment. Consequently, they could not tolerate the concerted attempts by the early Hasidic theoreticians to spread the knowledge and practice of Jewish mysticism as widely as possible. The net consequence of this fear and suspicion of Hasidic-sponsored hefker, namely, its populist transcending of the normal boundaries of accepted religious conduct, was a strengthening of precisely those conventional religious limits on the part of the Mithnagdim.

So, Nadler concludes:

> The Mithnagdim did not dispute the fundamental teachings of Jewish mysticism in principle. They shared...the religious conviction that God is immanent in the created universe and that it is possible for the ideal man...to commune with the divine presence inherent in the world. The Mithnagdim harbored...a very pessimistic view of the common man of their day; they believed that he was simply unable...ever to attain such a mystical state...In sum, the Mithnagdim allowed man no genuine mystical experiences in this life....In sharp contrast to Hasidism's quest for the unitive life...Mithnagdism seems to have been intent on raising and fortifying those borders...Because of this very limited assessment of the human condition, the Mithnagdim restricted their attention almost exclusively to carefully controlled and well-defined religious disciplines...The Mithnagdim...offered the individual Jew no path of redemption from his estranged, shattered existence in this world and no remedy for his divided nature and afflicted spirit. Mithnagdism absolutely forbade man from attempting to overcome his inherent inadequacies...[becoming] obsessed with human ineptitude and spiritual alienation. In response to the perceived Hasidic threat...the Mithnagdim fortified to an unprecedented degree the limits of spiritual attainment and the boundaries of acceptable religious conduct.

Enough time has passed to allow us to form a judgment on the disputes of two hundred years ago: Hasidism has shown its quality and character. When I consider the collapse of Habad into a degenerate pseudo-messianism, the remarkably superficial knowledge of Torah characteristic of its religious leadership, the traits that the Hasidic communities bear in common with their counterparts in other religions – cheap grace, distributed by worshipped men – I find perspicacious and compelling the deep forebodings of the GRA and those for whom he spoke. Hasidism promised a Jewish version of eighteenth century panglossism, and the GRA said so. Too bad Mithnagdism had no Voltaire, for in the end, Mithnagdism paid Hasidism an undeserved, unearned compliment: Mithnagdism took Hasidism seriously as a religious heresy, rather than dismissing it as the social aberration that is all that, within Judaism in the authentic, dual-Torah, it was and is.

In many ways Nadler's work – a vastly recast and revised dissertation – defines the model of a first-rate monograph on an important subject. It is both specific, rich in close reading of texts, and also broad and general in its explicit articulation of the stakes, the issues, the consequences. It is lucidly argued and carefully drafted. But we should not miss Nadler's special accomplishment. Rabbinic Hebrew follows its own rules of expression and nuance, cites and alludes and embodies all those obscurities that pass for learning in the intertextualist realm. So it is not easy to follow what is at stake in the prose that Nadler's sources present. Nadler works his way through this arcane, recondite, mandarin writing and makes of it an intelligible medium of argument of plausible and important propositions. The technical achievement of figuring out what is going on in difficult texts matches the intellectual achievement of framing the whole in terms that bear consequence for a wide audience interested in the history of Judaism within the history of religion – work that makes a difference, indeed, a huge difference.

Jacob Neusner
University of South Florida and Bard College

11

Shavit's *Athens in Jerusalem*

Yaacov Shavit, *Athens in Jerusalem. Classical Antiquity and Hellenism in the Making of the Modern Secular Jew*. Translated by Chaya Naor and Niki Werner. London and Portland (OR), 1997: The Littman Library of Jewish Civilization. xv + 560 pp.

In this well-translated book, Professor of the History of the Jewish People at Tel Aviv University, Yaacov Shavit here extends to secular Jews the commonplace proposition that Classical Antiquity nourished the Enlightenment. To present as monumental and new what is an entirely familiar notion – everybody knows about Tchernichowsky's Hellenism in his Hebrew poetry for example – Shavit gussies up his ho-hum hypothesis with massive exercises of irrelevant research. In the racist premise that "Athens and Jerusalem, Greeks and Jews, represent two distinct and different human entities," he asks, "Did Athens have any impact on the shaping of modern Jewish culture." To pursue the problem he has fabricated for himself, therefore, he has to frame an account of "the Greek soul" and "the Jewish soul," yielding such constructs as "the modern Jewish historical consciousness" (p. 375).

Silly talk of souls and collective consciousness should not obscure that Shavit pursues a serious program: "the purpose of this survey is to present the structural similarity between the complex intercultural relations that existed between Judaism and the Hellenistic civilization in the ancient world and those that exist between Jews and Western culture in the modern age. It is this similarity that motivated the historical study of these past relations between Jews and Hellenists as a model for the relations between Jewish and Western culture in the modern era" (p. 299). And again, "from the late eighteenth century onwards two modes of historical comprehension and insight were created. The first was an idealistic mode, the fruit of a confrontation between two abstract entities

– Judaism versus classical Greece...The second was an empirical historical mode, in which Hellenism was perceived as a historical cultural reality, syncretistic and diversified. Historical research addressed the complex relationship and cultural interferences between the cultural...reality in the Hellenistic era...This led to a new understanding of Jewish history and Judaism; Judaism was perceived as a pluralistic, dynamic, even syncretistic entity" (p. 11). Shavit intends the work to "cast light on...intellectual history and the history of Jewish culture in modern times...the emphasis is on historical reflections and perceptions and images of the past and their role in collective historical memory" (p. 12).

The problem is, Shavit loses his way in a morass of irrelevant topics, as a review of the contents of the work shows. Shavit divides the work into three "mirrors:" [I] waking the dead: Greece ad an ideal and an exemplar; Hellenism and Hebraism: the two poles of the world; Israel and Greece: revising a legendary past; "Greek Wisdom" as secular knowledge and science; Japheth in the Tents of Shem, the reception of the classical heritage in modern Hebrew culture; the moral dimension: commonality and particularity; worlds without compromise: reconstructing the disparities; have Jews imagination" Jews and the creative arts; [II] the nature of the Hellenistic mirror; Judaism and Hellenism in Palestine and Alexandria, two models of a national and cultural encounter; Homeric books and Hellenistic culture in the world of the sages; [III] back to history: the secularization of the ancient Jewish past; the children of Japheth (Aryans) and the children of Shem (Semites): race and innate nationalism; the people and its land: country, landscape, and culture; a "polis" in Jerusalem: the Jewish state; the new Jewish culture: ideal and reality; what has Athens to do with Jerusalem? Much of the book proves tedious and irrelevant to the quite provocative thesis announced at the outset.

While Shavit explicitly disclaims the intent to provide "even a brief description of the relationships between Judaism and paganism in ancient times or between Judaism and Western civilization in modern times," in fact the bulk of the book does exactly that. In nearly the whole of part II and much of the rest, Shavit finds himself attempting to characterize a world he has said he would not discuss. So he surveys a small sample of secondary scholarship on a variety of topics, and only limited portions – the only persuasive ones – address topics that Shavit knows firsthand. Alas, the book amazes by its superficiality. Shavit ignores a variety of works that contradict points he wishes to make, e.g., "no philosophical concepts permeated the Talmud under the Greek influence," a proposition systematically criticized in books that (fortuitously) do not appear in Shavit's bibliography. I may state flatly that, when it comes to Rabbinic Judaism, Shavit is simply an amateur.

So Shavit has turned the familiar notion that Hellenism influenced some secular thinkers of Jewishness into an excuse for a tiresome and mechanical exercise in pseudo-scholarship. Shavit wanders far afield to fill up his scorecard. He even lists (p. 473) the untreated topics that he thought of using as "mirrors and inverted mirrors" to "reflect additional aspects of" what he calls "modern Jewish history." The list encompasses stupefying irrelevancies, e.g., the continuity between Hellenistic antisemitism and modern secular antisemitism, Jewish and Greek attitudes towards women, Greek and Jewish diasporas and homelands, religion and state in Judaism and the State of Israel and in Greece, "do the Jewish and Greek cultures both belong to the realm of Mediterranean culture," "what of the parallel between the development of the modern Greek and modern Hebrew languages?" and so on and so forth. How these subjects pertain to "the making of the modern secular Jew" Shavit does not say.

The upshot is that Shavit has found for himself an excuse for collecting and arranging a great deal of information and passing his opinion on it. But if the book is tedious, diffuse, and for long stretches simply pointless, within the nearly 600 pages readers will find about 200 pages that really do investigate how modern ideologists of Jewishness drew upon, or responded to, ancient Greek culture, as some did. Here, not surprisingly, the book's bibliography shows that Shavit has turned out original scholarship. This marginally-competent book could have used an editor, and its author, a measure of humility.

Jacob Neusner
University of South Florida and Bard College

12

Brody's *Geonim*

Robert Brody, *The Geonim of Babylonia and the Shaping of Medieval Jewish Culture*. New Haven and London, 1998: Yale University Press. ISBN: 0-300-07047-0. 384 pp. $40.

Professor of Talmud at the Hebrew University, Jerusalem, and well-known for his editions and study of Geonic writings, Dr. Brody here provides a systematic compendium on the literature of and concerning the Geonim, the Rabbinic authorities of ca. 500-1000 C.E., an age in the history of Judaism awaiting its systematic reconstruction. For what he has accomplished, Brody deserves only praise. He introduces the pertinent sources and points to the relevant scholarly treatment of them; no one will ignore this exceptionally useful work when taking up its subject.

Brody divides the book into three essentially unrelated parts: the historical setting, the classical Geonic period, and Se'adyah Gaon and after. And the three parts themselves cohere only loosely The historical setting deals with these topics in order: defining the Geonic period (Savoraim and Geonim); the primary sources (Epistle of Sherira Gaon, account of Nathan the Babylonian, the Genizah); the Geonic academies, continuity and change; the multifaceted role of the Gaon; the exilarchate; the struggle against heresy (Anan and the origins of Karaism, issues of contention between Karaites and Rabbanites, Rabbanite reactions); competition with the Palestinian center; ties with the diaspora (the sphere of Babylonian hegemony, Palestine and Egypt, the Maghreb, Europe). The presentation of "the classical Geonic period" takes up the literary sources: the intellectual world of the Geonim (knowledge of languages, areas of interest, the supernatural, attitudes towards authority); the Talmudic sources (oral versus written Talmud, interpretation and application of the Talmud); extra-Talmudic oral traditions; the responsa literature; the She'iltot (the genre, form and structure, the She'iltot of R. Ahai, the sources of the She'iltot, the influence of the She'iltot); the earliest legal codes (Halakhot Pesuqot, Halakhot Gedolot). Finally comes a set of essays dealing with Se'adyah: Se'adyah Gaon, revolutionary champion of tradition (Se'adyah's career); the halakhic monographs; Talmudic exegesis and methodology; theology; biblical exegesis; linguistics and poetry. Clearly, the classical, and correct, program of *Wissenschaft des Judenthums* governs; nothing can be done before these questions are answered.

Alas, as the survey of the contents shows, this is not so much a coherent book, with a cogent program, as a set of discrete research reports, a sequence of free-standing topical papers, encyclopaedia-articles really, some of them more, some less persuasive. The chapters tend to a certain (merciful) brevity and follow a simple formula: survey of sources, low-level paraphrase of their allegations or contents, and not much more than that, except where Brody has done original work. The best of the studies – the ones that draw on his own research – show confidence and mastery and historical imagination, the others summarize the work of third parties, encompassing, also, Brody's often captious outsider-opinions. What he knows first hand, he knows well; but his opinions outrun his knowledge in many areas. The treatment of Karaism is entirely a survey of secondary scholarship, and the presentation of Talmudic literature does not even survey scholarship beyond the most sectarian limits. Indeed, in not a few of the areas where he relies on secondary accounts, alas, Brody does not do a thorough job even of bibliography. Here he gives not so much an opinion as a mere local prejudice: the books omitted are the ones his crowd apparently will not read. That is why many of the treatments are not only incoherent but shallow; the wild incoherence of the presentation of Se'adyah suffices to make the point that Brody does not do philosophy or history of ideas.

An account of "the shaping of medieval Jewish culture" certainly could have come forth. That is shown by Brody's conclusion, a perfunctory, three-page "epilogue," which can well serve as the opening lines of the coherent book, as distinct from collection of topical essays, demanded by Brody's misleading title, with its concern for Jewish culture: "One might say that this was the last formative age of a unified Rabbanite Jewish culture...Those who have written on this period have rightly emphasized two related phenomena: the transformation of the Babylonian Talmud from a literary corpus to a legal 'code,' which...could serve as an authoritative guide to religious practice...In addition, the Geonim...were engaged in a bitter and ultimately successful struggle against an even more fundamental challenge...to Rabbinic Judaism, mounted by a variety of sectarian movements..." But none of this affects the logic of the book; it is tacked on, but ought to have stood at the head and dictated the program of the whole. And, it may be noted by the careful reader, the vitality of the prose of the epilogue contrasts with the lifeless prose characteristic of the shank of the book. Where things began to get interesting, Brody stopped work.

Consider then what Brody misses or treats in a superficial and trivial way. He writes about the most important period in the history of religion for monotheism (inclusive of dualism): Christianity in the Near and Middle East, Judaism, Zoroastrianism, and Islam. That is to say, in the same period as that of the Geonim of Babylonia, in the same place and within the same political framework, Islam confronted both Judaism and Christianity with a challenge at once political and intellectual; the regnant religion, Zoroastrianism, began its long, slow decline by perspicaciously writing down its heritage of religious classics; and the now-well-established Christianity of the eastern Roman Empire renewed itself in the crucible of the Muslim *défi*. In Brody's hands, Zoroastrian supplies no analogies (compare, on this same period, this writer's *Judaism and Zoroastrianism at the Dusk of Late Antiquity. How Two Ancient Faiths Wrote Down Their Great Traditions*), Islam scarcely made any profound difference to Judaism or more than an adventitious and practical impact upon it, and in Brody's mind Christianity rarely supplied analogies to clarify the situation of Judaism. It would be difficult to imagine a more complete failure of historical imagination, a more pedestrian recapitulation, in a more parochial manner, of writings that took shape in a time of enormous upheaval. Working within an intellectual ghetto, Brody has succeeded in making boring the single most interesting period in the history of Judaism from late antiquity to the nineteenth century.

But if the failures may characterize an entire academic community, the successes belong to the author himself. These are those of industry, erudition, and systematic inquiry into primary and some secondary sources. Whether the discussion is grounded in personal mastery of sources or merely superficial survey of secondary work, the book gathers a massive amount of information and organizes it accessibly. So, in the balance, Brody's book is definitive and opens many doors. Providing a survey of sources and learning on a variety of relevant subjects, Brody has written what will stand for a generation as the definitive account of the sources: thorough on the principal subjects, broad in scope, and accessible. Here is the starting point for all future research on its subject. Now others, with richer capacities for framing important questions and constructing a coherent historical account of culture can take over and turn the sources into the cultural history that eludes Brody's grasp.

So, as I said, Brody has also provided a research-tool of inestimable value, and no library of Judaism will miss this reference-work. In the balance, then, we must be glad for what we have been given. The philology in hand, others, with different gifts and capacities, may now turn to history and culture.

Jacob Neusner
University of South Florida and Bard College

13

Rubin's *Telling and Remembering*

Steven J. Rubin, ed., *Telling and Remembering. A Century of American Jewish Poetry.* Boston, 1998: Beacon Press. 499 pp. $27.50.

The two hundred poems Professor Rubin, University of South Florida English and writing professor, has assembled, with perspicacious introductions, allow us to listen to the eloquent voices of sensitive spirits. "The unacknowledged legislators of mankind," poets see our condition more deeply and express, in a more refined use of the American language than the rest of us are able to do, the meaning of our lives. Arranged chronologically, from Emma Lazarus, b. 1849, to Robyn Selman, b. 1959, the poems provide a glimpse and a survey of the American Jewish spirit. Not a poet nor even a critic of poetry, it was with innocent and ignorant appreciation that I read every one of them. I would not imagine to criticize the poetry, for I do not know bad from good, but to me, they all are good, even though some spoke to me more particularly than others.

But I know how to read a book of Judaism, and in this document of Judaism, few of them have much of a Jewish message, and scarcely more than one or two, a Judaic one. Rubin has created a major document of American Judaism, an artifact and a monument, and in these pages, in America we see what we Jews have been and have become. The picture that the poets portray, the mirror that in their souls they hold up for us – this is what I find of broad general interest in this first-rate exercise of taste and judgment.

Since poets transform common experience into uncommon insight and do so with magical language, I took a special interest in one question: what experience does Judaism – not merely being Jewish, but the religion, Judaism – afford to the poets for the body of their experience and reflection? The Jewish poets of America accurately reflect, and reflect upon, everyone's ordinary experience: immigration, Holocaust, ethnic identification. They embody us all, using their (in many cases, formidable) mastery of language to speak to us all, to render the particular into the exemplary.

Ah, but what they have not experienced – what they leave out! They mirror the remarkable emptiness of American Jews' Jewishness: they have little to say about Judaism, with which, by the evidence of their poetry, they simply do not engage. These are chefs who know potatoes but no spices. Scripture, the written Torah, speaks to only a few of them. The yearning for encounter with God of the Qabbalah, the soaring intellect, reaching Heaven, of the Talmud, the intense conscience of prophecy – little of the heritage of sanctity and moral regeneration captured by the word "Torah" affects these poets. And if they do not enter into the inner resources of the Torah, that is to say, Judaism, who is going to?

The poets, as a group, speak of ordinary things in an extraordinary way, but, overall, mostly of themselves. They rarely invoke experience that transcends private life, on the one side, or public culture, on the other. Here is no Emily Dickenson, seeing in Amherst the very heart of human being. That is why they testify to the commonplace condition. The immigrants' children speak of the immigrants, capturing the pathos of their unrealized dream. The next generation talks of alienation and isolation, the one beyond, the horrors of realized evil. And all of them talk of themselves, thinking to transcend the particular – my this, my that, throughout.

Some show us what our American language can do, some surprise by the banality of their usage, but many amaze by the commonplaceness of their message. And few startle us with that insight of genius that would recast the inner life of the faith through the special perception of the poet. That is not to complain with what the American Jewish poets do achieve, which is to capture and recast in powerful language and evocative images the experience of us all, death or hope or discovery, for instance. It is to point out that, though poets they may be, they're not much as Jews. By their testimony they show their ordinariness. They hear little of the music, see details out of all context, understand vaguely or not at all what Jewish is all about, which is Judaism. That is what transforms sound into music, squiggles into art, details of this and that into massive moments of meaning.

My complaint with the poets is not that they make mistakes, although some of the mistakes are egregious. How little does one have to know to have Aqiba's students carry him out of Jerusalem in the time of siege? The poet means Yohanan ben Zakkai, and to those that know, it makes a huge difference; it is like calling not George Washington but

Abraham Lincoln the Father of his country. How thin, how desiccated, an experience of being Jewish must one have had to invoke only the Holocaust when thinking Jewish? I look in vain for the magic of God encountered in the here and now of the Sabbath, I hoped to encounter words capable of giving body to the wonder of the Sukkah, to the imagination's triumph over time and space of the Seder. Great artists not only paint well, but through paint they impart a new vision to beauty. These poets rarely invoke the counterpart, for Jews, of beauty, which is holiness and sublimity.

Here we have some masters of language (among many users thereof), with an enormous capacity for eloquence and evocation – and nothing to say about the subject of their poetry! It is as though a composer has challenged the technical skills of the Boston Symphony Orchestra for a complex composition devoted to a Coke commercial: there is an incongruity between the technical gifts and the use to which they are put. That is not so of them all, Cynthia Ozick standing for the handful of those of profound Judaic sensibility. But for the most of the poets in these pages, we have a composer of enormous technical gifts who ends up giving us boring and unsurprising variations on Twinkle, Twinkle Little Star would find his match in these pages: poets yes, but as to Jewish – there's no there there.

Contrast these johnny-one-notes with their Israeli counterparts, Bialik or Tchernichovsky of the old generation for instance. Bialik transformed the entire treasure of Judaic writing of two thousand years into the gems of his own devising, he could say whatever he wished to say in language that evoked eternity. He knew. He felt. He understood. And he could sing. Nor do we have to refer only to the founders of the language. How has Hebrew poetry responded to the Holocaust, by contrast to the strident, shrill, and empty scream that passes for poetry here? My knowledge of Israeli poetry is scarcely even elementary, but I could not help comparing the American Jewish Holocaust poetry with the intense, bitter, devastating poetry of Uri Tzvi Greenberg, whom I encountered in his poetry when I was young, decades ago before the Holocaust was invented and we did not know how to feel about those still-fresh wounds. He had the power of language to confront God, as the prophets would, and to tell God, having chosen the gentiles in place of the Jews, not to forget to bless the gentiles' pigs or to respond to the arrogant clanging of their bells. Now there is a Holocaust poet – and among Israeli Hebrew poets, he is only one. But he cared enough to hate, and he did not have to invent meretricious symbols lacking all resonance in reality.

If the Israeli Holocaust poets are writing Jewish and even Judaic poetry, and they are, then the American Jewish poets, in the aggregate, are doing something else. In the Jewish and the Judaic contexts if the Israelis are men, we are monkeys – grotesque imitations, meretricious imitators, players of games, not Jews but virtual-Jews. If I do not speak of counterparts in Yiddish or in Spanish or French or Russian, it is because I do not have the knowledge. But I wonder whether Jewish poets in Yiddish or the other Jewish languages (as American in these pages is asked to serve as a Jewish language) work out of so abbreviated an agendum of experience, so impoverished a vocabulary of encounter as do most of these. American Jewish poetry, seen in the aggregate, eloquently tells us how the poets feel this morning, but as to the tale cannot make us care, who are Jews.

That is what I learn from Professor Rubin's masterful collection. He has created a document of American Judaism, and no one who asks about the Jewish spirit in America will want to miss this anthology.

Jacob Neusner
University of South Florida and Bard College

14

Kaplan and Dresner's *Abraham Joshua Heschel*

Abraham Joshua Heschel. Prophetic Witness. By Edward K. Kaplan and Samuel H. Dresner. New Haven & London, 1998: Yale University Press. 402 pp.

In a life full of paradox and crisis, Abraham Joshua Heschel, 1907-1972, embodied the fate of Judaism in the twentieth century. In his person, he lived through the principal experiences, intellectual, religious, and political, that have defined the condition of the Jews and set forth the issues with which the Judaic faith has had to contend. The first half of his life story, told in these pages, underscores the challenges of a life in interesting times, lived in particular through the medium of intellect. Because of Heschel's broad influence as a political icon of the left, presented as he is here as a prophet redivivus, Heschel's life, rather than his thought, attracts attention today. Some of his students, including this writer, took the path to the right, most to the left, and the far left of American politics at that. But long after his left-liberal politics lose all relevance for generations that define the political imperatives differently, his religious ideas, framed in terms of knowledge of God through revelation in the Scriptures, will continue to shape the life of piety and faith for thoughtful people, and that is why he rightly deserves a major biography.

Heschel was an unlikely candidate for a position at the center of American Judaism, its theology and its politics. To get there he had to abandon or vastly reconfigure his own heritage, his nationality, his ethnicity, his modes of thought and expression, even the language he spoke and the clothes that he wore. The simple outline tells the story of a man whose adaptations to challenge required remarkable courage. He started within the most isolated of the Orthodox Judaisms in Poland, got himself a secular education while continuing Orthodox practice and faith in Lithuania, affiliated with Liberal (Reform) Judaism in Germany, then the USA, and ended up at the seminary of Conservative Judaism in New York City. And through the passage from language to language, culture to culture, country to country, he continued to pray three times a day and thank God for every bite of bread, to study the Torah as God's revealed word and to set forth what he learned as teaching of that same living tradition. It is hard to point to a more successful story of renewal of an ancient tradition through the encounter with contemporary intellect and sensibility than Heschel's.

His life began in a politically isolated community of Yiddish speaking Jews in Poland, not speaking Polish or imagining a role for himself in Polish politics, lived in Germany through the 1920s into the late 1930s and saw the first stages of what became the Holocaust (he lost his mother and sisters and many other relatives in the tragedy). He ended up in the USA as a principal voice in, first the movement lead by Martin Luther Kings, Jr., marching in Selma, then in the anti-Viet Nam politics of the American left. During his American years, 1940-1972, he produced a series of systematic works, framed within the philosophy of religion, as a philosophy of Judaism, as well as important studies of principal figures in the theology and law of that religion. His final works showed the beginnings of a major theological enterprise, as his confrontation with German philosophy gave way to a systematic theological undertaking, only marginally realized.

It is difficult to imagine a life more burdened with crises of the world and of the spirit, beginning with a movement out of an intense, socially-tight, community of the Hasidic faithful and within a very few years into German Liberal Judaism. But Heschel was no ordinary Hasid, a mere follower of some holy man, he was a prince of the realm. And he did not then go off to Germany and clip off his beard and side curls, he found his way into the intellectual heart of German Liberal Judaism and taught at the US counterpart, Hebrew Union College, and at the somewhat more traditional Conservative school in NYC as well. And in Liberal, Reform, and Conservative Judaism Heschel did not then adopt the standard position of rationalism and secular apologetics characteristic of those Judaisms. He preached nothing other than a philosophical form of Hasidism, much as did Martin Buber. So too, a victim of the anti-Semitism of the age, that of German National Socialism, and part of a religion that Soviet Communism absolutely prohibited, Heschel found for himself a leading position in the nascent American left of the Civil Rights and Viet-Nam era.

That is the life story, half of which – the years from 1907 through 1940 – is narrated here. Heschel was born into the aristocracy of Hasidism in Poland, a Judaism that fostered direct encounter with God through a variety of media of prayer and pious expression, musical, narrative, and the like, and held that certain men mediated between God and man. Heschel traced his genealogy directly to principals among those men. He left the social world of Hasidism without abandoning its pattern of pious living, giving up the clothing and the intense social life but not the activities of prayer and study. Out of a world that valued only Torah-study – that is, systematic learning only of the holy books of Scripture, Talmud, and Hasidic classics – in his high school years he left his mother's house in Warsaw (his father having died when he was ten) and went off to Vilna, where got himself a secular education, in the Yiddish language. From Vilna he proceeded to the University of Berlin and the Reform Institute for Higher Learning in Judaism of the same city, so identifying himself with secular Western philosophy, which he studied, and into the language of which he formulated a philosophized Hasidism. So he made choice after choice, moving from a world bounded by the faith to the ambiguities of the cultural union of German philosophy and Judaic classics negotiated by German Liberal Judaism, from Yiddish to German, from a politically-neuter university to intense activism (a story not pertinent to the first half of his life). In so doing, he bypassed German Orthodoxy, identifying with the Liberal Institute for Higher Learning and avoiding the German-Orthodox Rabbinical Seminary scarcely three blocks away in Berlin.

What makes Heschel important is the books he wrote in the USA, where he framed a reading of the Judaic religious tradition that advocated religious observance in practical terms alongside direct encounter, even confrontation, with the secular challenges to religiosity posed by Western philosophy and culture. But his intellectual achievements, however, formidable, do not account for the attention paid to his name today, twenty-five years after his death, when many of the most constructive enterprises in other-than-Orthodox Judaism in the USA identify with him and use his name to signal their character, the Heschel Day Schools for example. And while some of his students carried his intellectual legacy rightward, to others among them, including the primary author of this book, represented him as a prophet in their own image of prophecy. So the remarkable range of human experiences that Heschel encountered finds its match in the broad catholicity of responses to Heschel's life-story, on the one side, and (in lesser measure) life's work, on the other.

How well do Kaplan and Dresner tell the tale? The bulk of the research was done by Samuel H. Dresner, professor of philosophy at the

Jewish Theological Seminary of America and for a long time pulpit rabbi, Heschel's student first at Hebrew Union College in the earlier 1940s, then at JTSA, and his leading disciple and interpreter. The book was written by Edward K. Kaplan, professor of French and comparative literature at Brandeis, who first met Heschel at the political phase of his career, in 1966, when Heschel was one with the Berrigans. The collaboration of researcher and writer has produced a book with the strengths and weaknesses of each of the partners. On the one hand, the work is lovingly researched, pages and pages of data being lovingly filled with information of marginal interest – empty filler really. We hardly need to be told the geography of the Warsaw neighborhood where Heschel grew up, for example, or be given potted tours of Weimar Berlin. Some of the anecdotes are of dubious provenience and no responsible scholar will have included a fair number of them. Heschel's correspondence, stories of people who knew him, the lives of people who crossed his path – the flood of information, lovingly preserved, hardly makes for compelling reading. But for the first systematic biography, I suppose, that was not the governing criterion of relevance, and Dresner's research, complemented by Kaplan's, forms the starting point for all future work on the man. But it suffices to say, all the hard questions are yet to be asked. Why, for example, did a teen-age boy leave his father's religious world and his mother's house and strike out on his own, changing the very clothing that he wore along with his life's curriculum? Kaplan has little to say on that critical question, and nothing compelling to contribute. What accounts for Heschel's assiduous cultivation of Buber in the years after Buber told Schocken Books not to publish Heschel's doctoral dissertation on the prophets – politics or something he thought there was to be learned? Kaplan does not speculate.

Like all of us, as the principal author Kaplan reveals the strengths and weaknesses of his field, which is French and comparative literature and not philosophy, philosophy of religion, theology, let alone Scripture and Talmud, philosophy and mysticism, Hasidism, secular Jewish intellectualism, let alone the classics of Judaism on which Heschel worked. The strengths of Kaplan's writing underscore his weaknesses. Heschel wrote some Yiddish poetry, and Kaplan's analysis and exposition of Heschel's poetry invariably proves persuasive and lively. But Kaplan's grasp of issues of German philosophy in the first third of the twentieth century is wooden and superficial, and his narrative becomes clunky and dull. The contrast between his lively prose in dealing with Heschel's poetry and his dutiful, lifeless, and tiresome paraphrase in dealing with his philosophy tells the tale. Indeed, when it comes to Heschel's serious efforts to contribute to philosophy – his philosophical reading of the scriptural prophets, a reading framed in dialogue with psychology and phenomenology – Kaplan's presentation scarcely rises above the reportorial. Kaplan can say what Heschel said, but he does not tell us a great deal about the intellectual challenges that Heschel addressed, the generative issues and how he responded to them. It would be unfair to say that Kaplan possesses no qualifications for the work, since he rightly enjoys the main one: he was willing to devote years of his life to the task. But no one can doubt that a great deal of work remains to be done to place Heschel into the philosophical and theological context in which he pursued his work.

Heschel in the years recounted here spent so much of his energies simply surviving the shift he made from the Hasidic world of Poland to the philosophical world of Germany, he was so preoccupied with problems of founding a career, his opportunities for academic writing so limited, that the wonder is, how he produced anything anyone might want to read a whole lifetime later. But, as Kaplan and Dresner make plain, Heschel participated in the advanced issues of European philosophy of a certain order; he made himself an equal in dialogue with Martin Buber, thirty years his senior; he established for himself a major presence in German Liberal Judaism, and he laid the foundations for what would be – but in the first thirty years certainly was not – a great life of mind. In these thirty years he laid the foundations for a major edifice of thought, but had he died in the Holocaust, he would not be remembered today.

What Heschel did in the years treated here was reinvent himself, recast his intellect in new forms, and identify with a Judaism that would accommodate his aspirations to participate in Western thought with the heritage of Hasidism, its faith and piety alike. In doing so, Heschel accomplished the key-task. That is to say, Heschel turns out to have saved his own life by his turn from Hasidism to Reform Judaism. When the prophetic president of Hebrew Union College, Julian Morgenstern, undertook to rescue the lives of the scholars of Judaism of Germany, then Austria and elsewhere, in a heroic, last minute effort that laid the foundations for American Jewish scholarship from then on, Heschel was on his list. The final chapter of this book certainly proves the most gripping, as Morgenstern's desperate attempt to save Heschel's life despite the State Department's hostility to any such project plays itself out in documents that, even now, contain their own suspense.

That is the story – from Hasidism to Reform Judaism, from the rebbe's circle to the philosophers' way – that Kaplan and Dresner tell. They stop in the middle, they cram the pages with marginally-relevant data, a lot of it clearly chosen to add color to a thin narrative, and Kaplan's prose sometimes lacks precision let alone art. Still, if the book gives off a certain hagiographical odor, if it is about a third longer than it should be, and if it stops where it should start, nonetheless, we have gotten this far in the study of the most interesting and complex life of Judaic intellectual activity in modern times. The exposition completed in these pages gains in interest as Heschel's life unfolds, and not only in interest but in competence. So if the second volume is ever done, we may be sure that it will contain the justification for such an elaborate project that the first lacks. That is to say, the important work awaits: the account of Heschel's intellectual biography – the only one that matters.

Professor Jacob Neusner, University of South Florida & Bard College, edited, with his son, Noam Neusner, *To Grow in Wisdom. An Anthology of Abraham Joshua Heschel.* New York, 1989: Madison Books.

JACOB NEUSNER
University of South Florida and Bard College

South Florida Studies in the History of Judaism

240001	Lectures on Judaism in the Academy and in the Humanities	Neusner
240002	Lectures on Judaism in the History of Religion	Neusner
240003	Self-Fulfilling Prophecy: Exile and Return in the History of Judaism	Neusner
240004	The Canonical History of Ideas: The Place of the So-called Tannaite Midrashim, Mekhilta Attributed to R. Ishmael, Sifra, Sifré to Numbers, and Sifré to Deuteronomy	Neusner
240005	Ancient Judaism: Debates and Disputes, Second Series	Neusner
240006	The Hasmoneans and Their Supporters: From Mattathias to the Death of John Hyrcanus I	Sievers
240007	Approaches to Ancient Judaism: New Series, Volume One	Neusner
240008	Judaism in the Matrix of Christianity	Neusner
240009	Tradition as Selectivity: Scripture, Mishnah, Tosefta, and Midrash in the Talmud of Babylonia	Neusner
240010	The Tosefta: Translated from the Hebrew: Sixth Division Tohorot	Neusner
240011	In the Margins of the Midrash: Sifre Ha'azinu Texts, Commentaries and Reflections	Basser
240012	Language as Taxonomy: The Rules for Using Hebrew and Aramaic in the Babylonia Talmud	Neusner
240013	The Rules of Composition of the Talmud of Babylonia: The Cogency of the Bavli's Composite	Neusner
240014	Understanding the Rabbinic Mind: Essays on the Hermeneutic of Max Kadushin	Ochs
240015	Essays in Jewish Historiography	Rapoport-Albert
240016	The Golden Calf and the Origins of the Jewish Controversy	Bori/Ward
240017	Approaches to Ancient Judaism: New Series, Volume Two	Neusner
240018	The Bavli That Might Have Been: The Tosefta's Theory of Mishnah Commentary Compared With the Bavli's	Neusner
240019	The Formation of Judaism: In Retrospect and Prospect	Neusner
240020	Judaism in Society: The Evidence of the Yerushalmi,Toward the Natural History of a Religion	Neusner
240021	The Enchantments of Judaism: Rites of Transformation from Birth Through Death	Neusner
240022	Åbo Addresses	Neusner
240023	The City of God in Judaism and Other Comparative and Methodological Studies	Neusner
240024	The Bavli's One Voice: Types and Forms of Analytical Discourse and their Fixed Order of Appearance	Neusner
240025	The Dura-Europos Synagogue: A Re-evaluation (1932-1992)	Gutmann
240026	Precedent and Judicial Discretion: The Case of Joseph ibn Lev	Morell
240027	Max Weinreich *Geschichte der jiddischen Sprachforschung*	Frakes
240028	Israel: Its Life and Culture, Volume I	Pedersen
240029	Israel: Its Life and Culture, Volume II	Pedersen
240030	The Bavli's One Statement: The Metapropositional Program of Babylonian Talmud Tractate Zebahim Chapters One and Five	Neusner

240031	The Oral Torah: The Sacred Books of Judaism: An Introduction: Second Printing	Neusner
240032	The Twentieth Century Construction of "Judaism:" Essays on the Religion of Torah in the History of Religion	Neusner
240033	How the Talmud Shaped Rabbinic Discourse	Neusner
240034	The Discourse of the Bavli: Language, Literature, and Symbolism: Five Recent Findings	Neusner
240035	The Law Behind the Laws: The Bavli's Essential Discourse	Neusner
240036	Sources and Traditions: Types of Compositions in the Talmud of Babylonia	Neusner
240037	How to Study the Bavli: The Languages, Literatures, and Lessons of the Talmud of Babylonia	Neusner
240038	The Bavli's Primary Discourse: Mishnah Commentary: Its Rhetorical Paradigms and their Theological Implications	Neusner
240039	Midrash Aleph Beth	Sawyer
240040	Jewish Thought in the 20th Century: An Introduction in the Talmud of Babylonia Tractate Moed Qatan	Schweid
240041	Diaspora Jews and Judaism: Essays in Honor of, and in Dialogue with, A. Thomas Kraabel	Overman/MacLennan
240042	The Bavli: An Introduction	Neusner
240043	The Bavli's Massive Miscellanies: The Problem of Agglutinative Discourse in the Talmud of Babylonia	Neusner
240044	The Foundations of the Theology of Judaism: An Anthology Part II: Torah	Neusner
240045	Form-Analytical Comparison in Rabbinic Judaism: Structure and Form in *The Fathers* and *The Fathers According to Rabbi Nathan*	Neusner
240046	Essays on Hebrew	Weinberg
240047	The Tosefta: An Introduction	Neusner
240048	The Foundations of the Theology of Judaism: An Anthology Part III: Israel	Neusner
240049	The Study of Ancient Judaism, Volume I: Mishnah, Midrash, Siddur	Neusner
240050	The Study of Ancient Judaism, Volume II: The Palestinian and Babylonian Talmuds	Neusner
240051	Take Judaism, for Example: Studies toward the Comparison of Religions	Neusner
240052	From Eden to Golgotha: Essays in Biblical Theology	Moberly
240053	The Principal Parts of the Bavli's Discourse: A Preliminary Taxonomy: Mishnah Commentary, Sources, Traditions and Agglutinative Miscellanies	Neusner
240054	Barabbas and Esther and Other Studies in the Judaic Illumination of Earliest Christianity	Aus
240055	Targum Studies, Volume I: Textual and Contextual Studies in the Pentateuchal Targums	Flesher
240056	Approaches to Ancient Judaism: New Series, Volume Three, Historical and Literary Studies	Neusner
240057	The Motherhood of God and Other Studies	Gruber
240058	The Analytic Movement: Hayyim Soloveitchik and his Circle	Solomon
240059	Recovering the Role of Women: Power and Authority in Rabbinic Jewish Society	Haas

240060	The Relation between Herodotus' *History* and Primary History	Mandell/Freedman
240061	The First Seven Days: A Philosophical Commentary on the Creation of Genesis	Samuelson
240062	The Bavli's Intellectual Character: The Generative Problematic: In Bavli Baba Qamma Chapter One And Bavli Shabbat Chapter One	Neusner
240063	The Incarnation of God: The Character of Divinity in Formative Judaism: Second Printing	Neusner
240064	Moses Kimhi: Commentary on the Book of Job	Basser/Walfish
240066	Death and Birth of Judaism: Second Printing	Neusner
240067	Decoding the Talmud's Exegetical Program	Neusner
240068	Sources of the Transformation of Judaism	Neusner
240069	The Torah in the Talmud: A Taxonomy of the Uses of Scripture in the Talmud, Volume I	Neusner
240070	The Torah in the Talmud: A Taxonomy of the Uses of Scripture in the Talmud, Volume II	Neusner
240071	The Bavli's Unique Voice: A Systematic Comparison of the Talmud of Babylonia and the Talmud of the Land of Israel, Volume One	Neusner
240072	The Bavli's Unique Voice: A Systematic Comparison of the Talmud of Babylonia and the Talmud of the Land of Israel, Volume Two	Neusner
240073	The Bavli's Unique Voice: A Systematic Comparison of the Talmud of Babylonia and the Talmud of the Land of Israel, Volume Three	Neusner
240074	Bits of Honey: Essays for Samson H. Levey	Chyet/Ellenson
240075	The Mystical Study of Ruth: *Midrash HaNe'elam* of the Zohar to the Book of Ruth	Englander
240076	The Bavli's Unique Voice: A Systematic Comparison of the Talmud of Babylonia and the Talmud of the Land of Israel, Volume Four	Neusner
240077	The Bavli's Unique Voice: A Systematic Comparison of the Talmud of Babylonia and the Talmud of the Land of Israel, Volume Five	Neusner
240078	The Bavli's Unique Voice: A Systematic Comparison of the Talmud of Babylonia and the Talmud of the Land of Israel, Volume Six	Neusner
240079	The Bavli's Unique Voice: A Systematic Comparison of the Talmud of Babylonia and the Talmud of the Land of Israel, Volume Seven	Neusner
240080	Are There Really Tannaitic Parallels to the Gospels?	Neusner
240081	Approaches to Ancient Judaism: New Series, Volume Four, Religious and Theological Studies	Neusner
240082	Approaches to Ancient Judaism: New Series, Volume Five, Historical, Literary, and Religious Studies	Basser/Fishbane
240083	Ancient Judaism: Debates and Disputes, Third Series	Neusner
240084	Judaic Law from Jesus to the Mishnah	Neusner
240085	Writing with Scripture: Second Printing	Neusner/Green
240086	Foundations of Judaism: Second Printing	Neusner

240087	Judaism and Zoroastrianism at the Dusk of Late Antiquity	Neusner
240088	Judaism States Its Theology	Neusner
240089	The Judaism behind the Texts I.A	Neusner
240090	The Judaism behind the Texts I.B	Neusner
240091	Stranger at Home	Neusner
240092	Pseudo-Rabad: Commentary to Sifre Deuteronomy	Basser
240093	FromText to Historical Context in Rabbinic Judaism	Neusner
240094	Formative Judaism	Neusner
240095	Purity in Rabbinic Judaism	Neusner
240096	Was Jesus of Nazareth the Messiah?	McMichael
240097	The Judaism behind the Texts I.C	Neusner
240098	The Judaism behind the Texts II	Neusner
240099	The Judaism behind the Texts III	Neusner
240100	The Judaism behind the Texts IV	Neusner
240101	The Judaism behind the Texts V	Neusner
240102	The Judaism the Rabbis Take for Granted	Neusner
240103	From Text to Historical Context in Rabbinic Judaism V. II	Neusner
240104	From Text to Historical Context in Rabbinic Judaism V. III	Neusner
240105	Samuel, Saul, and Jesus: Three Early Palestinian Jewish Christian Gospel Haggadoth	Aus
240106	What is Midrash? And a Midrash Reader	Neusner
240107	Rabbinic Judaism: Disputes and Debates	Neusner
240108	Why There Never Was a "Talmud of Caesarea"	Neusner
240109	Judaism after the Death of "The Death of God"	Neusner
240110	Approaches to Ancient Judaism	Neusner
240112	The Judaic Law of Baptism	Neusner
240113	The Documentary Foundation of Rabbinic Culture	Neusner
240114	Understanding Seeking Faith, Volume Four	Neusner
240115	Paul and Judaism: An Anthropological Approach	Laato
240116	Approaches to Ancient Judaism, New Series, Volume Eight	Neusner
240119	Theme and Context in Biblical Lists	Scolnic
240120	Where the Talmud Comes From	Neusner
240121	The Initial Phases of the Talmud, Volume Three: Social Ethics	Neusner
240122	Are the Talmuds Interchangeable? Christine Hayes's Blunder	Neusner
240123	The Initial Phases of the Talmud, Volume One: Exegesis of Scripture	Neusner
240124	The Initial Phases of the Talmud, Volume Two: Exemplary Virtue	Neusner
240125	The Initial Phases of the Talmud, Volume Four: Theology	Neusner
240126	From Agnon to Oz	Bargad
240127	Talmudic Dialectics, Volume I: Tractate Berakhot and the Divisions of Appointed Times and Women	Neusner
240128	Talmudic Dialectics, Volume II: The Divisions of Damages and Holy Things and Tractate Niddah	Neusner
240129	The Talmud: Introduction and Reader	Neusner
240130	*Gesher Vakesher:* Bridges and Bonds The Life of Leon Kronish	Green
240131	Beyond Catastrophe	Neusner

240132	Ancient Judaism, Fourth Series	Neusner
240133	Formative Judaism, New Series: Current Issues and Arguments Volume One	Neusner
240134	Sects and Scrolls	Davies
240135	Religion and Law	Neusner
240136	Approaches to Ancient Judaism, New Series, Volume Nine	Neusner
240137	Uppsala Addresses	Neusner
240138	Jews and Christians in the Life and Thought of Hugh of St. Victor	Moore
240140	Jews, Pagans, and Christians in the Golan Heights	Gregg/Urman
240141	Rosenzweig on Profane/Secular History	Vogel
240142	Approaches to Ancient Judaism, New Series, Volume Ten	Neusner
240143	Archaeology and the Galilee	Edwards/McCullough
240144	Rationality and Structure	Neusner
240145	Formative Judaism, New Series: Current Issues and Arguments Volume Two	Neusner
240146	Ancient Judaism, Religious and Theological Perspectives First Series	Neusner
240147	The Good Creator	Gelander
240148	The Mind of Classical Judaism, Volume IV, The Philosophy and Political Economy of Formative Judaism: The Mishnah's System of the Social Order	Neusner
240149	The Mind of Classical Judaism, Volume I, Modes of Thought:: Making Connections and Drawing Conclusions	Neusner
240150	The Mind of Classical Judaism, Volume II, From Philosophy to Religion	Neusner
241051	The Mind of Classical Judaism, Volume III, What is "Israel"? Social Thought in the Formative Age	Neusner
240152	The Tosefta, Translated from the Hebrew: Fifth Division, Qodoshim, The Order of Holy Things	Neusner
240153	The Theology of Rabbinic Judaism: A Prolegomenon	Neusner
240154	Approaches to Ancient Judaism, New Series, Volume Eleven	Neusner
240155	Pesiqta Rabbati: A Synoptic Edition of Pesiqta Rabbati Based upon all Extant Manuscripts and the Editio Princeps, V. I	Ulmer
240156	The Place of the Tosefta in the Halakhah of Formative Judaism: What Alberdina Houtman Didn't Notice	Neusner
240157	"Caught in the Act," Walking on the Sea, and The Release of Barabbas Revisited	Aus
240158	Approaches to Ancient Judaism, New Series, Volume Twelve	Neusner
240159	The Halakhah of the Oral Torah, A Religious Commentary, Introduction and Volume I, Part One, Between Israel and God	Neusner
240160	Claudian Policymaking and the Early Imperial Repression of Judaism at Rome	Slingerland
240161	Rashi's Commentary on Psalms 1–89 with English Translation, Introducion and Notes	Gruber
240162	Peace Indeed	Garber
240163	Mediators of the Divine	Berchman
240164	Approaches to Ancient Judaism, New Series, Volume Thirteen	Neusner
240165	Targum Studies, Volume Two: Targum and Peshitta	Flesher
240166	The Text and I: Writings of Samson H. Levey	Chyet

240167	The Documentary Form-History of Rabbinic Literature, I. The Documentary Forms of Mishnah	Neusner
240168	Louis Finkelstein and the Conservative Movement	Greenbaum
240169	Invitation to the Talmud: A Teaching Book	Neusner
240170	Invitation to Midrash: The Workings of Rabbinic Bible Interpretation, A Teaching Book	Neusner
240171	The Documentary Form-History of Rabbinic Literature, II. The Aggadic Sector: Tractate Abot, Abot deRabbi Natan, Sifra, Sifré to Numbers and Sifré to Deuteronomy	Neusner
240172	The Documentary Form-History of Rabbinic Literature, III. The Aggadic Sector: Mekhilta Attributed to R. Ishmael and Genesis Rabbah	Neusner
240173	The Documentary Form-History of Rabbinic Literature, IV. The Aggadic Sector: Leviticus Rabbah and Pesiqta deRab Kahana	Neusner
240174	The Documentary Form-History of Rabbinic Literature, V. The Aggadic Sector: Song of Songs Rabbah, Ruth Rabbah, Lamentations Rabbati, and Esther Rabbah I	Neusner
240175	The Documentary Form-History of Rabbinic Literature, VI. The Halakhic Sector: The Talmud of the Land of Israel A. Tractates Berakhot and Shabbat through Taanit	Neusner
240176	The Documentary Form-History of Rabbinic Literature, VI. The Halakhic Sector: The Talmud of the Land of Israel B. Tractates Megillah through Qiddushin	Neusner
240177	The Documentary Form-History of Rabbinic Literature, VI. The Halakhic Sector: The Talmud of the Land of Israel C. Tractates Sotah through Horayot and Niddah	Neusner
240178	The Documentary Form-History of Rabbinic Literature, VII. The Halakhic Sector: The Talmud of the Land of Israel A. Tractates Berakhot and Shabbat through Pesahim	Neusner
240179	The Documentary Form-History of Rabbinic Literature, VII. The Halakhic Sector: The Talmud of Babylonia B. Tractates Yoma through Ketubot	Neusner
240180	The Documentary Form-History of Rabbinic Literature, VII. The Halakhic Sector: The Talmud of Babylonia C. Tractates Nedarim through Baba Mesia	Neusner
240181	The Documentary Form-History of Rabbinic Literature, VII. The Halakhic Sector: The Talmud of Babylonia D. Tractates Baba Batra through Horayot	Neusner
240182	The Documentary Form-History of Rabbinic Literature, VII. The Halakhic Sector: The Talmud of Babylonia E. Tractates Zebahim through Bekhorot	Neusner
240183	The Documentary Form-History of Rabbinic Literature, VII. The Halakhic Sector: The Talmud of Babylonia F. Tractates Arakhin through Niddah and Conclusions	Neusner
240184	Messages to Moscow: And Other Current Lectures on Learning and Community in Judaism	Neusner
240185	The Economics of the Mishnah	Neusner
240186	Approaches to Ancient Judaism, New Series, Volume Fourteen	Neusner
240187	Jewish Law from Moses to the Mishnah	Neusner

South Florida Academic Commentary Series

243001	The Talmud of Babylonia, An Academic Commentary, Volume XI, Bavli Tractate Moed Qatan	Neusner
243002	The Talmud of Babylonia, An Academic Commentary, Volume XXXIV, Bavli Tractate Keritot	Neusner
243003	The Talmud of Babylonia, An Academic Commentary, Volume XVII, Bavli Tractate Sotah	Neusner
243004	The Talmud of Babylonia, An Academic Commentary, Volume XXIV, Bavli Tractate Makkot	Neusner
243005	The Talmud of Babylonia, An Academic Commentary, Volume XXXII, Bavli Tractate Arakhin	Neusner
243006	The Talmud of Babylonia, An Academic Commentary, Volume VI, Bavli Tractate Sukkah	Neusner
243007	The Talmud of Babylonia, An Academic Commentary, Volume XII, Bavli Tractate Hagigah	Neusner
243008	The Talmud of Babylonia, An Academic Commentary, Volume XXVI, Bavli Tractate Horayot	Neusner
243009	The Talmud of Babylonia, An Academic Commentary, Volume XXVII, Bavli Tractate Shebuot	Neusner
243010	The Talmud of Babylonia, An Academic Commentary, Volume XXXIII, Bavli Tractate Temurah	Neusner
243011	The Talmud of Babylonia, An Academic Commentary, Volume XXXV, Bavli Tractates Meilah and Tamid	Neusner
243012	The Talmud of Babylonia, An Academic Commentary, Volume VIII, Bavli Tractate Rosh Hashanah	Neusner
243013	The Talmud of Babylonia, An Academic Commentary, Volume V, Bavli Tractate Yoma	Neusner
243014	The Talmud of Babylonia, An Academic Commentary, Volume XXXVI, Bavli Tractate Niddah	Neusner
243015	The Talmud of Babylonia, An Academic Commentary, Volume XX, Bavli Tractate Baba Qamma	Neusner
243016	The Talmud of Babylonia, An Academic Commentary, Volume XXXI, Bavli Tractate Bekhorot	Neusner
243017	The Talmud of Babylonia, An Academic Commentary, Volume XXX, Bavli Tractate Hullin	Neusner
243018	The Talmud of Babylonia, An Academic Commentary, Volume VII, Bavli Tractate Besah	Neusner
243019	The Talmud of Babylonia, An Academic Commentary, Volume X, Bavli Tractate Megillah	Neusner
243020	The Talmud of Babylonia, An Academic Commentary, Volume XXVIII, Bavli Tractate Zebahim A. Chapters I through VII	Neusner
243021	The Talmud of Babylonia, An Academic Commentary, Volume XXI, Bavli Tractate Baba Mesia, A. Chapters I through VI	Neusner
243022	The Talmud of Babylonia, An Academic Commentary, Volume XXII, Bavli Tractate Baba Batra, A. Chapters I through VI	Neusner

243023	The Talmud of Babylonia, An Academic Commentary, Volume XXIX, Bavli Tractate Menahot, A. Chapters I through VI	Neusner
243024	The Talmud of Babylonia, An Academic Commentary, Volume I, Bavli Tractate Berakhot	Neusner
243025	The Talmud of Babylonia, An Academic Commentary, Volume XXV, Bavli Tractate Abodah Zarah	Neusner
243026	The Talmud of Babylonia, An Academic Commentary, Volume XXIII, Bavli Tractate Sanhedrin, A. Chapters I through VII	Neusner
243027	The Talmud of Babylonia, A Complete Outline, Part IV, The Division of Holy Things; A: From Tractate Zabahim through Tractate Hullin	Neusner
243028	The Talmud of Babylonia, An Academic Commentary, Volume XIV, Bavli Tractate Ketubot, A. Chapters I through VI	Neusner
243029	The Talmud of Babylonia, An Academic Commentary, Volume IV, Bavli Tractate Pesahim, A. Chapters I through VII	Neusner
243030	The Talmud of Babylonia, An Academic Commentary, Volume III, Bavli Tractate Erubin, A. ChaptersI through V	Neusner
243031	The Talmud of Babylonia, A Complete Outline, Part III, The Division of Damages; A: From Tractate Baba Qamma through Tractate Baba Batra	Neusner
243032	The Talmud of Babylonia, An Academic Commentary, Volume II, Bavli Tractate Shabbat, Volume A, Chapters One through Twelve	Neusner
243033	The Talmud of Babylonia, An Academic Commentary, Volume II, Bavli Tractate Shabbat, Volume B, Chapters Thirteen through Twenty-four	Neusner
243034	The Talmud of Babylonia, An Academic Commentary, Volume XV, Bavli Tractate Nedarim	Neusner
243035	The Talmud of Babylonia, An Academic Commentary, Volume XVIII, Bavli Tractate Gittin	Neusner
243036	The Talmud of Babylonia, An Academic Commentary, Volume XIX, Bavli Tractate Qiddushin	Neusner
243037	The Talmud of Babylonia, A Complete Outline, Part IV, The Division of Holy Things; B: From Tractate Berakot through Tractate Niddah	Neusner
243038	The Talmud of Babylonia, A Complete Outline, Part III, The Division of Damages; B: From Tractate Sanhedrin through Tractate Shebuot	Neusner
243039	The Talmud of Babylonia, A Complete Outline, Part I, Tractate Berakhot and the Division of Appointed Times A: From Tractate Berakhot through Tractate Pesahim	Neusner
243040	The Talmud of Babylonia, A Complete Outline, Part I, Tractate Berakhot and the Division of Appointed Times B: From Tractate Yoma through Tractate Hagigah	Neusner
243041	The Talmud of Babylonia, A Complete Outline, Part II, The Division of Women; A: From Tractate Yebamot through Tractate Ketubot	Neusner

243042	The Talmud of Babylonia, A Complete Outline, Part II, The Division of Women; B: From Tractate Nedarim through Tractate Qiddushin	Neusner
243043	The Talmud of Babylonia, An Academic Commentary, Volume XIII, Bavli Tractate Yebamot, A. Chapters One through Eight	Neusner
243044	The Talmud of Babylonia, An Academic Commentary, XIII, Bavli Tractate Yebamot, B. Chapters Nine through Seventeen	Neusner
243045	The Talmud of the Land of Israel, A Complete Outline of the Second, Third and Fourth Divisions, Part II, The Division of Women, A. Yebamot to Nedarim	Neusner
243046	The Talmud of the Land of Israel, A Complete Outline of the Second, Third and Fourth Divisions, Part II, The Division of Women, B. Nazir to Sotah	Neusner
243047	The Talmud of the Land of Israel, A Complete Outline of the Second, Third and Fourth Divisions, Part I, The Division of Appointed Times, C. Pesahim and Sukkah	Neusner
243048	The Talmud of the Land of Israel, A Complete Outline of the Second, Third and Fourth Divisions, Part I, The Division of Appointed Times, A. Berakhot, Shabbat	Neusner
243049	The Talmud of the Land of Israel, A Complete Outline of the Second, Third and Fourth Divisions, Part I, The Division of Appointed Times, B. Erubin, Yoma and Besah	Neusner
243050	The Talmud of the Land of Israel, A Complete Outline of the Second, Third and Fourth Divisions, Part I, The Division of Appointed Times, D. Taanit, Megillah, Rosh Hashannah, Hagigah and Moed Qatan	Neusner
243051	The Talmud of the Land of Israel, A Complete Outline of the Second, Third and Fourth Divisions, Part III, The Division of Damages, A. Baba Qamma, Baba Mesia, Baba Batra, Horayot and Niddah	Neusner
243052	The Talmud of the Land of Israel, A Complete Outline of the Second, Third and Fourth Divisions, Part III, The Division of Damages, B. Sanhedrin, Makkot, Shebuot and Abldah Zarah	Neusner
243053	The Two Talmuds Compared, II. The Division of Women in the Talmud of the Land of Israel and the Talmud of Babylonia, Volume A, Tractates Yebamot and Ketubot	Neusner
243054	The Two Talmuds Compared, II. The Division of Women in the Talmud of the Land of Israel and the Talmud of Babylonia, Volume B, Tractates Nedarim, Nazir and Sotah	Neusner
243055	The Two Talmuds Compared, II. The Division of Women in the Talmud of the Land of Israel and the Talmud of Babylonia, Volume C, Tractates Qiddushin and Gittin	Neusner
243056	The Two Talmuds Compared, III. The Division of Damages in the Talmud of the Land of Israel and the Talmud of Babylonia, Volume A, Tractates Baba Qamma and Baba Mesia	Neusner
243057	The Two Talmuds Compared, III. The Division of Damages in the Talmud of the Land of Israel and the Talmud of Babylonia, Volume B, Tractates Baba Batra and Niddah	Neusner

243058	The Two Talmuds Compared, III. The Division of Damages in the Talmud of the Land of Israel and the Talmud of Babylonia, Volume C, Tractates Sanhedrin and Makkot	Neusner
243059	The Two Talmuds Compared, I. Tractate Berakhot and the Division of Appointed Times in the Talmud of the Land of Israel and the Talmud of Babylonia, Volume B, Tractate Shabbat	Neusner
243060	The Two Talmuds Compared, I. Tractate Berakhot and the Division of Appointed Times in the Talmud of the Land of Israel and the Talmud of Babylonia, Volume A, Tractate Berakhot	Neusner
243061	The Two Talmuds Compared, III. The Division of Damages in the Talmud of the Land of Israel and the Talmud of Babylonia, Volume D, Tractates Shebuot, Abodah Zarah and Horayot	Neusner
243062	The Two Talmuds Compared, I. Tractate Berakhot and the Division of Appointed Times in the Talmud of the Land of Israel and the Talmud of Babylonia, Volume C, Tractate Erubin	Neusner
243063	The Two Talmuds Compared, I. Tractate Berakhot and the Division of Appointed Times in the Talmud of the Land of Israel and the Talmud of Babylonia, Volume D, Tractates Yoma and Sukkah	Neusner
243064	The Two Talmuds Compared, I. Tractate Berakhot and the Division of Appointed Times in the Talmud of the Land of Israel and the Talmud of Babylonia, Volume E, Tractate Pesahim	Neusner
243065	The Two Talmuds Compared, I. Tractate Berakhot and the Division of Appointed Times in the Talmud of the Land of Israel and the Talmud of Babylonia, Volume F, Tractates Besah, Taanit and Megillah	Neusner
243066	The Two Talmuds Compared, I. Tractate Berakhot and the Division of Appointed Times in the Talmud of the Land of Israel and the Talmud of Babylonia, Volume G, Tractates Rosh Hashanah and Moed Qatan	Neusner
243067	The Talmud of Babylonia, An Academic Commentary, Volume XXII, Bavli Tractate Baba Batra, B. Chapters VII through XI	Neusner
243068	The Talmud of Babylonia, An Academic Commentary, Volume XXIII, Bavli Tractate Sanhedrin, B. Chapters VIII through XII	Neusner
243069	The Talmud of Babylonia, An Academic Commentary, Volume XIV, Bavli Tractate Ketubot, B. ChaptersVII through XIV	Neusner
243070	The Talmud of Babylonia, An Academic Commentary, Volume IV, Bavli Tractate Pesahim, B. Chapters VIII through XI	Neusner
243071	The Talmud of Babylonia, An Academic Commentary, Volume XXIX, Bavli Tractate Menahot, B. Chapters VII through XIV	Neusner
243072	The Talmud of Babylonia, An Academic Commentary, Volume XXVIII, Bavli Tractate Zebahim B. Chapters VIII through XV	Neusner
243073	The Talmud of Babylonia, An Academic Commentary, Volume XXI, Bavli Tractate Baba Mesia, B. Chapters VIII through XI	Neusner

243074	The Talmud of Babylonia, An Academic Commentary, Volume III, Bavli Tractate Erubin, A. ChaptersVI through XI	Neusner
243075	The Components of the Rabbinic Documents: From the Whole to the Parts, I. Sifra, Part One	Neusner
243076	The Components of the Rabbinic Documents: From the Whole to the Parts, I. Sifra, Part Two	Neusner
243077	The Components of the Rabbinic Documents: From the Whole to the Parts, I. Sifra, Part Three	Neusner
243078	The Components of the Rabbinic Documents: From the Whole to the Parts, I. Sifra, Part Four	Neusner
243079	The Components of the Rabbinic Documents: From the Whole to the Parts, II. Esther Rabbah I	Neusner
243080	The Components of the Rabbinic Documents: From the Whole to the Parts, III. Ruth Rabbah	Neusner
243081	The Components of the Rabbinic Documents: From the Whole to the Parts, IV. Lamemtations Rabbah	Neusner
243082	The Components of the Rabbinic Documents: From the Whole to the Parts, V. Song of Songs Rabbah, Part One	Neusner
243083	The Components of the Rabbinic Documents: From the Whole to the Parts, V. Song of Songs Rabbah, Part Two	Neusner
243084	The Components of the Rabbinic Documents: From the Whole to the Parts, VI. The Fathers According to Rabbi Nathan	Neusner
243085	The Components of the Rabbinic Documents: From the Whole to the Parts, VII. Sifré to Deuteronomy, Part One	Neusner
243086	The Components of the Rabbinic Documents: From the Whole to the Parts, VII. Sifré to Deuteronomy, Part Two	Neusner
243087	The Components of the Rabbinic Documents: From the Whole to the Parts, VII. Sifré to Deuteronomy, Part Three	Neusner
243088	The Components of the Rabbinic Documents: From the Whole to the Parts, VIII. Mekhilta Attributed to Rabbi Ishmael, Part One	Neusner
243089	The Components of the Rabbinic Documents: From the Whole to the Parts, VIII. Mekhilta Attributed to Rabbi Ishmael, Part Two	Neusner
243090	The Components of the Rabbinic Documents: From the Whole to the Parts, VIII. Mekhilta Attributed to Rabbi Ishmael, Part Three	Neusner
243092	The Components of the Rabbinic Documents: From the Whole to the Parts, IX. Genesis Rabbah, Part One, Introduction and Chapters One through Twenty-two	Neusner
243093	The Components of the Rabbinic Documents: From the Whole to the Parts, IX. Genesis Rabbah, Part Two, Chapters Twenty-three through Fifty	Neusner
243094	The Components of the Rabbinic Documents: From the Whole to the Parts, IX. Genesis Rabbah, Part Three, Chapters Fifty-one through Seventy-five	Neusner
243095	The Components of the Rabbinic Documents: From the Whole to the Parts, X. Leviticus Rabbah, Part One , Introduction and Parashiyyot One through Seventeen	Neusner
243096	The Components of the Rabbinic Documents: From the Whole to the Parts, X. Leviticus Rabbah, Part Two, Parashiyyot Eighteen through Thirty-seven	Neusner

243097	The Components of the Rabbinic Documents: From the Whole to the Parts, X. Leviticus Rabbah, Part Three, Topical and Methodical Outline	Neusner
243098	The Components of the Rabbinic Documents: From the Whole to the Parts, XI. Pesiqta deRab Kahana, Part One, Introduction and Pisqaot One through Eleven	Neusner
243099	The Components of the Rabbinic Documents: From the Whole to the Parts, XI. Pesiqta deRab Kahana, Part Two, Pisqaot Twelve through Twenty-eight	Neusner
243100	The Components of the Rabbinic Documents: From the Whole to the Parts, XI. Pesiqta deRab Kahana, Part Three, A Topical and Methodical Outline	Neusner
243101	The Components of the Rabbinic Documents: From the Whole to the Parts, IX. Genesis Rabbah, Part Four, Chapters Seventy-six through One Hundred	Neusner
243102	The Components of the Rabbinic Documents: From the Whole to the Parts, IX. Genesis Rabbah, Part Five, A Methodical and Topical Outline; Bereshit through Vaere, Chapters One through Fifty-seven	Neusner
243103	The Components of the Rabbinic Documents: From the Whole to the Parts, IX. Genesis Rabbah, Part Six, A Methodical and Topical Outline; Hayye Sarah through Miqqes, Chapters Fifty-eight through One Hundred	Neusner
243104	The Components of the Rabbinic Documents: From the Whole to the Parts, XII., Sifré to Numbers, Part One, Introduction and Pisqaot One through Seventy-one	Neusner
243105	The Components of the Rabbinic Documents: From the Whole to the Parts, XII., Sifré to Numbers, Part Two, Pisqaot Seventy-two through One Hundred Twenty-two	Neusner
243106	The Components of the Rabbinic Documents: From the Whole to the Parts, XII., Sifré to Numbers, Part Three, Pisqaot One Hundred Twenty-three through One Hundred Sixty-one	Neusner
243107	The Components of the Rabbinic Documents: From the Whole to the Parts, XII., Sifré to Numbers, Part Four, A Topical and Methodical Outline	Neusner
243108	The Talmud of the Land of Israel: An Academic Commentary of the Second, Third, and Fourth Divisions, I. Yerushalmi Tractate Berakhot (Based on the Translation by Tzvee Zahavy)	Neusner
243109	The Talmud of the Land of Israel: An Academic Commentary of the Second, Third, and Fourth Divisions, II. Yerushalmi Tractate Shabbat. A. Chapters One through Ten	Neusner
243110	The Talmud of the Land of Israel: An Academic Commentary of the Second, Third, and Fourth Divisions, II. Yerushalmi Tractate Shabbat. B. Chapters Eleven through Twenty-Four and The Structure of Yerushalmi Shabbat	Neusner
243111	The Talmud of the Land of Israel: An Academic Commentary of the Second, Third, and Fourth Divisions, ÎII. Yerushalmi Tractate Erubin	Neusner
243112	The Talmud of the Land of Israel: An Academic Commentary of the Second, Third, and Fourth Divisions, IV. Yerushalmi Tractate Yoma	Neusner

243113	The Talmud of the Land of Israel: An Academic Commentary of the Second, Third, and Fourth Divisions, ÎV. Yerushalmi Tractate Pesahim A. Chapters One through Six, Based on the English Translation of Baruch M. Bokser with Lawrence Schiffman	Neusner
243113	The Talmud of the Land of Israel: An Academic Commentary of the Second, Third, and Fourth Divisions, ÎV. Yerushalmi Tractate Pesahim B. Chapters Seven through Ten and The Structure of Yerushalmi Pesahim, Based on the English Translation of Baruch M. Bokser with Lawrence Schiffman	Neusner

South Florida-Rochester-Saint Louis Studies on Religion and the Social Order

245001	Faith and Context, Volume 1	Ong
245002	Faith and Context, Volume 2	Ong
245003	Judaism and Civil Religion	Breslauer
245004	The Sociology of Andrew M. Greeley	Greeley
245005	Faith and Context, Volume 3	Ong
245006	The Christ of Michelangelo	Dixon
245007	From Hermeneutics to Ethical Consensus Among Cultures	Bori
245008	Mordecai Kaplan's Thought in a Postmodern Age	Breslauer
245009	No Longer Aliens, No Longer Strangers	Eckardt
245010	Between Tradition and Culture	Ellenson
245011	Religion and the Social Order	Neusner
245012	Christianity and the Stranger	Nichols
245013	The Polish Challenge	Czosnyka
245014	Islam and the Question of Minorities	Sonn
245015	Religion and the Political Order	Neusner
245016	The Ecology of Religion	Neusner
245017	The Shaping of an American Islamic Discourse	Waugh/Denny
245018	The Ideaglogy and Social Base of Jordanian Muslim Brotherhood	Boulby
245019	Muslims on the Americanization Path	Esposito/Haddad
245020	Protean Prejudice: Anti-semitism in England's Age of Reason	Glassman
245021	The Study of Religion: In Retrospect and Prospect	Green

South Florida International Studies in Formative Christianity and Judaism

242501	The Earliest Christian Mission to 'All Nations'	La Grand
242502	Judaic Approaches to the Gospels	Chilton
242503	The "Essence of Christianity"	Forni Rosa
242504	The Wicked Tenants and Gethsemane	Aus
242505	A Star Is Rising	Laato
242506	Romans 9–11: A Reader-Response Analysis	Lodge
242507	The Good News of Peter's Denial	Borrell